Pelican Books
Kitchen Sink or Swim?

Deidre Sanders was b... County Grammar School and ... read English. She first worked for *Medical News*, the *Sun* newspaper and *Nova* magazine. After a year travelling in the West Indies and South America with her husband, she worked on the *Sunday Times* magazine and then moved to *Woman's Own*, where she edited the 'At Your Service' consumer rights column for several years, campaigning on many subjects, often connected with women's problems. She received a Consumer Writers' Award for her work, and in 1977 was awarded a Jubilee Medal. In 1978 she joined the *Daily Star* as their problem columnist, and took on her present job as the 'agony aunt' of the *Sun* newspaper in 1980.

Her daughter, Susie, was born in 1976 and she and her husband have adjusted their working lives in order to care for her equally. She has also written, with her husband and some friends, *Would You Believe It?*

Jane Reed has spent all her working life in magazines. In 1970 she became Editor of *Woman's Own* which became Britain's leading weekly magazine for women in the mid-seventies. In 1979 she moved from editing to publishing six of IPC's monthly titles, *Woman and Home, Ideal Home, Homes and Gardens, Woman's Journal, Successful Slimming* and *Mother*, for two years. In 1981 she took over as Editor-in-Chief of *Woman* magazine, which has a massive circulation. She is frequently on the radio and television and is Chairman of the Editorial Committee of the International Federation of Periodical Publishers. Her last book was about living in London.

Deidre Sanders with Jane Reed

Kitchen Sink, or Swim?

Women in the Eighties: The Choices

Penguin Books

Penguin Books Ltd, Harmondsworth, Middlesex, England
Penguin Books, 625 Madison Avenue, New York, New York 10022, U.S.A.
Penguin Books Australia Ltd, Ringwood, Victoria, Australia
Penguin Books Canada Ltd, 2801 John Street, Markham, Ontario, Canada L3R 1B4
Penguin Books (N.Z.) Ltd, 182–190 Wairau Road, Auckland 10, New Zealand

First published 1982

Printed and bound in Great Britain by
Cox & Wyman Ltd, Reading
Set in Linotron Times by
Rowland Phototypesetting Ltd,
Bury St Edmunds, Suffolk

Contents

*To Gwen, who should have benefited
from the ideas in this book,
and Susie, who will*

Our thanks above all to Rick Sanders for all his help in editing the interviews. We are also grateful to Elizabeth Bargh for her help with the early research, and to Jane O'Neill and Simone Waldock who patiently typed and retyped.

Introduction

I spent most of the seventies working on *Woman's Own* magazine, then under the editorship of Jane Reed. The second half of that decade saw the Equal Pay and Sex Discrimination Acts come into full force, as well as improved maternity rights and better provisions for women under the state pensions scheme, allowing for the fact that they might spend up to twenty years at home full-time caring for dependants. I specialized in covering women's rights and related problems, and was enthusiastically encouraged by Jane to write special supplements and features. They aimed to tell women what they were now entitled to, make sure they got it, and to draw attention to large loopholes and problems remaining – such as the almost complete lack of back-up care for the children of women who need to work.

It was extremely satisfying to see a mass circulation women's magazine steadily move from encouraging women to stick to stereotyped roles to being a force for greater opportunity and freedom for women. A campaign that we organized against the way the income-tax system discriminates against married women attracted the support of 7,000 readers. The changes achieved were small but seemed in themselves significant straws in the wind. Changes might come slowly, but they would come. The movement towards greater equality and freedom of choice for women was inexorable – and stimulating.

As the seventies ended Jane and I both left *Woman's Own* in different directions, and coincidentally everything we had in our small way worked for in this field during the previous years seemed to start being dismantled.

It became increasingly clear to us that tremendous forces were gathering which could push women out of the work-force altogether, quite apart from dashing any hopes that old injustices would be put right.

We saw with alarm that as the eighties got under way a groundswell in public opinion surfaced in the letters pages of newspapers, in radio phone-in programmes and in television debates with increasing regularity as unemployment figures rose. It has even taken to the streets. In the winter of 1981 we watched a man walk stoically up and down the rain-soaked streets of a small Scottish town. He was wearing a home-made sandwich board upon which he had carefully painted the words: GET WOMEN BACK IN THE HOME AND GIVE THE MEN THEIR JOBS.

It was at this point that Jane asked me to pull all our thinking together into a book. And although that's how it started, my researches and interviews have led us down a rather different path. What began as a review of 'the way women are' is now linked with constructive suggestions for the way men, women and children might live in the future.

To many the sandwich-board slogan is the obvious, common-sense solution to many evils. 'Millions of jobs now filled by wives only working for unnecessary luxuries like a colour TV, holidays in Spain and a second car would be freed for men who need the work to support their families' . . . 'It is well known that as more and more married women have gone out to work the divorce rate and juvenile delinquency figures have soared' . . . 'In these days of the Pill women shouldn't have children unless they are prepared to give up a few years of their life to care for them' . . .

Journalists writing about the problems of working women have always received a steady trickle – it's now a flood – of such letters suggesting that they would all be solved (and a good many other evils besides) if women didn't work at all, or at least not while their children are young or there are old folk in need of care.

Women's rights are often seen as somehow linked with a breakdown in moral values and partly responsible for a medley of social ills: vandalism, mugging, baby-battering, old people dying neglected and alone, one-parent families, sexual licence.

Women's rights are commonly believed to be achieved only at the expense of the well-being of everyone else – elderly parents, husbands, children.

The Conservative government which came to power at the end of the seventies, though led by a woman, never looked as though it was going to give the lie to such ill-founded beliefs. Far from being a champion of women, it cut public expenditure in a way which often hit women particularly hard. Patrick Jenkin, then Secretary of State for Social Services, intoned in a television debate, 'If the Good Lord had intended us all having equal rights to go out to work and behave equally, He really wouldn't have created men and women.'

Katharine Whitehorn's *bon mot* in the *Observer*, 'Ah then, if the Good Lord had intended Patrick Jenkin to think, He wouldn't have made him bone from ear to ear,' lifted the spirits but, with men like that in a position to wreak havoc on the services affecting working women, the future for women in the eighties to us looked terrifying.

Our most recent background talks with government officers confirm this. Because they see no organized campaign for equal pay, for instance, they believe there is no call for it. They honestly seem to think women are content to earn 25 per cent less than men; that there is no pressing need to introduce amendments to the Equal Pay Act to allow this most blatant inequality to be removed; that women are easily able to make provision for family care if they want to continue working; and that it is simple for them to 'keep their hand in' with interesting part-time work if they prefer to spend more time at home with their children.

It isn't only this government. While Mrs Thatcher's administration have had a knack of unleashing statements that leave normally mild women choking, we shouldn't kid ourselves that life would be all that much different for women in the early eighties under a Labour government, or probably even an SDP administration, though they *say* the right things.

The Labour administration had begun cutting social service budgets long ago. Labour too were looking for ways to shift some of the costly 'caring' back into the home and the family. Mr Callaghan: 'The nature and strength of the family and our attitude towards it will influence our attitude to care for the old and the weaker members of society . . . and the woman usually is the centre of the family.'

The problems both administrations ran into were far from entirely of their own making. There does need to be some radical shake-up in the organization of society and of our working lives.

Sooner or later the economic tide will turn, but it is unlikely to bring a return to full employment. Hot on the heels of the recession is microtechnology, bringing with it new patterns of employment. For instance, a work-force that is inevitably slimmed down by the recession is re-equipped with new technology when the business picks up; fewer hands are needed to work it, fewer redundant workers are re-employed.

In other words there are going to be too many people chasing too few jobs – as they are presently structured – for the foreseeable future.

So three powerful forces are on the move against women working. There's the recession itself, scything down jobs at a rate which has shocked all but those who had been tagged Jonahs for their doomful prophecies. There's the job-gulping onward march of new technology. And there are government policies which cut back jobs done by women and the services without which it is next to impossible for them to work, given the present attitude that all the caring needed for those too weak to help themselves is women's responsibility alone.

As one comfortable industrialist said to Jane: 'It is a time when women must be prepared to make sacrifices.' What sacrifices, she asked, was he planning to make?

However, it is obviously not much use standing forlornly waving the flag of Women's Rights, hoping the chaps will do the decent thing and play fair with the ladies. This is a grim battle for survival.

It isn't a question of *rights* that makes us so sure a kitchen-sink policy for women is not the right answer (at the time of writing there are nearly two million men out of work and their 'right to work' hasn't done them much good) but of the terrible *wrongs* we fear may be done, not only to women but their children and menfolk, too, if this is mistakenly adopted as the solution. That fear led to this book being written. We felt we had to try to do something.

To start with, let's scotch the idea that women work for pin money, for unnecessary luxuries. There are nearly four million women of working age who have no man to support them; they are unmarried (of these 300,000 care for elderly and infirm parents), widowed, divorced or separated, often with children. There are fewer than nine million women working altogether, so these unsupported women make up a good proportion of all the women at work.

When women have a husband, these days one wage is often just not enough to keep the family. *There would be two and a half million more children living below the poverty line if it wasn't for women working*.

Quite apart from the financial argument, we should not pretend that life at home full-time is *always* a rich and satisfying life for a woman. It may be, if she has a pleasant home, friendly neighbours, outside interests of her own, and enjoys joining in with the playgroup and other wives' activities.

We are absolutely *not* knocking the value of full-time motherhood. It is a terrific and satisfying career for those who enjoy it. We believe the responsibilities of parenthood should be taken very, very seriously.

But what about the hospital consultant whom we interviewed, a mother of three, who would *never* have been a consultant if she hadn't carried on working? Do we really want no women with current experience of motherhood in influential positions?

And what about those who, like one mother interviewed, are on the eleventh floor of a high-rise block, where every sound thunders through the walls and the only contact with neighbours is when they complain about the noise their child makes, and who can't even afford to replace their make-up to put on a bit of a face for the world?

Is it really necessarily bad for children if their mother has a job – and remember that two out of five working women work part-time? Eighty-three per cent of children on the NSPCC's 'at risk' registers have mothers at home full-time, compared with only 49 per cent generally. Psychiatrists regard the modern nuclear family as a psychological and emotional pressure cooker, and have found that a job is a valuable outlet and protection against depression. For a woman to be depressed is not good for her children or husband.

Certainly our impression after reading scores of thousands of readers' problem letters is that many perfectly good marriages go downhill because of the totally different life-styles of the couple once the wife is at home full-time with small children and the husband out at work all day – a long day too; since men under thirty with children work four times as much overtime as childless husbands of the same age. Roughly a third of all divorces involve couples with pre-school children.

Convinced that a 'back to the kitchen sink' movement for women was not the answer to the nation's unemployment problems, we pondered what an answer – or partial answer – might be.

We read books and talked to experts, but also we travelled all over the country with tape-recorders to talk to the women, and sometimes their husbands and children, who are living lives that many of us, padded round with comfortable jobs, homes and life-styles, can only theorize about.

Some were men and women who had written to us. A handful were known to us. Others we found by contacting places of work where people were being made redundant, professional organizations, trade unions, self-help groups and counselling services.

We are very grateful to the men and women who were prepared to trust and confide in us. After all, to the vast majority we were complete strangers. In almost all cases we have changed their names in this book to protect their privacy. Where we haven't, we interviewed them on this understanding.

In each chapter we have followed our theoretical argument

with a selection of these interviews which we hope will both illustrate and strengthen our case.

We also drew on three other sources. While at *Woman's Own* magazine, we commissioned a survey by Gallup Poll focusing on the child-care problems of working women and followed it with a campaign for 'Fair care for children and a fair deal for Mum'. There was a tremendous response from readers. Letters poured into the office, and we have quoted from a few of these containing telling personal experiences.

There are extracts from a few letters from among the thousands sent to me in my role as problem-page editor of the *Sun*.

Finally, we have quoted a few interviews from the Equal Opportunities Commission survey report, *The Experience of Caring for Elderly and Handicapped Dependants*.

In all these cases we obtained the consent of the people concerned and have changed their names. First we worked our way through what we thought we knew, making sure that we had got the picture right. Women are being pushed back into the home. This has been possible largely because their position at work has never been one of strength. For all concerned, the home is not necessarily the best place for women to spend all their time, especially compulsorily. We found a rather unexpected strand assumed increasing significance. This was that it isn't so much *maternal* deprivation that children in countries like ours suffer from so much as *paternal* deprivation.

The more consistent link between juvenile delinquency and parental behaviour isn't whether the mother worked, but inadequate fathering.

Not only that. Fathers who, as is too common, don't get very involved in the upbringing and day-to-day routine of caring for their children later regret it – when it is too late. Marriages are happier, too, when couples share both working and child-care fairly equally.

Sharing the child-care has certainly been a happy personal experience. I had my daughter, Susie, in 1976. My husband was as interested in her as I was *and* prepared to put in as long hours looking after her, even as a tiny baby. Since my husband is a writer and able to arrange his hours of work to a large extent, and *Woman's Own* allowed me to work more flexible hours, we were able to share Susie's care fifty-fifty. Even though this meant late nights at the typewriter, neither of us would have chosen to do it any other way.

But at the moment that sort of arrangement is rare and possible only for a lucky few who can arrange their working lives that way. Could it become a realistic option for many?

In the final chapter we explore the ways society might encourage the spread of shared work and home responsibilities. We look at a way of funding it and at how it could work, for parents and children and *happy* families. If the concept seems too futuristic to be taken seriously, remember that at the moment we are paying millions of pounds to people to stay at home full-time, unemployed, regardless of whether they have anything much to do there, while others work full-time and overtime and don't have enough time for their children.

Most mothers working part-time find the balance of work and family life very satisfactory – the main drawback is the lousy pay of most part-time work. Isn't it time we made it financially possible for fathers to have a similar option to choose a life healthily balanced between work and the family? Isn't it time we gave children a chance to see more of their dad? Doesn't this make more sense than saying all the women should be at the kitchen sink all day and all the men at the factory?

1. Women under Attack

The movement of women back to the kitchen sink has begun.

After three decades during which women steadily moved into the work-force, in 1980, for the first time for thirty years, the number of women known either to be working *or looking for work* fell markedly. In December 1979 there were nearly ten million women either working or registered unemployed. By March 1981 there were just over nine and a half million. Almost half a million women had given up and gone home.

Add to those the up to 200,000 who would have been expected to join the official work-force during that period had the trend of the past decade continued, and it makes well *over* half a million women who melted out of the work-force just during the first fifteen months of the 1980s.

By the summer of 1981 the Equal Opportunities Commission were calculating that there were at least one million women who were unemployed, in that they would normally have wanted a job, but who were not on the unemployment register.

That's the handy thing for government, any government, faced with a recession and rising unemployment. When a man loses his job, he stays in the unemployment statistics as an uncomfortable reminder of his plight. When a woman loses her job, there's a fair chance that sooner or later she will redefine herself – or at least can be officially redefined – as a housewife, uncounted in the embarrassing official tally of those out of work. Many women never sign on as unemployed, and the Department of Employment found back in 1976 that nearly 30 per cent of women who did sign on looking for long-term work left the unemployment register within six months without a job – more than left with work. For every 1 per cent rise in unemployment there is a 0.7 per cent fall in the percentage of women who are officially recorded to be in work or looking for work. Those who vanish from the statistics (or never join them) still need and/or want to work but they have lost hope.

We expect women along with men to be losing their jobs in a recession, but why do they give up even staking their claim to work?

It is a phenomenon rapidly increasing in the eighties rather than totally new. It has long been known that there is a large pool of unregistered female unemployment, but during the seventies this pool was thought to be slowly but steadily emptying itself into the numbers of women actually employed or officially registered as looking for work.

One of the main reasons was held to be that changes in National Insurance regulations meant that more married women were paying full National Insurance contributions and so could claim unemployment pay if registered.

When statistics showed women's registered unemployment almost trebling from 260,000 to 763,000 between the end of 1975 and June 1981, we were at first reassured that that didn't *really* mean that three times as many women were out of a job as before. At least part of the increase was put down to more women finding it worth their while to register.

But as more work was done on the statistics, it became clear that not only had the numbers of women officially out of work trebled, but the numbers of women who were not registered as unemployed, but who would like to work if there was enough work to go round, were increasing, too. The tide of the eighties is flowing *into* that pool of unregistered female unemployed, not out of it.

In 1976, when official unemployment was around 1,350,000, of whom roughly one million were men, we conducted a survey through *Woman's Own* magazine and found that there were then 750,000 unregistered unemployed women – which took the nation's total to more than two million out of work, split roughly fifty-fifty between men and women. The then Labour government were no keener officially to acknowledge the 'real' total than is the Conservative government today.

While more married women do now pay full National Insurance contributions and so have an extra incentive to sign on, nearly two thirds don't. As official unemployment moves nearer three million, it is being cautious to estimate that there are at least one million unregistered unemployed women, women wanting to work if . . . If there were jobs to be found . . . if they hadn't been made to feel guilty at the idea of wanting a job while there are so many men out of work . . . if (ironically) their own husband wasn't out of work, on the dole.

The wife of an unemployed man is more likely to be a full-time housewife than a woman whose husband is in work – 70 per cent of the wives of the unemployed are at home compared with 50 per cent of women married to men in work. This is partly because regions of high unemployment for men also have few jobs for women, but also because of the way social security benefits are structured.

If her husband is claiming unemployment pay it is not worth a wife earning more than £12 a week (at rates from November 1981). If he is claiming supplementary benefit (unemployment pay ends after one year out of work, and many need to claim supplementary benefit before this) her earnings above £4 a week are deducted from his benefit. In other words, it is not really worth the wife's while working unless she can earn enough to support the whole family – which few can – and until the end of 1984 a female breadwinner in a couple will not be able to claim Family Income Supplement, which tops up the earnings of low-paid men with families.

It adds up to a massive incentive for wives not to work – the system encourages a couple to live entirely on the dole. In addition, there may be pressure from husbands who, on losing *their* jobs, want their working wives to stay at home full-time to look after them.

As well as this link with male unemployment, the early eighties have seen many other forces prising women out of the work-force.

What before the 1979 election had been promised by the Conservatives as cuts in town-hall bureaucracy seemed after the election rather to take the form of cuts in services affecting women. Either as employees of those services their jobs were threatened (in health, education and social services three in four workers are women) or cuts in services meant that someone else had to take up the caring role, and that someone else was almost inevitably a woman. Complete lack of any outside help might well mean that a woman had to give up even a part-time job which took her out of the home. Talk of services previously provided by the state being supplied by the voluntary sector in effect meant that women were expected to do for nothing what they or someone else had been paid to do previously. Suddenly the question was not whether women would have equal rights to work, but whether they would work at all.

Was this uneasy feeling among women just paranoia, I asked Baroness Young, Secretary of State for Education, in an interview at that time, or was there a concerted campaign by the government to get women out of the work-force, since it could have such a beneficial effect on the unemployment statistics?

'I don't think this is a policy of the government at all,' she answered. 'The attitude of the Conservative Party on this is that there really ought to be a voice for women, and if they want to go out to work or if they need to go out to work, they should be able to do so.'

Yet in both education and social services there have been cuts which have had a devastating effect on women. Early in the government's life, the EOC pointed out how far-reaching could be the effects of planned government cuts in education totalling £705,000,000:

1. *Student grants for mature women:* Many education authorities require a record of full-time employment before they will give study grants. The inevitable cuts in discretionary grants would affect women returning to the job market after a period looking after children, at home. Also, the majority of students on para-medical, social services and arts courses are women; grants are not mandatory for these courses, so cuts in discretionary grants would be more damaging to women. Cutbacks in the

TOPS scheme, an important source of retraining, would hit mature women. Cuts in in-service training for teachers would affect the married woman who returned to work.

2. *Nursery education:* The massive £4,000,000 cut planned for the nursery education programme of 1979/80, and the widely canvassed idea of not taking rising-fives into primary schools, would affect women, as nursery school staff are predominantly female. Female primary school teachers, already losing out to male teachers in senior posts in primary schools, would be hit hardest.

Working women would have more difficulty in finding nursery places for their pre-school children, which means they would have to take at least five years away from work, keeping them out of touch with new developments and behind their male colleagues in status and salary.

3. *Part-time teachers:* Reductions in supply teachers and part-time teaching posts mainly affect women, yet it is a false economy for education administrators to get rid of these jobs in favour of full-time teachers, as many are career teachers keeping their hand in while their families are young.

4. *Changes in school hours:* Though the single-session school day (with its implications for the single and working parent) was not to be introduced, several local education authorities were proposing changes in school hours to cut heating and lighting bills, which would place working parents under an additional strain in making after-school and holiday care arrangements.

5. *School meals:* The removal of the local authorities' duty to provide school meals would mean lay-offs in the supervisory and catering staff, which is almost entirely female.

6. *Adult education:* Traditionally staffed by part-time female teachers and used by women students (students' ratio of female to male is 3:1), cuts here would affect women disproportionately. Mature women, who often lack confidence in their abilities, use adult education as an intermediate and essential step to further education and training.

7. *Higher education:* Cuts in higher education would mean reductions in the arts and humanities, where women are heavily concentrated because of inadequate careers education in schools at the pre-option stage.

8. *Further education:* Traditional areas of employment for girls do not provide apprenticeship schemes or day release, so reductions in full-time courses would particularly affect girls training in nursery nursing, hairdressing and secretarial skills.

In the event, in the first half of 1980, the National Union of Public Employees identified more than 20,000 school-meals jobs already lost and warned about possible eventual job losses of up to 300,000 among school-meals staff. Northamptonshire cut the school-meal staffing level by 30 per cent. Dorset dismissed 800 dinner ladies when it axed meals for primary school children, for example. The hardship and personal suffering which can lie behind what sound like fairly small-scale cuts in employment (women's part-time employment at that) became apparent when I went to Dorset to talk to just two of them – Annie, trying to live on her widow's pension of £16.78, and Margaret, who hadn't been outside her gate for days – whose interviews appear at the end of this chapter.

A survey by the Child Poverty Action Group (CPAG) at the end of 1980[1] found that one education department in the South-West was planning to abolish 250 school assistants' jobs in the near future. The department fully expected that many of the women assistants would continue to give help in the school on an unpaid voluntary basis.

If unemployment don't get you, your conscience will! Women may be hit directly by job losses or indirectly by pressure to take on responsibility for services previously provided by local authorities. Someone like Margaret could be so lonely she would take the work simply for the company. But is this fair? Quite apart from the question of whether it is exploiting Margaret, it may be doing someone like Annie, who *must* support herself, out of a job.

Teaching posts have gone. Leicester reduced its teaching

force by 258, for example, and nursery-school assistants from 113 to seventy-three. Warwickshire lost 240 teaching posts. In the Newcastle area, Joanna, whose story is on page 43, has found that even though she re-trained to the extent of getting a degree, and her work has been praised by head teachers, she cannot get a permanent post. 'I've got twenty years of work left and I'm really not very optimistic about my future,' she says.

While 2 per cent of full-time teaching jobs were cut between June 1979 and September 1980, 30 per cent of part-time posts disappeared.

The CPAG survey found that the next round of cuts in social services would affect jobs – and since social services are predominantly staffed by women, a reduction in employment opportunities for women would result. A councillor on one social services committee where social-work aides were being reduced commented: 'As a source of employment for women in the borough it was a very important source of jobs and the number of applications was always enormous . . . the aides' jobs were also important since they were a form of using community resources which were previously untapped, but nevertheless should not become a voluntary task.'

The job losses in the areas of social work, part-time domestic help in old people's and children's homes, clerical staff and care assistants for the frail elderly in residential homes may not total a large number of jobs in any one borough, but they represent an important loss of income for a good many families.

By cutting the number of hours worked, local authorities can make real savings – but here again they rely on women's consciences and the moral obligations they feel towards people in their care. The needs of a house-bound old lady must be met in one hour instead of two hours a week, the paper work in the education department must be fitted into nine hours rather than twenty-six. Meals for school children suddenly have to be prepared in two hours rather than three. 'You just can't do it in the time,' said one helper, 'however much you rush around.' The inevitable result is that those workers put in more hours than they are paid for. As one said, 'It's moral blackmail.'

Attacking women's job opportunities on another front, the University Grants Committee issued an edict that from 1 August 1980 public money could no longer be spent on crèches or nurseries either directly or indirectly. Both students and staff with children would no longer receive any assistance with child-care costs.

Such facilities are vital to an increasing number of students. The age range of college students is steadily rising because more and more are gaining extra or different qualifications as their only way to stay employed. Quite apart from the problems of the recession, with the fast changing pace of modern technology men and women can expect to re-train for new careers two or three times in a lifetime – a degree in a different subject could have given Joanna transformed options in her working life.

We are not blaming *all* the difficulties faced by women on the Conservative government under Mrs Thatcher. The squeeze on local authority budgets began years ago under a Labour administration. In the words of one director of social services, 'Labour left us with no excess fat. We've had to cut to the bone.' However, it's a government which, considering it's headed by a woman, has managed to capture for itself an astonishingly bad press among women.

Patrick Jenkin seemed to voice Conservative thinking when he said:[2] 'Some mothers have to go out to work either to make an essential contribution to family finances but perhaps also for their own fulfilment. I accept that where parents wish to work or have to work there should be facilities for their children. I do not accept that these facilities should be provided free by the state . . . If they are made available at public expense too readily, then they can all too easily be seen as the expression of a philosophy which preaches that parents can do what they like and it is the duty of the state to look after the children.'

. . . To them that hath shall be given, and from them that hath not shall be taken away . . .

This completely ignores the fact that the women whose earnings are most needed are just those whose earnings are not enough to pay the full cost of good child-care, and that we haven't even got enough good child-care facilities in this country to cater for the needs of lone parents. And the prospects for mothers wanting to work are getting worse.

The 1980 Employment Act, while allowing all women the right to have time off with no loss of pay for ante-natal care and maintaining the right to six weeks' maternity pay and twenty-nine weeks' leave after the birth of a baby, introduced new procedures which effectively made it more difficult for a woman to return to her job.

Women in firms with fewer than six workers have lost the right to return to their job after having a baby, yet women are very likely to work in small firms; 80 per cent of retail workers for instance – a traditional female occupation – are employed in firms of ten or less.

A survey published in *New Society* in 1980[3] showed that in the early cuts the already notoriously inadequate provision for children under five was the second most affected type of service.

Nottinghamshire was closing two day-nurseries, but it had the most generous provision among the counties. Dyfed was making no cuts in existing day care – it had none. Long-awaited and counted-on day care centres were being postponed, perhaps indefinitely. For example, Coventry had deferred building a new day-nursery and reduced the staff in nine existing nurseries by one officer each – presumably with the result that each nursery could take fewer children, since the ratio is governed by law.

As the interview with Linda shows, closing down nurseries or not opening them at all means that divorced or deserted wives will have to live on supplementary benefit rather than being able to earn their own living – which seems small saving – and that mothers who live dangerously near the edge of breakdown may tumble over. Being forced to take children into local authority care doesn't seem much of a financial saving either, quite apart from the huge emotional cost usually paid by the child for the rest of his or her life.

The Child Poverty Action Group study found that twenty-two authorities were increasing charges for day-nurseries, though day-nursery places are only given to the most hard-pressed of parents. Not one local authority was making plans to expand provision for the care of under-fives. In order merely to stand still in relation to the increasing numbers of frail elderly, handicapped children reaching adulthood and children of one-parent families, an increase of 2 per cent would be needed in spending on these services. The government, however, had proposed that local authority expenditure in 1980/81 should be reduced overall by 4 per cent and that a disproportionate reduction of 6.8 per cent should be made in spending on social services.

The *New Society* survey showed the people most affected by the cuts were the elderly. The disabled, mentally ill and handicapped rated few mentions, 'but so little is spent on them there is little to save,' said *New Society*.

Typical economies included, in Cumbria: 'defer opening of multi-purpose day centre, £85,000'; in Coventry: 'delay opening day centre for elderly, £26,000'; in Croydon: 'closure of old people's home, £41,000'. Wakefield saved £95,000 on staff costs and raised £150,000 by increasing charges for home helps.

Only a tiny minority of authorities were managing to meet the Department of Health and Social Security minimum standard of twelve home helps per 1,000 people aged sixty-five or over in their population. As many as half the counties were thought to have reduced the level of their home-help service in 1980. *New Society* found that eight had even begun to charge clients existing on supplementary pension, while the CPAG found that a quarter had made general increases of £2–£5 per week for home-help services.

Increased charges may make the services more economic to run in the short term, but with such impoverished clients it takes only a small rise in cost – or just the imposition of any charge at all – to price the service out of their reach.

But according to Mr Jenkin, 'The family must be the front-line defence when Gran needs help . . . All experience shows that trying to help people outside the family context can bring poor results with heavy costs.'[4]

But what kind of care can the family provide when they are

unemployed and the support services are disappearing day by day?

The problem is that the government seems to want to have its cake and eat it. It wants to cut back on the social services provided by the state, on *formal care*, and talks cosily about caring in the context of the family, *informal care*, but is unwilling to provide any of the essential back-up needed if people are to look after their own elderly, sick and disabled. Lily (page 54) had to give up work to care for her mother because there was no help available to enable her to go on working, yet she can't get even an hour's home help to give her a break, though her own health is far from good. If the strain placed on the carers – women almost invariably – is too great, physical or mental crack-up could follow. The costs to the community then will be even greater, in economic, social and moral terms.

And somehow we could take all this more easily if we felt the government knew what it was doing. Has it thought about the long-term consequences as it merrily scythes down the seed corn of our social services? It appears not.

The House of Commons Treasury and Civil Service Committee, investigating the possible effects of cutting 102,000 Civil Service jobs by 1984, found that the government was 'unable' to say what services would be hit. The Social Services Committee, looking at the effects on the health service of planned cut-backs in personal social services, reported that 'we have seen no assessment by the government of the social and economic effects of ending or reducing services'.

What this last committee did find, ironically, was that some 11,500 *more* jobs had been created, but mainly to cope with extra benefit payments and increase *man*power for law and order . . .

As well as these fierce social and family pressures on women to go back into the home full-time, and the jobs cut because of government policy, many women's jobs have been demolished, along with men's, by the recession itself.

Department of Employment official statistics for the UK show male unemployment doubling from the end of 1975 – the last recession – compared with the trebling of female unemployment by the end of 1981. While the number of men out of work rose from 940,500 to 2,105,100, the number of women registered unemployed rose from 260,300 to 835,600.

Table 1: Official unemployment in the United Kingdom.

1977	*Men*	*Women*
March	1,028,500	355,000
June	1,050,800	399,200
September	1,124,300	484,800
December	1,060,700	420,100
1978		
March	1,058,400	402,600
June	1,022,900	423,100
September	1,041,100	476,600
December	962,500	401,800
1979		
March	1,005,500	396,800
June	930,200	413,700
September	936,100	458,400
December	934,200	421,200
1980		
March	1,025,100	452,800
June	1,132,400	527,300
September	1,378,800	660,600
December	1,585,700	658,500
1981		
March	1,783,200	701,500
June	1,917,900	762,600
September	2,104,600	894,200
December	2,105,100	835,600

Source: *Department of Employment Gazette*

Officially, in the five years up to 1981, women's employment did not seem to suffer numerically as much as men's, but while women constitute only 28 per cent of the officially unemployed *we should not forget those 1 million unregistered women looking for jobs.*

Including them, 47 per cent of the unemployed were women.

Among school-leavers, official figures show that girls have at least as many problems finding work as boys. In July 1980, 343,000 boys and 295,000 girls left school and were available for employment. In September, 32 per cent of the boys and 34 per cent of the girls were still without work.

Men's jobs in general may be seriously affected because it is heavy industry which is feeling the worst effects of the recession first, while women's jobs are concentrated more in the service industries, but there are special pressures on women's jobs, too.

Four million working women are working part-time. The first people to go when a work-force is being cut back are often the part-timers, regardless of length of service. In late 1981 an industrial tribunal ruled that, since most part-timers are women, this constitutes unlawful discrimination – though only when the women have children who could be considered to prevent them working full-time.

Even so, laying off part-time women is often thought not to be in the same league as making full-time workers redundant. It's much cheaper too. Redundancy pay depends on a worker being employed for more than sixteen hours a week and working for that employer for two years or more. Because of interruptions to have a family, women are far less likely to qualify even if they work more than the required number of hours per week.

'Last in, first out' is a common rule of thumb when an employer is deciding which employees to lay off, and it is a guide-line that the union is likely to agree with. Women are much more likely than men to fall foul of this ruling.

Above all, the pressure on employment generally is encouraging more people to think that it is men being kept in work that is important – that it makes more sense now for women to return to the kitchen sink.

That this is simplistic nonsense is illustrated by just a few cases. Sandra (page 55), a divorced mother, was living with her four-year-old on supplementary benefit. 'For a year I couldn't get a nursery place,' she said. 'Now that I have that, there are no jobs. The last one I tried for, I was the 107th applicant that morning.' Since Jim had been made redundant (page 60) his wife Mary had been the family's breadwinner, earning nearly £6,000 a year, but now she was being made redundant too. Muriel, unmarried, self-supporting and caring for her eighty-six-year-old mother, had been made redundant (page 66) three years short of retirement age after working thirty-two years for the same small firm.

But the pressure on employment, and so on women to get out of the work-force, is not going to let up. Even if we pull out of the recession, there is every reason to believe that the pressure on jobs will be continued and increased by the combination of a growing potential work-force with the rapid development of microtechnology – the chip taking over people's jobs.

In *The Collapse of Work*[5] Clive Jenkins and Barrie Sherman (of the Association of Scientific, Technical and Managerial Staffs) pointed out that in round terms the number of extra workers in the UK entering the labour market up to 1991 is forecast as 2.5 million. Just to keep unemployment down to the 'unacceptable' level of 2 million would require our economy to sustain an average rate of growth of 4 per cent a year every year for the next eleven or twelve years. 'We have never managed to grow at even 3.5 per cent for any three consecutive years since the war,' commented Messrs Jenkins and Sherman.

And to that add the job-destroying potential of microtechnology. Japan is investing about £35 *billion* (not million) into its computer industry in the decade 1975–85. They are spending £1.5 *billion* a year on awareness and training alone, compared with about £20 million budgeted in this country.[6]

In 1970 the average twenty-inch colour set contained two integrated circuits; by 1977 Japanese sets had four integrated circuits. Owing to the changes in production this engendered – on average an 80 per cent reduction in other parts – staff levels were cut by 50 per cent. The big seven Japanese manufacturers reduced their work-force from nearly 48,000 to 25,000, while the number of colour TV sets made rose from 8.4 million in 1972 to 10.5 million in 1976.

British manufacturers either had to copy the Japanese or go

out of business altogether. Employers and unions were faced with the choice – either adopt the new technology and reduce your work-force accordingly or all lose your jobs. Philips closed its Lowestoft factory employing 1,100. The 1,400 workers at their Croydon factory, to which the work was transferred, can now make the necessary 500,000 sets a year.

The colour TV market also illustrates the way the British tend to under-estimate the impact of new technologies and the speed with which they will take effect. In 1965 the BBC and ITV were asked to estimate the number of colour TV sets that would be in operation in Britain by 1975. The BBC estimated 750,000, ITV 2 million, but were worried that they were on the high side. In fact, there were 8 million.

While this increased demand for microtechnologically produced goods creates more employment, the very method of production is in the short term reducing manning levels overall.

The jobs forecast to be at risk are:

Manufacturing: assembly-line work on electro-mechanically controlled devices from carburettors to thermostats; unskilled jobs involved in moving, cleaning or stacking parts or materials which will no longer be needed; unskilled work in despatching departments; welding, painting, joining and so on.

Clerical: routine typing, filing, general office work and switchboard operations (30 to 40 per cent reduction).

Management and administration: jobs needed to organize components, processes and employees, which are being reduced; and filing or processing forms.

Retail and services: supermarket checking-out, jobs in wholesaling, fork-lift truck driving etc.

Technical: jobs connected with new equipment – in the short term there will be an explosion of such jobs, but in the long term there will be fewer, since the new technology is simpler and more reliable.

It has been estimated that the new technology will create at least one million jobs in the next few years in Britain, France, West Germany and the United States. But the USA will take almost two thirds of these. Britain's share will depend on how we respond to the challenge. This seems to lie at the heart of the conflicting views about the effect of new technology on employment. Some believe it will cause the collapse of work, huge unemployment; others see it as the latest wealth-bringing development – the third industrial revolution.

It is true that new technology certainly has the potential to bring us greater wealth for less effort, but that is if our industry takes full advantage of it. If it doesn't, the industry of other countries will take over our markets with products manufactured more economically as a result of the new technology.

If we are to take advantage of this revolution, it needs far-sighted and courageous planning from government, employers and unions. In this, so far, we seem to be lagging behind.

In France, for example, the government is planning to supply free viewdata sets to every phone user, having worked out that it is cheaper to do that than to print and continually have to update telephone directories. Subscribers will be able to use the computer system themselves, and have their computer-consciousness pushed forward by a decade.[7]

According to the government's own figures, published in the Bank of England's quarterly bulletin by the beginning of 1981, British industry had suffered in the previous three years the biggest loss of competitiveness we have ever seen. The more chance unions have to monitor the use of new technology in this country, the higher grow their estimates of the unemployment it is going to cause.

In 1979 the New Technology Committee of APEX (the Association of Professional, Executive, Clerical and Computer Staff) predicted a fall in office jobs (women's work) of a quarter of a million by 1983. In December 1980 an updated report predicted that by 1983 at least half a million jobs will have disappeared from the labour market for ever, owing to the 'irresponsible implementation of new technology'. Bluntly, a firm faced with an ever shrinking and depressed market doesn't use its new technology to enable its work-force to be more productive, or to pay its workers the same wage for working fewer hours. It uses it to save itself wage costs – as Doris and

Diana found, even though both were willing to re-train and Diana had worked in computers for twenty-two years. 'Now they can call it up on a VDU, they don't need us any more,' she says.

Unions feel that this is a back-door method of introducing the new technology. Firms say they must make workers redundant because of the recession, and having done that, wheel in the word processors, so that, even if business does pick up, those jobs are lost for ever.

One of the many examples quoted by APEX was of a large chemical company which in 1980 declared 140 workers redundant, including thirty staff grades, 'ostensibly because of lack of orders. On the Monday following the departure of these employees, equipment for a computerized stock-control system appeared in the offices, without any consultation with staff or union. Orders also appeared to revive within weeks.'

On whether more men or more women are going to be pushed out of the work-force in future, views are varied, not to say diametrically opposed. Some believe that employment in the manufacturing industry – mostly male – is going to contract the most, while service industries – mostly female labour – expand. Others believe that strenuous efforts will be made to prevent this trend from continuing. Men will see that they get the lion's share of the jobs remaining. The 'two nations' that some forecasters fear – a smaller number of workers employed for a well-paid forty-hour week while millions of families struggle on state benefits pitched at present poverty levels – would also involve far fewer women working outside the home.

But in the present climate, even if more women do work, their doing so will be regarded grudgingly. Which could mean that, although a woman may be the family's only breadwinner, because there is no work for the man, she gets bad pay, since 'women only work for pin money', do 'women's work' etc. This is already happening in the north-east.

The level of informed concern in the future of women was shown by a high-level conference organized for October 1980 by the British Council of Productivity Association on The Challenge to Equal Rights: Recession and the New Technology, aimed at senior executives and planners. It had to be cancelled when a week before it was due to take place the organizers found they had only one delegate.

As an internal report in the Equal Opportunities Commission was nicknamed: 'Missus, you've had your chips.'

*

The personal stories that lie behind some of the unemployment statistics give the lie to the assumption that sacking women doesn't matter in the way that making men redundant does. As we travelled, talking to people from Dorset to Newcastle, the message was the same. Depriving working women of their livelihood, their family's income, causes hardship. It is just as frustrating for a woman to have to work way below her capacities as it is for a man. Women are just as upset as men at being made to feel they are only fit for the working scrap-heap at forty or fifty. And time and time again their stories showed that, in spite of pious statements about concern for workers being made unemployed, employers are often very brutal in the way they handle redundancies.

Women don't just work for pin money. Making them redundant isn't a comparatively painless operation. For this fifty-year-old widow, whose job was ended as a result of cuts in public expenditure, redundancy has meant the wreck of her pension plans after a lifetime's hard work, as well as leaving her on the breadline now.

Annie (Dorset)

I was made redundant when the County Council decided to stop school meals for children under thirteen years old. My income now is my widow's pension of £16.78 a week. What it boils down to is that I have got to have a job of some sort to support myself. It's either that or live on social security.

I'm fifty next week and you're a bit limited at that age. The chances round here are really grim. Still, I've got to work until

I'm sixty. I'd hoped in my own mind that I'd be able to continue till then with the Council – I'd paid superannuation with them – and with their pension and my widow's pension I'd have had enough to live on. This redundancy has really destroyed my plans for the future.

If someone's prepared to employ me, whatever it is, I'll have a go. But quite honestly I never thought it would come to this. I thought that while I had my health and strength I could easily cope with everything and earn a living. It has brought me down to earth to realize that this is what can happen.

I was widowed twenty years ago and left with one son, David, who is now twenty-two. I was twenty-nine and my husband was thirty-four when he died. He was a market gardener. We were only married for four years, and really those four years brought to me all the joys and sorrows that most people have in a lifetime.

When I left school at fourteen I very much wanted to be a professional cook, but it was the tail end of the war, so there was no hope of further education. You just had to do what was available nearby.

First I became a mother's help and then I went into school meals. I was classed as a general kitchen assistant – doing all the washing up and that at the old grammar school. It was fascinating to me – looking back, it was the start of school meals. I remember I had the rather fantastic wage of 15s. a week. That sounded generous then, but it didn't pay in the holidays, and it was a bit meagre spread over. I kept at it because it was all experience and led into school meals generally. But when I was eighteen I realized I couldn't go on living off the wage and got a job on an airfield canteen. It was hard, long hours. Then we got caught up in the Berlin airlift, when we were open twenty-four hours a day, which was exciting. I finally stayed there, working very long hours, until 1950, when I became ill. I suppose I worked myself to a standstill, and it took its toll, but even so it was an experience. I was twenty then, and went back to being a mother's help.

After that I took a job as a shop assistant on a service base. It wasn't me, but I soon adapted, and I was meeting service people. I stayed there until I married in 1956. I didn't work for the first six months, but then I went part-time to the village bakery and grocers until I had David. I liked working, and bought my own washing machine out of it. But then we settled down to more of a family life. I always assumed I would stop work, with a baby. We didn't go in for high living, so I didn't feel it a hardship to give up and be in my own home.

When my husband died we were living in a tied cottage which was owned by an elderly lady; we stayed there until she died, when David was five, living on my widow's pension of £3 10s. 0d. My husband had been earning about £7, not a great wage, but we had quite sufficient to live on.

When we lost the tied cottage, we came back here to live with my parents, and in 1965, without thinking I had a chance, I applied for the general kitchen assistant's job at the new canteen here in the village school. David was seven then, at school. I did get the job, and once I'd done it for a while, I felt really secure.

I loved the job – the atmosphere of being with children, taking over when the cook was doing her college course, taking everything in my stride, being really a part of the school. It was a good job for a mother, too, always being at home when my son was – the best sort of job. We had all walks of life in our village school. It was nice that the children would come to you with their own little personal problems.

They were all very appreciative of their meal; it meant a lot to the children as well as the parents. They all stayed for lunch – nobody went home.

I stayed at this school right up until two months ago, when I was made redundant. Now all they do is provide a free meal for those children who are entitled. Where we always did the very best we could, nutritional standards have now been flung out of the window. By the end, I had become cook, and I made sure there was always one roast a week, sometimes two. I knew the children didn't like liver, for example, but rather than replacing it with sausages, I used to make sure they got fish, chicken or fresh meat.

Next week I'll register unemployed. I couldn't do it before because all the upset and upheaval has given me a skin infection; but now my doctor has signed me off so I can look for work. But I didn't get any sick benefit. I did manage to get my eighteen weeks' redundancy money last week.

If I hadn't been a person that's always had to be careful and always known that I had to pay the bills . . . well, I've never had what I class a social life, I've never really wanted to, and I've never been able to. I've been contented with having neighbours. The only hobby I have is bellringing, which is not expensive, and something a single person can do. I've always felt bad intruding on things that are for couples.

I have a small car, but a car round here isn't a luxury, because public transport is getting worse and worse. They're planning to cut it even further down. You can't get buses to go to work round here – yet the only person on our estate who's managed to get a job in the village is a widower who does jobbing around. If he wanted to improve himself he'd need a car. You've got to have a car to get to work.

My luxury is my telephone, which is my lifeline. My elderly parents live here, and it means they can phone if something happens and it's the last thing I would give up. If I can get a job which will support the phone and the car I shall be very happy. My parents have only their retirement pension of £41.50 between them.

The chances around here are really grim, though. I'm fifty and you're a bit limited at that age. In the end I'll have to accept whoever will accept me. I'll be willing to train for anything, but obviously people are going to go for someone who'll stay for more than ten years. Still, I've got to work until I'm sixty.

At first the Council seemed to offer several options – reduction in hours, voluntary redundancy or voluntary retirement – but for that you had to be fifty, and I was a few weeks short of that, then, so I ended up working twelve weeks' notice on shorter hours. They treated it as a redundancy notice. I was given all these supposed options and then I was made redundant. 'You're forty-nine and you'll be treated as forty-nine,' they said.

My son David is an electrician. He doesn't earn a fantastic wage, but he lives here with us. He's always very anxious to pay his way, but I'm not going to live off him. He wouldn't see me want for anything, but he's twenty-two and his life ahead of him. I hope one day he'll marry and have a family of his own – that's something I really look forward to, and he's going to need every penny. I don't want to sponge off him.

I'll try to get something – to be independent to get to work and support myself, that's the main aim. I'll have a go at anything. But quite honestly I never thought it would come to this.

*

A wife's earned income, though small, is a vital contribution to the family budget when the husband's earnings are low. And in rural areas, when there are no jobs to bring women together, they may spend days on end in almost total isolation. Like Annie, Margaret used to work in the school-meals service and has been made redundant. Her husband is a casual labourer and her daughter is on short-time. The loss of Margaret's job means a doubt about how the family is going to cope with bills such as electricity. She hasn't been outside her own gate for three days, and there are only two buses a week from her village.

Margaret (Dorset)

I used to help dish up and serve out the dinners at our village primary school, and do the washing up. It was hard work, but oh I do miss it. We were all made redundant in July.

I was very lucky to get the job – I started it eight years ago. My daughter was at school there, and her father and me used to help out over there a lot, building the swimming pool, raising money and that. There was a long waiting list to get a job as a dinner lady. Jobs were scarce even then in this part of the world. Being right out in the country, it's very difficult for women to get to where there's work unless they have a car. There's only two buses a week into town from our village. Anyway, I got the job because they knew me so well, I think.

Since I was made redundant I have realized what a good job I had. I used to moan sometimes about what hard work it was. I used to get bad hands from all the washing up, or a bad back or legs – it was very hard work – and think, 'I wish I didn't have to go today.' But I miss seeing the children, getting out of the house, mixing with a bit of company and having a laugh, as well as the money.

Now, for instance, I haven't been outside the gate for three days. It's not so bad while the weather's good and I can get it out of my system with the gardening. I dread when it's dark in the morning, dark in the evening, and my husband and daughter are both out all day.

But I'm definitely going to miss the pay packets. I used the money – it was about £66 a month take-home pay – to help out with big bills – like getting in half a ton of coal for the winter. I always used it to pay the electricity bill. That's money well spent.

What I earned helped. My husband's got no trade. At the moment he's got a job repairing farm machinery. He's gifted with things like that. He likes outdoor work. His father was a decorator, handyman and gardener – he'd try anything – and he used to help him.

My husband was a farm worker but the lady who owned the farm died and he was out of work for three months. We had to live on supplementary benefit, like we did when he had an accident with the machinery down there and was home. We certainly needed my money then.

He seems quite settled in this job. The only trouble is that he does get very dirty. He's looked in the paper to see if there is something better, but there just aren't the jobs about.

My daughter works. She's a secretary with a local firm, but she's had her hours cut back to a three-day week. She's finding it hard now – well, we all are. She's got a little car to get to work because the work bus goes from another village some way from here, so she was still left with the problem of getting over there.

Now her money's been cut back she doesn't know whether she can afford to keep running the car, and then she'll be stuck for getting to work. I don't think town people realize the problems of life in places like this.

I'd like another job, if I could find one, but even if you find one, it's getting to it that's the problem. I'd go back to doing housework and cleaning, if necessary – I used to do it before I got the job at the school. There were two jobs going at houses in the village before we were made redundant, and I would have applied if I had known what was going to happen. All the wives round here are after jobs like that, the chance may not come again for a long while.

But it was all done so quickly. They had cut back our hours the year before – I used to work from 10 a.m. to 2.30 p.m. but in the end I was only doing 12 to 2.45 p.m. Then about three weeks before the end of term they told us that things looked black for September, but nothing specific. Then the next day they sent out letters saying that we were all going to be made redundant. I reckon they had them all printed already. They knew what was going to happen.

My husband is very sad about it. He thought it was a good thing for me to work. The hours used to fit in with our daughter when she was at school – I was always home when she was. When once I was thinking of packing it in, he said, 'I think you're doing the wrong thing.' It got me out, you see. At one time, when we lived in an even more remote spot than we do now, we had to move because I was bad with my nerves, I got miserable in myself.

I miss the children. We used to take the meals out to them on trolleys. They really used to enjoy their dinners, the little ones. They weren't fussy. I suppose they'd left home at 8.30 in the morning and that's a long time to go without hot food, isn't it? They used to come in at 12 and really love it.

There's a lovely little kitchen over there. They built it some time after I started work there. It seems such a shame for it to be wasted. It's just as we left it – we didn't even have the chance to clean it properly because we were on such short hours. I should love to be going back there next week. I'd be a totally different person.

*

During the sixties and seventies women were told that if they could not get good jobs it was their fault for not working for qualifications. They should aim high. Going back to work after having a family, this teacher did all the right things. She got a degree, her work has been praised by head teachers, but as public expenditure cuts prune the teaching force she still cannot get a permanent job. Are our schools so wonderful, our country so rich in talent, that we can afford to throw talent and application on the scrap-heap? Or does this waste not matter because she is a woman?

Joanna (Newcastle)

1970 found me newly moved into this house with two tiny babies. That was fine until I realized I had left behind all my work colleagues, my friends, all the people who knew me as Joanna. I only ever met people who knew me as the children's mother or my husband's wife and I was getting fed up with that. I couldn't phone anybody up when I felt low and say how about a pint because they didn't see me in that light.

My husband moved up here to take a job at the poly, and I just came with the family, to lead a family life. By then I'd been working five years as a teacher – my last job was acting head of English in a secondary modern.

After two years of looking after the tribe, as it were, my next-door neighbour, who was a trained infant teacher and had two younger children of her own, said she could manage four children as well as two, why didn't I apply to be a supply teacher because they were desperate? As it happened, I was able to fit in with what they wanted, and the situation became constant. Every year I got a bigger work load – they were happy to offer me more time until finally I was working about three quarters of the timetable, teaching remedial work, English to O level, working in the social studies department.

But in 1974, when my children were six, they decided to phase out all part-time staff. Rather than rush into any job I could get, in competition with all the people coming out of colleges, I decided what I should do was improve my qualifications, because my husband's job looked insecure at that time, for one thing.

I was accepted by the university, and took a B. Phil., which we regarded as a good in-service degree for a teacher to obtain.

While I was off on the course, I did permanent supply teaching for a year at the High School, teaching O-level English – which suited me fine because the research I was doing for the degree was about sixth-form girls. I wrote it up and got the degree, with exams too, not just research. It was such a slog – at one point I couldn't believe I was going to manage it. But I kept thinking of my mother, who had worked so hard and never achieved very much apart from the kitchen sink, who had always given me inspiration to do my best. She wasn't the sort of person who would want you to give up just because you're a girl, or to think that being married and having a home and two children was enough.

Having got my degree, I started applying for work in that hard winter of '79. All kinds of problems, endless caretaker strikes, children on half-time because there was no heating. I was looking around, answering adverts, and didn't hold out much hope. But in the summer term I landed a temporary appointment. I did that for the term, as asked, and was well received. The head said he'd never had such a mature supply teacher and felt as though I'd been there for years. I think that's relevant, because I obviously wasn't a nuisance to him. Supply teachers do sometimes have to be spoon-fed.

My children then must have been nine or ten. When September came, I had no work. I'd applied for several jobs and not even got interviews. Feeling very despondent, I got in touch with the county English adviser – having previously worked in secondary modern schools, it was difficult to know where I fitted into the comprehensive system.

I laid my cards on the table and said look, I've just done this B. Phil., I've got all my experience, I'm applying for middle school jobs in the county. I don't get interviews. Am I applying for the wrong things? (I was only applying for basic scale 1 jobs. Before I had my family I was on a responsibility post.)

He looked at my credentials and said, 'I'm afraid you don't have the right qualifications.' I said I was a qualified teacher. 'Ah yes,' he said, 'but it's an all-graduate profession now, and we don't interview people without a degree.' I said I had a degree, a B. Phil. in educational studies. 'Oh,' he said, 'that's not the sort of degree we want. That really doesn't count for first entrants into the profession.'

What about my experience? I said. What about all these good references I can call on from head after head who's been delighted with what I've done? Doesn't that count?

'No,' he said, 'not really, because we have this policy of appointing graduates, and there's not really a lot of hope for you.'

I was very low. I mean, I couldn't have felt worse. My husband said not to worry, something would turn up, and in fact on the first day of September a local headmaster – I'd applied to his school for a job and not been interviewed – phoned and said he needed a supply teacher to do two mornings a week. He had to fight the county to keep me – they were cutting back heavily – and as a special dispensation they agreed I could do two mornings' social studies a week. Then he needed someone to cover a whole class for a term because one of his teachers was leaving. I didn't hold out much hope of getting the job permanently, but even so it seemed the best thing to do. So I taught a class of ten-year-olds for a term and did well enough.

This is one of the problems with the profession – you've no way really of finding out if you're any good. You've got no measure. If you go to your head and ask if you're doing all right, in one sense you're on equal terms with him, especially if you're the same age – it's just that he's a man and got through to his promotion, and you've stopped off by the way, and you don't know what good you're doing. You've either got a job or you haven't, and if you haven't you don't know why. You can be praised and congratulated and told you're doing the right things, but when it comes to an interview you just don't fit. Your face isn't right and for some reason you don't get any further.

Anyway, that job finished, and I was asked to do a term's health education at my children's school – in effect I researched and created a whole new course for them, and again the head seemed totally delighted at what I'd done, and said so.

During that summer I applied for more jobs, got no interviews, not even a reply from some.

Then I was offered another temporary job, no length of time stipulated, doing remedial work. I said I'd like to apply for the job permanently. Oh no, they said, you haven't got a remedial qualification. But I'd taught remedial work already at the High School, and asked whether I could go on a course. They told me no, because they only allowed full members of staff on them. It's Catch-22. If you can't go on the course and get the upgraded qualification, then you can't apply for the job.

So now I do part-time work with a class of eleven-year-olds, all of whom are very slow, with a lot of problems, and they think I'm their teacher. We have a relationship. I might not have a piece of paper that says I know what I'm doing – I just happen to know what those children need in the classroom.

And yet there's a nagging feeling that perhaps I don't, because nobody supports my view by giving me an appointment. So all the time I've got this awful feeling that someone better is going to come and take over – somebody who is supposed to be better – which is a feeling no other teacher has. They're going to come in and say that the last teacher was only on supply, so she didn't know what she was doing, and once again the class that you've got to know, the discipline that you've established, has a very brief life, and you've got to come home with this vast empty space ahead of you. You don't know if someone's going to ask you to step in and teach so-and-so for a brief time, or what.

You can't plan your work or your leisure if you don't know how long it's going to last. So your whole approach, whether you put pictures up in the classroom, how much of an effort you make to get them to be polite and responsible, is affected. I don't want to go on like this for another twenty years.

Every time I'm coming to the end of a term's appointment I really have to force myself to keep going for the last few weeks. I have no will, no enthusiasm, I have to talk myself into going on. I get depressed, though I'm not the sort who has to be clinically treated for depression. But when I'm depressed I get angry, I get an unsettled feeling. I can't plan my life at all.

The point is that when I'm not on a permanent appointment, I'm not doing what I was trained for. Supply teaching is like being on permanent teaching practice – you're always under the scrutiny of somebody. There are little things like you can't go into a staff meeting on equal terms, because you don't really belong, and whatever you might have to say can be resented. You're seen as an usurper with no right to opinions, because you won't be there for long. All your professional feelings about your work are continually undermined.

I'm thirty-nine, so I've got twenty years of work left. But my confidence is undermined at every term end, and I'm really not very optimistic about my future. But surely there must be somewhere in this world where I could offer my talents?

*

Closing down a day-nursery isn't a nice neat way of forcing some working wives to stay at home where they belong, as some think. It means that divorced or deserted mothers will have to live on supplementary benefit rather than being able to earn their own living – which seems small saving – and that mothers who live dangerously near the edge of breakdown may tumble over the edge. Being forced to take the children into care doesn't seem much of a saving, either. The cuts hurt women at the kitchen sink, as well as those at work.

Linda (South London)

The worst case of all when they closed down our nursery was a young mum whose child had been at the day nursery since he was a baby. She had a good job in the City. When the nursery closed, she was offered an afternoon school place, but that didn't work – her mother looking after the boy in the mornings. She ended up taking time off work, losing her holidays, losing pay and in danger of losing her job. She was in a terrible state, very upset. The child missed all his friends so desperately, and was seeing other children, who lived across the magic line in the other borough, who all went to day-nursery, out with their nurses. The child was heartbroken, and couldn't understand why he wasn't allowed to be out with them. The child, who'd been more or less brought up in the nursery, had been physically kicked out. And the mother had to give up working.

It's terribly cruel to tell a girl who's found one system of surviving with a child she's had young and on her own to go and interview childminders. Young girls don't trust childminders – they've heard all the terrible stories, and of course not all minders are good, and there's virtually no check on them. So it's a great social skill and it takes steely nerves to go and look at childminders and size them up and say yes or no – but it's that or find something going badly wrong. It's a major drama.

I'm older, and I didn't realize until I talked to this young girl how hard it was for her. Even for me it was hard – but being older and more articulate and bossy I went down to the childminding organizer and said, 'I want a good one. I'm very fussy and I want a bloody good one.' And she – being middle-class and articulate, I could talk to her direct – she knew I was going to talk to the papers if she didn't get me a good one. Oh, she was completely on my side. She said rather earnestly, you know, it depends what you mean by 'good' and all that. But she found me what I needed. It was no accident that I got a good childminder and somebody else didn't. But still I can't go to work.

Now my eldest is at school and the youngest is with a childminder who has her in the mornings and takes her to nursery school in the afternoons. But of course she puts her own children first – I mean, she's an excellent childminder in every way, but she doesn't look after children after school at all, and in school holidays and half-terms she just does the odd day. So now it would be impossible for me to do any kind of regular job. I'd never be able to keep it.

Because I'm a graphic designer, I could perhaps get a full-time job which would pay me well enough to employ a nanny or au pair, but you don't get jobs like that without a massive responsibility and having to be there come wind or high water.

Long before all this started I was a passionate believer in mothers' right to work at least part-time, whether or not they're filthy rich, no matter how tiny her children are. But also that no mother should be forced to work full-time. Nobody seems to understand that. So they're all for a single mother on social security to be out working – you know, 'why aren't you earning your living?' – but while laying on you that you ought to be doing it, they make it as difficult as possible. And then as soon as you've got your income they try to make you feel guilty for leaving your children. These two currents run . . . and then you get the Patrick Jenkin sort of thing. Complete idiocy – what was it? If God had meant women to work he wouldn't have made them bear children or something. He's laughable. This is going on in the 1980s!

Closing the nursery for me makes the choice all or nothing, because part-time work won't pay for the right kind of care. I enjoy working, I wouldn't not work if I could help it. But I can't do both, not be a single parent and a full-time worker.

The summer before last, when both children were at the day nursery, I did work for six weeks, and though I enjoyed it, it was just too much. Now I realize that I won't try and earn my living fully until they're both at school. That sounds weak and wishy-washy, but it's realistic. I mean, you notice danger signals, and I'm old enough now not to ignore them. I'm not going to get wound up and start bashing the kids again, because that's what would happen. I'd be screaming at them all the time.

I'd just had my second child when my husband had a serious

nervous breakdown. We'd just moved into an old house which needed doing up, a slum really – there was only cold water and it was very dirty and squalid – when he left. I was juggling all sorts of financial problems – debts, bailiffs, mortgage people wanting to take the house back – everything all at once, plus a three-and-a-half-year-old and a four-month-old child.

The only place the stress was coming out was on the children. I didn't know where to turn and I found I was doing uncontrollable things. I was handling my children very very roughly and was in danger of severely injuring the baby.

That's where it all begins. I would have been a candidate for the bin if I hadn't had some help. It wasn't easy to get the day-nursery place. The fact that my husband had cracked up and I was a single parent wasn't enough. I had to wait until I was on tranquillizers myself – then I could be given a place as a medical case. Even then it took six months.

But the day nursery saved us. That's why, when they were going to close the nursery, we raised objections. We kept getting smarmy promises of 'Well, you're going to be looked after. I don't know what you're worrying about,' but we were thinking of the mothers who are going to need it next year – and it won't be there.

Day-nurseries are a very economical form of social work because they perform so many functions at once. It *must* be cheaper in the long run than families falling to pieces, which is inevitable and immoral, as well as uneconomic.

I think the attitude with the council was that it was bad for children to be away from the mothers, and therefore closing a day-nursery wasn't such a bad thing if it encouraged mothers to look after their children. They completely misunderstood that the whole idea of a day-nursery was to *help* mothers look after their children.

For one thing, not all mothers are adults. Giving a sixteen-year-old mother a childminder doesn't help her at all. But having her in a nursery as well as the child . . . she needs it. There was a whole mothers' club there. I used to go round there just to be out of my home, which was the stress area, and be near my kids. They were being looked after, but you could be there – it was encouraged. As I say, a very young mother could go there and look after her child co-operatively with the nursery nurses and learn how to look after the child. A childminder can't provide that. What you need is a foster mother to foster both mother and child, which they sometimes do, but it's a far better approach to have the child in a day-nursery, which keeps the mother's own dignity. The child isn't taken away from her, she's gradually learning to cope, and the child isn't in any danger.

I cornered one of the councillors in the ladies' loo at a council meeting and started talking to her about the nursery and my situation when my husband left and she said I should have got an au pair and that was it!

Then we tracked the head of the social services committee. She said, 'Well, I brought up four boys all by myself. What you should do is get a nanny.' This was the one who said that pound for pound the council would get better value from childminders. Absolutely no idea of what's going on at all.

It's not just a question of the rights and wrongs of this and that. You've *got* to take the stress away from some mothers, you know, and that's going to stop the child's stress. I'm thinking of some of the other mothers who had children at the day-nursery – there was one who was given a childminder, but it ended up with three different childminders in nine months. The childminder situation is very delicate and doesn't always work. Another mother was very young. When her child started at the nursery, it took a long time for her to settle and her asthma to go. She became firm friends with two other girls and was getting on fine, and the mother got a job – the first she'd ever had, because she had the child as soon as she left school. She got a proper job and was very happy – and then the day-nursery closed. She had to leave her job and the child's asthma returned.

They said it was her stress that caused the child's asthma, which may be true – but there's this punishment attitude, that your own inadequacies should be visited on your children.

I hate to think about the loss of the day-nursery, for the sake of new mothers. And now they're going to close another near here. I can't see how any other solution is going to be as good. Basically it kept families together, instead of allowing the problems to grow and ending up with many parents in the local mental hospital and children in care. It was a cheap method of front-line defence, as it were.

But nobody wanted to stand up and say they needed a day-nursery place – I mean, nobody'd want to stand up and say they'd drunk a bottle of whisky a day, you know. The people who needed it most tended to be the least able to stand up and say. So there was a lot of helplessness.

In the present economic situation the day-nursery is needed more rather than less. There must be more family break-ups when there's more stress. Blokes walking out left, right and centre, and this is certainly the area for it. Even for those of us who started in a fairly comfortable position, middle-class and educated, not too young, only two children and reasonably spaced – you know, where everything should have turned out OK. It's not just working-class people.

A mother might be in a wonderful house with central heating, but she's still at the bottom of her thing when she's at the bottom of it, coping no better than a fifteen-year-old sometimes. It must be true. And that blessed day-nursery place gets you through. It's not that you're hopeless or inadequate. But there are times in everyone's life, and it just so happens that it's usually when their children are two years old.

When we had the playgroup, you'd get a mother coming in for the first time, especially if they'd just spent the last three years alone with their first child, looking like something out of the trenches in the First World War. Slowly we saw them blossom as they gradually joined in, took responsibility in the playgroup, had a laugh and a few drinks with us – we used to have parties and picnics – and they suddenly realized there was more to life than a child, and they sort of filled out into human beings. But even with a perfectly decent husband and a lot of money and whatever, they still arrived looking like a tanker rolled over them, sub-human and hardly able to utter a word, so frightened. These were women who must have had good jobs, just apologizing for their existence, having had three years of a child at home bossing them around.

I'm not standing up and saying that state day-nurseries are the ultimate ideal. They seldom give what a child would get at nursery school, and why should some child not get to nursery school because they go to a day-nursery?

If a social worker or health visitor spotted a problem, a bad situation in the family or house, there was a lot of good done by removing the kids for a time each week so they could have a bit of fun, light, air and space and other children and stimulus – and the pressure of their constant demands lifted.

At first I thought that if I didn't actually work while the children were in the day-nursery, the places would be taken away. But when it was explained that I'd been allocated a place for medical reasons, that meant I was encouraged to go away and do whatever I bloody well liked. I used to go over the road into the pub, march in, order a pint of bitter, smoke two cigarettes and then walk off down the road feeling 'I'm a human being.' And because I was alone at home, that was the only time in my whole seven-day week that I ever had any kind of adult conversation and males and life around me. I mean, I had friends, but it was all domestic life . . . and that was the gay social whirl of having a pint by myself in a place where children were not allowed.

People asked us why we didn't take over the nursery and run it for ourselves, but that would have been the opposite of what the day-nursery was for. It was to take away some of your responsibility for a short space of time. It's not that we didn't know the benefits of parent-run playgroups and things like that. It's just that it was not what was needed at the time.

*

The government talks about elderly and disabled being cared for in the community rather than by the state, but has cut back the help available to those trying to do that, rather than extending the support available to them.

Lily (Leeds)

My mother is nearly eighty-five and has spinal and kidney trouble, and arthritis. She has been up in a dressing gown for the last three weeks but has been bedridden for much of the last two or three years. I had to give up work because mother got so that she couldn't be left all day. My wages weren't enough that I could pay someone to be with her all the time, and there is no help available so that you can go on working in this situation.

I save the state £80 a week – that's what it would cost to keep mother in a home – but when I asked about a home help I was told that there is none available.

I get out when I can. Mother has good and bad days. Sometimes I can go and sometimes I can't. We have our bread and eggs delivered, and a greengrocer comes every week. It is more expensive than the supermarket, and we can't really afford it, but it does help when I can't leave mother.

The only help we get is that the District Nurse comes in to give mother an all-over strip wash. My health is not so good really – I have chest and heart trouble. Mother is very heavy, and unsteady on her feet. Movements can cause her pain. I can't do it properly myself. The District Nurse used to come in once a week to bathe mother, but as part of the cuts from Christmas 1979 she has come in just once a fortnight.

Also, in the days when the nurse used to come once a week, if she couldn't come for some reason, they would send someone else. Now she only comes once a fortnight but there is no replacement if she cannot make it, so mother has to wait another fortnight. We'll be all at the ready so that she doesn't waste her time, but then she doesn't come and they don't let you know. Last September mother was bedridden for five weeks. I had a chest infection verging on pneumonia, and mother never got washed really properly for the five weeks. It was very distressing for her.

*

Even before public expenditure cuts began to bite, there was precious little back-up help for women, such as nursery care. This divorced mother waited months for a nursery place. But once she'd found that, she discovered that she had been overtaken by the recession. It certainly matters to this woman that she is unable to work and earn a living.

Sandra (Sheffield)

Living on supplementary benefit is so degrading, I'd much rather work. A few times I've got really down. I remember once standing on the balcony of our flat – it's on the eleventh floor – and thinking, 'You wouldn't feel anything if you went over there. It would be peaceful.' But then I thought, 'That's no good. What about Justin?'

I met his father, Paul, when I was twenty-six. He was working in a hotel where I was telephonist/receptionist. We had a big white wedding, the works, but when I was pregnant, about eighteen months or so later, it turned out that he was already married to someone down south. I soon realized that he was a compulsive liar.

We were managing a pub and restaurant but it got to the stage that when I went down into the bar at night I wouldn't chat to the customers because I didn't know if I was contradicting him. People who didn't know us wouldn't know who to believe. For example, when we went away to Jersey for a week, I found that he had told the staff we had been for a Mediterranean cruise. He got a divorce from his first wife and I tried to make a go of it, but in the end I decided I just couldn't manage that kind of life, and we split up when Justin was eighteen months old.

The people who owned the pub were – are – good friends but they felt it wasn't feasible for a woman to run the pub and restaurant alone. I stayed on for about four months sorting things out – Paul had got the finances into a terrible muddle – and then went to stay with my parents until I could get a place to live.

I asked to be put on the housing list and after a while I was sent details of a twelfth-floor flat. I didn't want to live in a high-rise flat because Justin was only two. I'd been told that they didn't put families with young children in them any more, so I turned it down. The next flat I was sent was this one on the eleventh floor – so I asked about it at the housing office. The man there said, 'I'm ever so sorry but that's all you're going to get offered. You have to be on the housing list for years to be offered a house or a flat in a low block.'

Anyway, I took it. It's noisy and windy but it's in quite a good area. The lifts do get broken when the kids are on holiday but they are pretty good about mending them quickly. I know I was lucky really, but I did get in a bit of a state. I've just never had to cope on this sort of income before. I know there are people who manage, but I can't.

At first I got unemployment benefit, and at least I could claim a rent rebate. After six months I had to go on to supplementary benefit but I had to pay full rent out of that. Now, for example, I get £20 a week supplementary benefit, £10 a week maintenance from Paul, and I get £6.50 child benefit, but my rent has gone up to £13.35 a week.

My parents subsidize us. My mother comes over each week, and stocks us up on food. She buys all Justin's clothes. I smoke quite heavily, but my mother buys all my cigarettes for me. Supplementary benefit leaves no money for extras. You read in the papers about all the things that people get on supplementary benefit, but you get sod all. This flat is decently furnished, but that was all bought with what money I had saved up from when I worked.

I haven't bought any clothes for two years. When I'm out shopping with my mother, I might say, 'That's a nice dress.' She's generous and she'll say, 'Well, go in and buy it.' At one time I'd have said, 'Oh, thanks, great,' but now I think, 'I can't spend £25 on a dress, I could do better things with the money.' But then I think, 'She's done enough for me already, I can't say, "Give me the money and I won't have the dress."' I end up losing all round, in a way.

I want to work to support us. Here I am, thirty-two and still dependent on my family. It's degrading living on social security. I don't think the government should have to support me – it's not their fault that my marriage broke up – but there should be more help with child-care. I love Justin, and I wouldn't swop him, but sometimes I look at him and think, 'If it weren't for you I wouldn't be having to live like this.'

For a year or more I couldn't get Justin into a nursery. At one point I got a letter from the social services saying that they were taking my name off the waiting list because they were keeping all the places for priority cases. I thought, 'What am I, if I'm not a priority case?' I know I don't keep asking for help, and needing a social worker, but that doesn't mean that I don't need a bit of assistance. I went down there to explain and they put his name back on the register. There is a nursery school near here where he could definitely have got a place, but that was no help for me getting a job because the hours are only 9 to 12 in the morning.

I tried to find a childminder, but the list of registered minders they gave me was no help. Two I phoned had given up doing it and the others were all full up. There is a desperate shortage of nursery care.

Last winter was dreadful. I got so low. I couldn't afford to heat the flat all day, so I used to take Justin round and round the shops all day in his buggy – at least the warmth was free, and I was so desperate to get out of the flat a bit. In the evenings while Justin is up I will put the fire on if it's cold – I don't see why he should suffer – but once he's gone to bed I snuggle up in a dressing gown and turn the fire off. Even so I got an electricity bill I just couldn't pay. My mother came over with the money when they arrived to cut us off. I asked at the social security office about money to pay the bill, but she said, 'You get a heating allowance in with your supplementary benefit.' I said, 'I do?' It's something like 60p or 90p a week. My winter bills average about £5 a week. It's impossible for me to put £5 a week away from what I get.

My dad paid for a phone to be put in, because sometimes I did get very, very low. That was when I thought of jumping off the balcony.

Justin's father has bothered to see him just once since he was eighteen months old. I got a court order for him to pay £35 a week maintenance – Paul's got a good job now – but he's never paid it. He's just kept paying the old order for £10 a week. It's going back to court, but I've since heard that he has married again and got his wife to give up work, presumably so that he can claim not to be able to afford £35 a week. Once the hearing's over, she'll probably go back to work. His family are assuming that's it as well – they don't even know the girl.

But it does mean that he has another home to maintain now. If I could get a job with decent pay, I wouldn't want maintenance from him.

Eventually I did get a nursery place for Justin, he can go from 8 a.m. to 6 p.m. But now I can't get a job because the job situation is so awful. I used to work with the GPO before my marriage, and I saw a job as a telephonist advertised in the evening paper. I rang at lunch-time the next day to inquire about the job and asked if they'd had a lot of applications. She looked at the list and said, 'You're the 107th.'

I must have applied for over seventy jobs. Of the ones where you have to fill in an application form which asks whether you have children and whether you are married or single, I'd say I don't even get a reply from about 90 per cent.

I get an interview from the others, and appear to get on well, until they ask whether I have any children. I don't like to lie and in any case they would find out. I stress that Justin is in a full-time nursery and that if he's ill my mother would come over to look after him, but it's no good. One person said it's company policy not to employ people with children under eight. I'm willing to bet, though, that there are plenty of men working there with children under eight.

At a couple of other jobs they said that they had had so many applicants that they could afford to take someone with no responsibilities, regardless of how good I might be at the job. A couple of jobs I've been too old for. One was as a receptionist/telephonist, and they wouldn't even interview anyone over twenty-five. I kept saying, 'Well, I look young,' but it was no good. They can pick and choose. They don't need us.

I can't bear to stay cooped up in here all the time, with the wind roaring round. During the days I always go out unless I have a lot of washing to do. I often go over to my grandma's and do her shopping and a bit of decorating for her, things like that. Occasionally friends with children come round, but it's the night-times I could really do with the company.

I used to get out more when my car was running. The family used to fill it with petrol for me and pay for the insurance. Something went wrong, and during the time it stood waiting down below while I tried to find the money to pay for the repair, it was vandalized. What they couldn't take, they damaged. I got £25 for it as scrap.

Without the car I find that I'm afraid to walk home alone after dark. We have our fair share of muggings and rapes even in this area. There are other problems, too. I can't afford to pay for a baby-sitter. I have friends who will help out, but I can't afford to go out unless somebody takes me, and then having a man paying for everything . . . I'm afraid I do find I suspect people's motives now. If men are being nice to me I feel, 'I know what you're thinking.' They're probably not, but I automatically react like that.

Even if I am asked out, there's the consideration of whether I have enough make-up left, because I can't usually afford to replace things, or have I something decent to wear. Other people may say I look nice, but I know I've had the clothes for years. I can't feel good knowing that I don't look my best.

There was a chance that I would remarry, but Justin reacted so badly to him that we just had to give up the idea. Justin has been changed by all this. He used to be a very outgoing little boy, but now he's shy and very jealous of my giving attention to anyone else. He never calls the flat 'home'. The week we moved in he wet the bed every night. I am afraid I smacked him when morning after morning he came in wet, and I knew all the bed would be wringing wet. I knew it was wrong of me but I felt so bad.

I do appreciate how well off I am, having a family like mine.

Lots of people have nobody behind them. But when I'm down it doesn't help to know that there are people who are worse off. Still, I think I've come to terms with all this better now. It's very depressing, but at least I'm sure now that I'll survive.

*

The recession is often seen as a crisis of male employment. Anyone who mentions problems of women's jobs vanishing can find they get some very antagonistic responses suggesting women should be giving up their jobs voluntarily anyway. But this wife was left as their family's only major breadwinner – with husband made redundant, daughter unable to find work since she left school, and son finishing an apprenticeship. Now she, too, is being made redundant.

Mary and Jim (Cheshire)

Mary: Even with Jim not working for the last eighteen months, we've not been short. Now I'm being made redundant, too, it's suddenly going to go from everything down to absolutely nothing. I can't see any way out, can't see any light at all.

Jim: I've been unemployed since I was made redundant from a security firm in May 1979. I've tried for numerous jobs since then, but there's nothing at all. I've not been bothered about the money – I mean some of the jobs I've been for offered £60 a week. But I found there were people turning up in posh suits and polished shoes for those jobs. You think for those wages you're just going to walk into the job, but no chance . . . even for those jobs there are twenty or thirty people after it. You've got to have something on top of everyone else, and so far it hasn't been me.

I would have sued the firm for wrongful dismissal, but I hadn't been there six months. Before that, I worked for Dunlops for sixteen years as a fork-lift driver. I was bored, I needed a change, and the security job – I was a parcels courier – I did enjoy. But it turned out that my branch wasn't making money. One way to save some was to get rid of some of us – the last in being the first to go. They sacked the manager too, and were talking about shutting the branch altogether. But they brought in a whole new system for the job I was doing, and I think it is paying now.

I wasn't there long enough to get redundancy pay. I did get unemployment pay but that's about to run out now.

Something that doesn't help is having high blood pressure. I think anxiety when I was at Dunlops was part of the cause – not anxiety in the sense of something being wrong, money or anything, but that the job didn't suit me. I was browned off – just anxiety in general preying on my mind. They've stabilized the blood pressure now, but it's still high – they can't get it down to a reasonable level. This hits me when I go for a job. One of the first things they do is test your blood pressure. They say 'sorry' straight away.

I'm forty-six, which I think also counts against me – I think they're liable to accept you up to about forty-five, but then I think they start looking for someone else.

Mary: We came to this place from Manchester in 1963. Under a regional development scheme there were subsidies for factories – there were plenty of jobs – and also to get a house, which we couldn't get in Manchester. We had two children and a third on the way. As soon as she was old enough, I started work – I've been working for fifteen years and I thought I would be till I was sixty. I'm a quality control inspector at Metal Box, earning £104 a week. But they're closing the works after Christmas.

We've done well, really – we've both been in work until Jim lost his job eighteen months ago.

Our children – Keith's twenty-one and married. He's doing quite well wiring up computers. A semi-skilled job and it pays good money. Wayne's at Rolls-Royce – he's twenty and just coming out of his apprenticeship next week. He lives at home. Then there's Dawn – she's nearly eighteen. She left school the same time Jim lost his job and has never had a job. She went to college, studying to be a typist/receptionist, she was going for a diploma, she found she was doing all the same things she did at school and it meant getting up early and going for the train, so she decided to pack it in. She's not been able to get a job since.

At first she was very fussy, saying she would only be a receptionist, but just recently she's been to the employment and says she'll take anything. The only qualification she has is an RSA in typing. She did get CSEs, but no O level or anything like that.

She's engaged now and wants to get married. It'll be love on the dole. Her boyfriend has had jobs, but not now. The last thing he had was one of those Manpower schemes which finished last Christmas. He's looking for labouring in the building trade, anything like that, but no luck. He wanted her to leave college in case she ran off with someone else. I didn't want her to leave college, but she was adamant. Her father didn't want her to go to college in the first place, but I said she had to have as much chance as the boys did.

Jim: I thought it was a waste of time, I didn't think she had the capabilities for college . . . and she was a girl, which entered into it, I suppose. I would have liked her to have gone for a job as soon as she finished school. At that time it was easier, and she'd probably have a job today. A lot of her friends went into factories, but she didn't want that. Now she says she'll take anything and has nothing. Mind you, when she was at college, I wanted her to stick it – I said at the time she was a fool to give up half way through.

Mary: I think she realizes now she'd have had a better chance if she'd stayed. But if all this had happened three years ago, it wouldn't have mattered, because she could have slotted in somewhere no matter what. But everything's changed, there's no jobs at all. According to the papers it's the same all over, but in a small place like this you notice it more. Just today we heard of another local firm that's packing up at the end of the month, a cosmetic company. Mostly young women labour, with just a few men for the machines.

And they're closing down my factory next month. I'll get redundancy pay. It works out at three weeks' money for every year and I've been there eleven years so for me it'll be £3,546.

When Jim's dole runs out we'll be theoretically entitled to supplementary benefit, but my income will stop that. We'll have over £2,000 – if we'd have been finished and maybe got only £1,000 we could have gone on social security right away. We have a bank loan outstanding, which will take about £500, and there's things we were going to buy anyway. But we've just refurnished and had the kitchen done and it's all paid for. If we'd waited a bit longer we could have had it as a debt, maybe.

I earn nearly £6,000 a year so my redundancy pay is nothing in comparison. Even with both of us drawing unemployment, and related earnings is going down by a third in January, that's not much. I expect I'll get about £30 a week unemployment pay, and then if Jim loses his dole . . . we shall be very hard up. It's things like the coal and electricity bills we shall feel the pinch on, with both of us at home. You can't sit there in the cold, can you?

We don't owe anything, everything's been paid . . . I don't know if that's a good or bad thing because we can't get any help.

Jim: The house is rented. We were thinking of buying it, but we've had it now. We've been reading that if you've bought your own house the only thing you can get is tax relief . . . so a lot of people who did buy council houses and are now unemployed are trying to sell them back to the council so they can get rent relief which is more than they would get in tax relief.

Mary: Everything's come at a bad time, just as we've more or less got the children off our hands and we were looking forward to be able to enjoy ourselves. We've never been abroad and neither of us smokes or drinks, for example, but now we just won't be able to do the things we hoped. Whether we'll start arguing or what, I don't know. But it does cause friction being at home. We'll probably be on to the children, you know . . . about having the hairdryer on every day and having a bath every day. Dawn gets £25.70 a fortnight supplementary benefit. She doesn't give me anything at the moment, but we'll have to change that. Wayne gives me £7 at the moment and the problem is that he said he would give me more when he comes out of his apprenticeship, and though I'll have to take it, it doesn't seem fair when Dawn is giving me nothing. But this will change, I'm afraid.

I know it's a bargain for them to live at home, for them, but we've been lucky up to now, we've both been working and we've not made any claims on them. They shouldn't suffer. But as soon as there are worries it produces extra strains. You go merrily on and don't think about it and then all of a sudden . . . you know, we've always tried to give them what they want, and I don't feel they should get involved, but I suppose they'll have to be with only Wayne working.

Dawn's already asked if she and her boyfriend can live here when they're married, but I've been firm about that and said no. I can see there being a lot of arguments. Fortunately, being such a small town, there's no problem here in getting a council house. A wait here means four weeks . . . there are plenty of houses. There's no work, you see, and a lot of moonlight flits. There's one estate, it's like an army camp – the houses are badly built, and you can reach from one to another – they've given houses to the boat people, to Asians, to all sorts. You can go down and get one of those houses tomorrow with no trouble at all. Even on a good established estate, the wait's only five or six weeks. When we were in Manchester, we waited for four and a half years . . . I could have dropped through the floor here when we came and they told us sorry, you'll have to wait, but it turned out to be only for a few weeks.

Jim: My wage just kept us going, but Mary's on top made a heck of a difference to what we could do. So I've never been the sort to say that women should stay at home – oh no, no.

Since Mary's been out at work, I quite enjoy the domestic side of things. It's not mixed up in my mind with being out of work. The only thing is, if I bake a cake, I don't feel like eating it. I would like the surprise if someone had done it for me, but if I've done it myself it's not the same. Mind you, I have an allotment, so it's seldom I do any cooking outside of winter. I spend all my time down there.

I know if I was stuck inside doing nothing it would get on my nerves. So in winter I turn to cooking and doing things, which helps me, you know, and it helps Mary.

Mary: When I was first working, I did all the housework, and then we had a big argument and I said I couldn't cope. So Jim started to help. I've been lucky that he's the type who's always got to be doing something – he's not one to get on your nerves because he's bored at home, like some men. It's been lovely sometimes to come home from work and find a meal ready. I do appreciate it. What will happen when we're both at home, I don't know.

Jim: Not working hasn't made me depressed, but it can be quite disillusioning. We'll see what it's like when Mary's at home after Christmas . . . then maybe I'll feel depressed. Now, if we have a coal bill we can pay it. After Christmas I know full well we'll either have to go short or use up the redundancy money.

Mary: We've come to terms with Jim not working. It doesn't bother me like it did, as long as the money's there. That's where the trouble will lie. At first I was shattered, I really was – it was a big blow, and I thought where on earth is he going to get another job. But after a while, we stopped bothering. I just went out and carried on and that was it. But I just don't know what'll happen after Christmas. It's the money.

*

When there's any talk of women and women's rights, single women often quite justifiably complain that their interests are ignored. The 300,000 who care for elderly and infirm relatives are rightly called the 'unsung heroines'. And when people are less anxious about female unemployment than male unemployment, they forget the single women, who don't expect anyone else to earn their bread for them. Muriel, who cares for her eighty-six-year-old mother, has been made redundant, three years short of retirement age, after thirty-two years working for the same small firm.

Muriel (Sheffield)

I first worked on a machine and then later went on to setting and supervising. When the slump came they got rid of the higher-paid people. I was next under the works manager. I earned about £72 a week and brought home about £50 of that.

I am getting about £1,500 to £2,000 redundancy, but it has been held up because at first they offered me another job, on a machine at £50 a week. But I would have brought home about £39 a week, and then it turned out that they still wanted me to do setting and supervising. They were offering me my old job back for less money. I refused. There was no guarantee that the firm wouldn't still fold, for they've got very little work, and if I had worked twelve weeks on the machine, I would have lost a quarter of my redundancy pay. Then they offered me part-time work, but that would have meant they could have sacked me after twelve weeks without notice.

It was a very small firm. It was good to work for the companionship. It was like a family, but it was us against them. It was the sort of firm that if there was any scheme going around that was to their benefit, they were very quick to find out all about it, but if it was to our benefit, they didn't want to know. But I enjoyed myself. I wouldn't have stayed there thirty-two years if I hadn't.

It was a break. In that sense, I do miss it. Since my mother had a fall, she's had to sleep downstairs here, where we've only got the one room – it's a council house. It does get all rather on top of you, the two of us in here all day. At work, I could talk to people and get a reply. Mother is getting on now. She's gone downhill these last two or three years. I wouldn't have chosen this, but I was the only child unmarried when my father had a stroke in 1948. I came home because the family wouldn't have had an income otherwise.

My father was off sick for five and a half years, then he worked more or less for five and a half years before he died, leaving me with my mother.

My oldest sister used to live over the back, and she was very good, would come in every day, but she died four years ago. I have another sister who lives in a disabled flat with her husband, and one who has slight heart trouble. She is well enough to go to Spain but she can't manage the five miles over here.

I have a younger brother. He's done well for himself, but we've seen him three times in twenty-four years.

I used to like going on holidays abroad. That was my luxury. I don't drink or smoke, I don't go out much. Reading is my pleasure. Looking after my mother, I had to get back home after work, so there wasn't much opportunity for developing a social life, making friends. But I had to give up the holidays. Last year I was going to go away. The social services could arrange for someone to come in morning and evening, but they couldn't say exactly what time. She could have been left from 5 o'clock in the evening until 9 in the morning. It's a long time, and I would have fretted, so I didn't go in the end.

I was ear-marking some of this redundancy pay for a holiday, because this year they have arranged for my mother to go into a home to give me a break, but I don't know now.

The first year off work I get unemployment pay, but after that I don't know. I will have my redundancy pay, and £3,000 I've saved – my lifetime's savings. Because of that I won't qualify for supplementary benefit, but I will have another two years to last until I'm sixty. I'd been paying into the earnings-related pension scheme for two years, but they say you have to be paying in for five years before it makes any difference. That's why I want to try to hang on to some of my redundancy pay.

I started work at fourteen and I've worked for forty-three years. I've never been out of work in my life. I don't think it's right at all. They keep on passing it round how much people get on social security but they don't at all. I'm going to have to spend my lifetime's savings. You don't mind spending when you know you can make it up, earn it again, but now I don't know I'll ever have the money to replace it. It's not a nice feeling. I do think after forty-three years the government should keep me just for the next three years.

*

While there have been claims, noticeably becoming more muted, that new technology would create new employment opportunities, when the advent of new technology is not accompanied by expanding markets, then the chip replaces workers, rather than enabling the same number of people to produce more. Much routine women's work is particularly vulnerable.

Doris (Middlesex)

I was with the company nine and a half years, and they didn't tell us about the redundancies until the week before – not even a week. There'd always been rumours, every year, but this year it happened.

They cut our department down from three typists to one. They said because of 'operational and organizational changes', but it was really the recession, too.

In my department they were going to bring in a new system, like a glorified Xerox, which runs off a number of documents in one go instead of separately as we used to type them. It's supposed to speed up the process. But sales are definitely down, which decreases the work load.

I was given to understand that the reason it was me that lost my job was because of my age. I'm fifty-three. Whether they thought I wasn't capable of using the new technology I don't know, but I've nothing against change. I like to learn new things. I'm out working because I want to work, and I've got another six years, while most young people only want to be in a job two or three years before they move off somewhere else. If I was old and my job was suffering, well fair enough, but I was told there's nothing at all wrong with my work.

It did seem to be the older people that were got rid of mostly.

The money isn't the only problem. I'm not the sort of person who likes to be at home, doing housework and shopping. I like to be out at work. I like the company and keeping my mind occupied.

It was a blow. It was so sudden. I think I could have adjusted better if it had been expected. You really don't understand how you're going to feel until it happens to you. And they were so petty about it all, they handled it very badly. It's going to happen and you can't stop it, but there's a humane way of doing it.

I don't like my own company. I don't like being here by myself. Housework and shopping isn't enough, it's just not enough. There's too many hours. I mean, I've got friends I can go and have a coffee morning with, but that's not what I want to do.

I'm looking for permanent work. At the moment I'm temping to fill in, but that finishes tomorrow, so I'm left without a job again. I'll ring the agency again, but it's a bad time.

I can live on my husband's wages. I mean, you have to if you're not working. But your standard does come down. We were preparing for when we retire, things we'd like to do, and we were saving up.

You go to work initially to look after the family and make sure they're catered for. Then when they get married and leave home, you hope to get something out of it yourself. Your standards should go up, not down.

*

As we started researching this book, the families we came across with two or more members suffering the effects of the recession were all in the industrial north and known unemployment blackspots. After six months, however, the disease had spread. Diana was made redundant because new technology has made her job redundant, and the company cannot find her new work to do, since their market is shrinking, not expanding. It might not have mattered so much but Diana's husband has been on short time for over a year now. Some weeks her twilight-shift part-time job, a classic 'mum's job', was providing not pin money but a larger share of the family income than her husband could earn. How will they cope on less than half the pay, with two small children to worry about?

Diana (Hertfordshire)

At head office, just the nine of us on my shift have been made redundant. We're all mums. It was the twilight shift, 6 p.m. to 10 p.m., when our husbands were home. They told us a few weeks ago. There was one job offered, and though I went for it, they gave it to a girl from the day shift who already had a job, who was less qualified for it than me. The union took it up as to why I didn't get that job and they said it was because I didn't seem interested in it. Which was rubbish. I really wanted that job.

I used to bring home about £60 for five nights a week. My husband used to earn what was quite a good wage, but he earns less now than he did three years ago. He's a cabinet maker, and they have been on short time for ages. They went without this year's pay rise just to get two weeks' guaranteed full-time work. He never knows from one week to the next, one day to the next, how much he will be working. He brings home anything between £50 odd a week and £80 something, so some weeks I've earned more than him.

Our children are eleven and eight. When I started work seven years ago my money was for luxuries, but as his wages have gone down and prices up, it's become so that it was for essentials, paying bills, housekeeping, the mortgage.

I've been looking for another job, but there's nothing.

Nothing definite has been said about why we're being made redundant, but it's a combination of new technology and lack of work.

I've been in computers for twenty-two years – get into computers, they said, and you can't go wrong! When we started we had to punch cards that were fed into the computer. Then we used tapes. Now it's all what they call 'on line'. It's fed into the computer and stays there. They can call it up on a VDU, and they don't need us any more.

When you're involved in it yourself you can see it all. They just don't need the people any more. Now you just have a little computer to do the job, whereas before it took machinery the size of a room. Before the present system came in – the one I'm working at – we had roomfuls of girls doing card-punching. Now the girls will do anything to get away from the punch room. They know it's bound to go.

There were nine of us on our shift but only other jobs for three. If I found a full-time job I'd work out a way to look after the kids. My friend said she'd have them for a time, so I could get round it. What would happen about the holidays I really don't know. I'll cross that bridge when I come to it. Just having a job is it. But there is no work around.

My main worry is that we'll only just about manage to live. My husband's wage depends on how much work there is to do – some weeks it's been as low as £50. If there's no work, he's not paid. I feel it's like going back to when we first got married, struggling to get things together. Life got better and all of a sudden we're back to struggling again.

In future, my child benefit is going to be housekeeping instead of new clothes for the kids. They're going to suffer. Some of the girls I work with need that money every Tuesday and without it they can't live. In the past, I've never had to be like that, but I can see me up there every Tuesday morning waiting to get it.

My big fear now is that my husband will be made redundant too. A few weeks ago they laid off quite a few. You don't know when it's going to be your turn. His company are meant to be good employers, but the furniture industry is right down. If people have got the money they're going to buy food not furniture. It's a real worry – nobody's job is secure at the moment.

Every night when he comes in through that back door and doesn't say anything about work, I think, 'Thank God, that's all right. Another day, then.'

2. Not So Equal at Work

Whatever fine-sounding laws we may have in the statute book, women haven't received all that much equality yet. This is why they and their jobs are so vulnerable to the pressures now being brought to bear to push them out of the work-force. If people – women in this case – aren't that sure of their right to work for a decent wage anyway, it's not *that* hard to shake their confidence and even to shake them out of the work-force altogether. And some never did want to join the work-force on equal terms anyway. It's one thing for a mother who is trained as a teacher or doctor to want to keep her career at least ticking over and a chance to earn some independent income. To a miner's wife equality can sound dangerously like a demand that she, too, should go down the pit.

There may indeed be a backlash to women's liberation, but that is not an indicator of extreme egalitarianism being practised between the sexes but of the small inroads that have really been made into the attitudes held by many, if not most, men and women in this country.

The quickest indicator of how far from equal at work women are is that in 1977 the average gross hourly earnings of all women workers aged eighteen and over, excluding the effects of overtime and shift work, were 75.5 per cent of the male equivalent; in 1980 this had dwindled to 73.5 per cent. This difference in pay reflects a wide range of pressures on women who go out to work.

There's no doubt that in themselves most women want to work. Even before the recession, there was no shortage of female labour, which might have pushed up the rates of pay. Employers rarely need to compete for women workers. In the 1970s alone, about one million more women entered the labour force.

Figure 1. Married women in work. (Catherine Hakim, *Occupational Segregation*, Research Paper No. 9, Department of Employment, Fig. 1, p 5.)

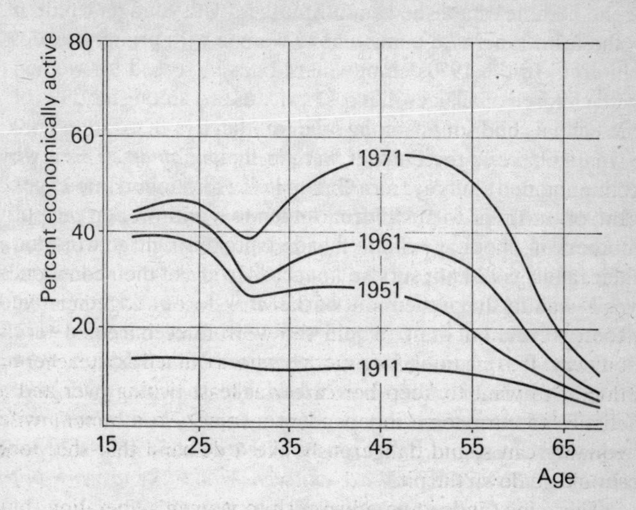

Today women make up around 40 per cent of the labour force. By 1977, 52 per cent of mothers were in employment, 58 per cent of all married women and 67 per cent of all women without dependants. However, other estimates indicate that the real figures may have been even higher, because mothers with young children are frequently intermittent workers and the percentage recorded as working will depend on how the statistics were collected. Many more may have worked or be expecting to work within, say, a six-month period than will be working the week the researcher calls. Janice (page 93) is typical of this pattern of working which tends to lead to dead-end jobs, and being vulnerable to redundancy on the last-in first-out principle.

What was clear was that increasing numbers of married women were either in or seeking employment, and this trend looked likely to continue until hit by the recession. What's more, while in the 1950s it was the women with children of secondary school age who started to return to work, during the 1960s the trend became established among mothers with younger children – the fastest increase being among women with primary school children. In the 1970s employment rates increased for women with children of all ages, but rose twice as fast among mothers of pre-school children as among other mothers.

In 1979, while the authors were both at *Woman's Own*, we commissioned a survey from Gallup Poll which found that 25 per cent of mothers with children under five and 42 per cent of mothers of school-age children had a paid job.[1] One quarter said their family could not survive financially without their earnings. While one in five would not work if it were not for economic necessity, four out of five would want to work even if there were no financial pressure. Among mothers without a paid job, even more mothers of under-fives would like to work than have actually managed to arrange it. *Twenty-seven per cent of mothers with under-fives would like to go out to work but don't, and 20 per cent of mothers of school-age children would like to work but can't get a job for one reason or another.*

At school, however, too many girls drastically under-estimate their future desire and need to work, even after they will have attained the goals of marriage and motherhood. They think of their working life as a short span to take them into at most their early twenties, when they expect to have their first child, but no further. In fact, quite apart from the fact that the majority of women living with their husbands work these days, and there would be three times as many families living in poverty if wives didn't work, one married woman in six finds herself alone at least for a time, often with dependent children to support. Louise (page 96) thought her dreams had come true when she was married at nineteen and expecting a few months later, but by the time the baby was six months old she was a single parent and hadn't the training that would have enabled her to support herself and her child.

Instead of acting as a counter-balance to traditional

stereotyped ideas the children will have picked up anyway (it's been found that parents even hold and talk to baby girls differently from baby boys) teachers too often reinforce these attitudes, probably unintentionally. Girls, even at pre-school and primary levels, are encouraged to develop verbal rather than mechanical or spatial skills and later are nudged into more 'feminine' subjects. Girls are expected to be more polite and acquiescent, whereas boys are expected and allowed to be more disruptive, individualistic and aggressive. Co-educational schools have been found to be if anything worse in getting pupils to cross traditional subject boundaries. This may be due to modelling as well as peer-group pressure. In a single-sex girls' school there is a better chance that sciences and maths will be taught by a woman rather than a man.

At eleven, girls are on average three months ahead on reading and writing, although boys do better at arithmetic. By fifteen, boys have caught up in reading and drawn ahead in scientific, mathematical and mechanical subjects. At thirteen or fourteen, boys more often choose physics and chemistry, and girls biology and languages. One in five girls has dropped science entirely by the fifth year.

Education is covered by the Sex Discrimination Act. In theory at least, schools are not supposed to divide pupils for subjects by sex, but there is still little positive action in schools to encourage pupils to make more informed choices. As Lady Howe, when deputy chairman of the Equal Opportunities Commission, pointed out, 'Nationally careers guidance is a disgracefully neglected subject. It is often a question of too little and too late. Careers should not be regarded as a peripheral part of the general timetable, usually squeezed in during the fifth year. They must be at the heart of all subject choices made at school.

'If a first-year girl prefers to opt for needlework and art instead of metalwork and technical drawing, she is not making an informed choice unless someone has explained to her what this may mean in terms of job and pay later on, and unless someone has taken trouble to ensure that it is a decision, and not merely a passive acceptance of prejudiced assumptions, how can

Figure 2. GGE O level passes (A-C grades only) by sex and selected subjects (summer examinations). England and Wales, 1978.

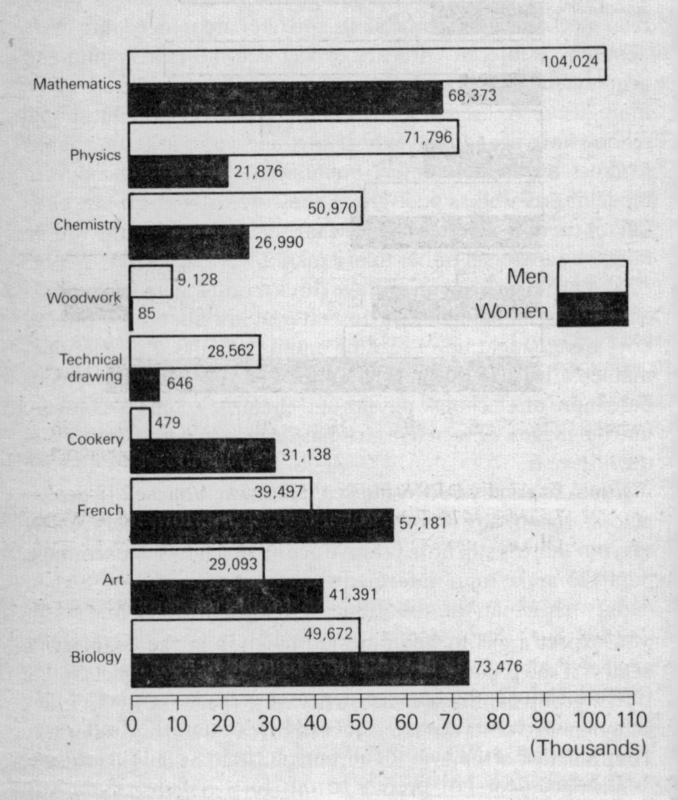

Source: England – DES *Statistics of Education*, Volume 2, *School Leavers, 1978.* Table 26. Wales – Figures supplied by Welsh Office.

Figure 3. GCE A level passes by sex and selected subjects (summer examinations). England and Wales, 1978.

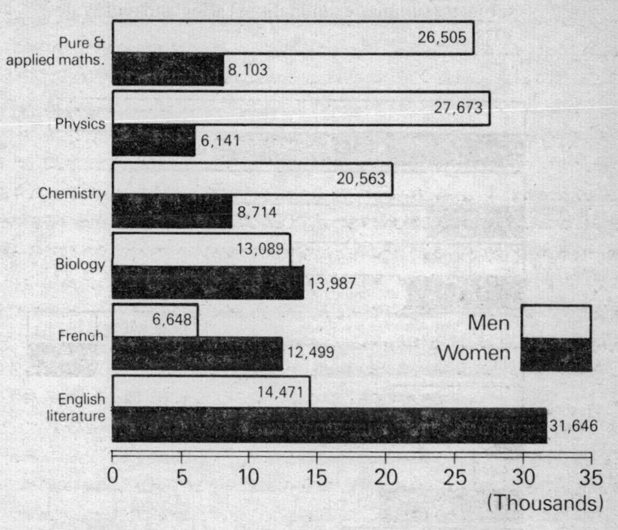

Source: England – DES *Statistics of Education,* Volume 2, *School Leavers, 1978*, Table 27. Wales – Figures supplied by Welsh Office.

you expect a girl to be interested in a job in the engineering sector, if she is not even given access to the basic subjects.'

The group of fifth-formers we talked to (page 100) at an Essex school proud of its academic record revealed some wonderfully contradictory attitudes – liberation tended to be only skin-deep. While one insisted she wasn't getting married before she was all of twenty-two – 'Well, I don't think so' – the choice careers still seemed to be working with animals and children, while the boys 'hog the computers'.

Mandy (page 103) did work with children – she became a mother's help. Only gradually she realized that the pay is too low

Figure 4. Full-time undergraduate students by sex and selected subjects (universities only). Great Britain, December 1978.

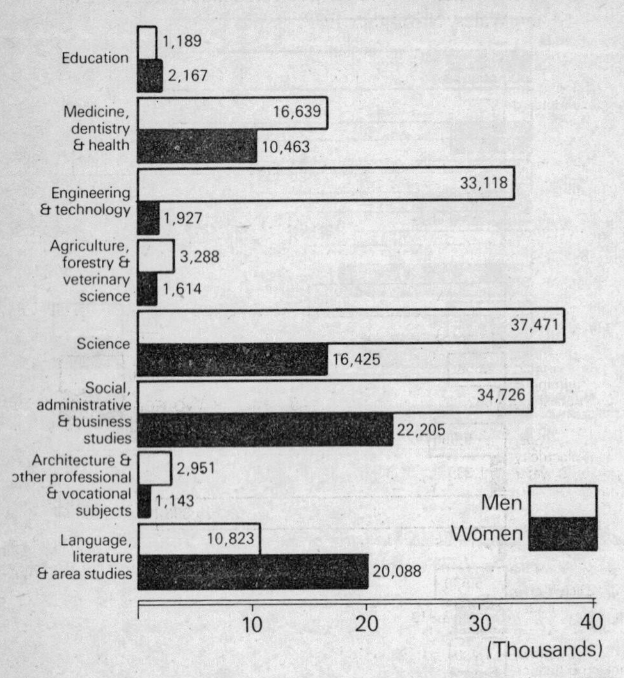

Source: DES *Statistics of Education*, Volume 6, *Universities 1978*, Table 1.

for saving and if you lose your job you lose your place to live. Such 'women's work' is a dead end.

Tables of O-level and A-level passes show sex discrimination well under way (pages 76, 77).

Tables for undergraduates and working youngsters attending day-release courses emphasize how girls are either training for less lucrative employment or not training at all.

Figure 5. Students aged sixteen to eighteen released by their employers during working hours to take part-time courses at maintained, assisted and grant-aided major establishments. By sex and selected industries. England and Wales, November 1978.

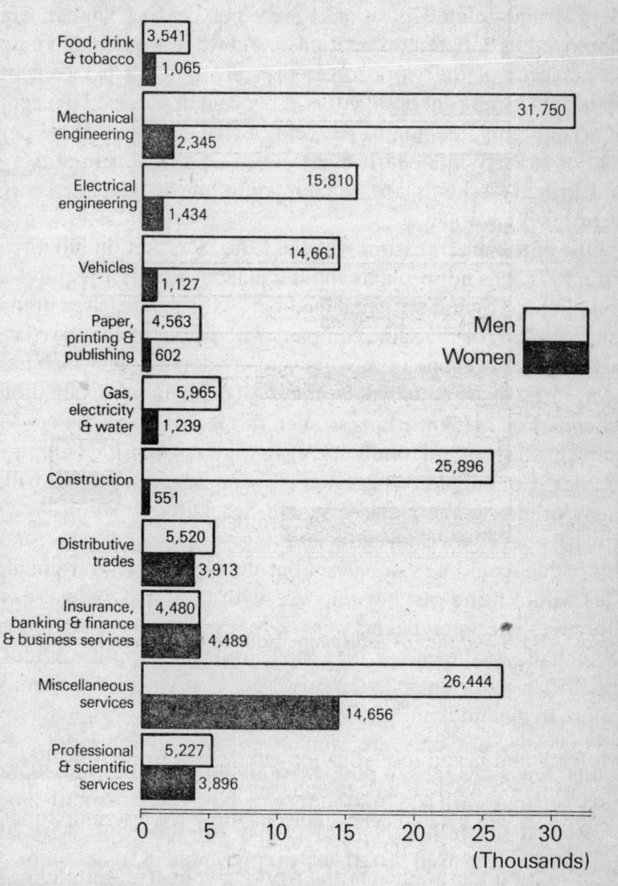

Source: DES *Statistics of Education*, Volume 3, *Further Education 1978*, Table 12.

As a result the work-force is still clearly segregated, with the men doing most of the higher-paid jobs in higher-paid industries and occupations. Over half of all female manual workers are employed in cleaning, catering, hairdressing and other personal services, while over half of all female non-manual workers are in clerical and related positions. Sixty per cent of women are employed in only ten occupations. And while women make up 40 per cent of the work-force, they are only 13 per cent of managers, 6 per cent of solicitors, 1 per cent of judges, 2 per cent of accountants, less than 1 per cent of civil engineers and 3 per cent of MPs. While nearly eight out of ten teachers in nursery and primary schools are women, only one in ten university lecturers is a woman.

One of the main reasons why the Equal Pay Act, in full force from 1975, has not brought about equal pay is that it requires a complainant to find an actual member of the opposite sex doing the same job for the same company with whom to compare her pay, or else someone of the opposite sex doing a job which has been rated as of equal value under a company job-evaluation scheme. For many working women this is near impossible – 45 per cent still work in totally segregated jobs. The Equal Opportunities Commission suggested an amendment (along with many others to the Equal Pay and Sex Discrimination Acts) which would give a claim to those doing work of equal value, and this 'value' could be established through an industrial tribunal. This would bring our law into line with the EEC's equal-pay directive. The amendments were not enthusiastically received in Whitehall. At the end of 1981 the European Commission took the British government to the European Court of Justice over its failure to amend the Equal Pay Act.

However, not only are women grouped in low-pay, low-status, low-skills jobs in poorly paid industries, they also work less overtime, earn less from shift-work bonuses, work part-time – often at lower hourly rates of pay for the same work as full-timers – and aren't so strongly represented in trades unions.

Most working women feel their first responsibility is towards their home and family. They look for work which will enable

Table 2: Women's gross weekly earnings as a percentage of men's in the same occupation. The comparison is between women at eighteen and men at twenty-one years.

	Women as a percentage of the occupational work-force	*Women's gross weekly earnings as a percentage of men's in the same occupation*
Non-manual		
(part) Clerical and related	75.0	71.7
Professional and related in education, welfare and health	65.8	70.1
(part) Selling	61.3	50.1
Professional and related supporting management and administration	13.8	73.3
Managerial (excluding general management)	12.9	61.8
Managerial (general management)	7.8	—
Professional and related in science, engineering, technology and similar fields	6.8	63.0
Manual		
Catering, cleaning, hairdressing and other personal services	76.3	69.0
Painting, repetitive assembling	47.8	64.2
Materials processing (excluding metal)	24.8	59.8
Making and repairing (excluding metal and electrical)	37.4	57.8
Processing, making, repairing and related (metal and electrical)	5.3	62.9
Product packaging and related Transport, operating, materials moving and storing and related	5.3	63.8

Source: Department of Employment *New Earnings Survey 1979*, Part E (1% sample), Table 135, pp. E46, and E47.

them to combine domestic responsibilities with work. The number of hours they work and where the job is are of paramount importance. Government estimates suggest that 40 per cent of all women workers work part-time and between 1971 and 1976 the number of female part-timers rose by 800,000 (a 30 per cent increase). Almost all the growth in employment in service industries between 1961 and 1971 was due to the 1.2 million extra women workers and *nearly all* these extra women workers were part-timers. Similarly in manufacturing, where full-time female employment *fell* by 16 per cent over the same period, part-time employment *increased* by 21 per cent. By 1977, 69 per cent of all working mothers were employed on a part-time basis, and mothers accounted for two out of every three part-time workers. In fact Britain has the highest percentage of part-time workers among their female work-force of any country in the western world. By 1976 one in six of the total work population in Britain was a female part-time worker.

While part-time work enables a woman to combine her domestic and work responsibilities, it very often disadvantages her at work. Marion, whom we met in the East End of London, works one day a week in a shop for a net profit of £4 (see page 112). Linda (page 115), who wrote to me at the *Sun*, works three evenings a week for £15.72. Part-time work in general is low-paid, low-status and unskilled or semi-skilled. The Gallup Poll survey for *Woman's Own* found that almost two thirds of working mothers (most of them working part-time) do semi-skilled or unskilled manual work compared with one third of women generally and only one-fifth of men. The mothers then averaged earnings of 90p per hour compared with current average rates of £1.48 for women generally and £2.49 for male workers. If we had been able to isolate a figure for the earnings of women without dependent children, the contrast would have been far greater, since the earnings rates for women generally included these low-paid mothers.

While to some extent this may be, as Mrs Thatcher suggested to us when we discussed the findings of our survey with her, because many mothers want only less demanding work without responsibility, the vast postbag we received as a result of the survey made it clear that there are many more mothers who would welcome better-paid, more stimulating work, if only it were on offer part-time. Barbara was one of thousands of mothers who wrote to us when we were campaigning, as a result of the survey, for 'Fair care for children and a fair deal for Mum'. We quote her letter (page 124) along with a few others. She was a cleaner in 1979 but 'trying to find a more interesting job'. I heard from her again in 1981. She was still a cleaner.

And not only have employers, and unions, a tendency to guard the better jobs for full-time workers, often identical work is paid at a worse hourly rate if done part-time rather than full-time.

This is another type of discrimination that slips through loopholes in the Equal Pay and Sex Discrimination Acts. In 1976 *Meeks* v. *the National Union of Agricultural and Allied Workers*, Mrs Meeks claimed unlawful sex discrimination because she worked as a part-time secretary and earned a lower hourly rate than the full-timers. She claimed discrimination against part-timers amounts to discrimination against women as most part-timers are women. The industrial tribunal rejected the claim, saying the Sex Discrimination Act does not apply to pay. It also said a claim under the Equal Pay Act could not succeed unless she could compare herself with a man doing the same job. There were no full-time male secretaries in her office.

Other cases to try to establish that part-time work should be paid pro-rata with full-time work have also failed, to date, though this is another loophole that the Equal Opportunities Commission would plug with their recommendations.

In the longer term, part-time work provides very little opportunity for training and promotion. Also, it restricts access to pension rights and fringe benefits, so that taken over a lifetime a woman's earnings turn out to be considerably less than a man's. Employers often look upon part-timers as 'fringe workers' who can be taken on or laid off with ease depending on the work available. Part-time workers are not covered by a number of statutory rights. For example people working less than sixteen hours a week (unless they work more than eight hours *and* have five years' continuous employment with the same employer) are not entitled to:

- redundancy payments from the state redundancy scheme
- claim against unfair dismissal
- payment for temporary lay-off
- pay statements showing how their earnings are arrived at
- certain maternity benefits – the right to return to work, maternity pay and a certain amount of protection against dismissal for pregnancy reasons

The career break is particularly difficult to navigate successfully. Our maternity rights are almost the meanest in Europe – only women in Ireland are entitled to less. If they do manage to get back to work, mothers are particularly vulnerable to poor rates of pay because there is so little provision for their children.

Adding together all nurseries, nursery schools, places with childminders and playgroups, there are places for something like 40 per cent of under-fives, while parents want places for two thirds of that age group. If 40 per cent sounds surprisingly good, you have to remember that a very large percentage of these places are part-time, ranging from five mornings a week in a reception class to one two-hour session *a week* in a playgroup. Playgroups have provided an invaluable service by giving children an opportunity for stimulating play and companionship, but their methods and times of operation actually mean that children of working mothers are *less* likely to attend them than other children, and what is called 'part-time' in connection with places for under-fives rarely covers the hours considered to be part-time by employers. When an employer does tailor hours to suit mothers, he usually expects to pay a lower rate for the job in exchange for being so amenable. You could call it blackmail. Few women's jobs pay well enough for them to be able to afford to pay privately for good substitute care for their children. Many women, like Annette (page 116), are forced to give up work altogether through lack of good back-up child-care facilities.

In the Gallup Poll survey for *Woman's Own* the working mothers with pre-school children gave as the *main* care used for their children while they were at work:

	Percentage
Local authority day-nursery	3
Employer's crèche	1
Local authority nursery school	1
Private nursery school	1
Playgroup	1
Paid childminder	8
Husband at home	64
Mother takes child to work	4
Unpaid friend or relative	8
No care	3
Other	6

Further working hours and/or times when these arrangements broke down for one reason or another were covered as follows:

	Percentage
Playgroup	1
Paid childminder	8
Husband at home	6
Mother takes child to work	6
Unpaid friend or relative	40
No care	11

Because they could only work during hours when their husband was at home, one third of these mothers of pre-school children were working evenings or nights – which could only be a strain on them, their health and energy and probably their marriage.

Of mothers who were not working but wanted to, one in ten had been forced to give up work because she could not make satisfactory arrangements for her children. (The 3 per cent of mothers who were working and left under-fives regularly without adult care clearly had not been able to make satisfactory arrangements. Sonia's story, page 121, shows the heartbreak that can be involved.)

One third of mothers wanting to work said that what was preventing them finding another job was the difficulty of finding work that fitted in with family commitments and/or employers' attitudes to mothers.

More than two thirds of mothers wanted places for their children in properly equipped and staffed nurseries or nursery schools. Only 5 per cent actually had such places.

Problems don't end when the children reach school age. After-school and school-holiday care, common in France and Sweden, is virtually unheard of here. A mother is caught in the Catch-22 that few well-paid (let alone interesting and responsible) jobs are available that fit in with school hours. Because the hours she can work are so inflexible, her bargaining powers with the potential employer – perhaps for a better rate of pay – are very limited. He knows she has little choice. If there is a good part-time job available, she may have to miss it because the timing is just half an hour out. Even if she should find one of the few stimulating, decently paid jobs within school hours, who is going to look after the children during the school holidays? While the number of mothers who have after-school and holiday play-scheme places for their children that actually cover working hours is so tiny as to be statistically insignificant, 96 per cent in the Gallup survey wanted holiday play-schemes for their children, and four out of five thought there should be after-school care.

It's estimated that there are about half a million 'latch-key' children – children who come home to an empty house or are left alone during the hours the parents work during the school holidays. Perhaps there are some parents who put material comfort before their children's welfare, but there isn't even the amount of care needed in this country to help single parents, let alone anyone else. What sort of a choice do 'caring' politicians, who claim to have the family's interests at heart, give mothers who must choose between a life of grinding poverty on supplementary benefit, which necessarily deprives their children, and leaving the children alone while they work to earn their family something like a decent – though it will not be luxurious – standard of living?

Quite apart from the practical problems faced by women trying to combine work and family responsibilities, and coping with employers' willingness to exploit their difficulties, the *expectations* that they will leave work at some time in order to have a family – the broken career pattern – reduces their lifetime earnings in a number of ways.

It may affect the decision whether or not to undertake extensive education or training. It may reduce the amount of on-the-job training a woman is prepared to undergo (a four-year apprenticeship may seem a waste of time if one is planning to start a family and leave anyway). Thirdly, the loss of experience and depreciation of skills during absence from the labour force will result in future lost earnings. The latter point is particularly important in occupations where there are very structured career paths and where the climb up the promotional ladder depends on continuous service.

Employers' attitudes towards employing women and offering them equal access to training opportunities don't help. Work is managed on the whole by men for men fulfilling traditional stereotyped roles. The rigid organizational structures in career paths, staffing structures, pension rights, hours of work, etc., give little room for flexibility. This is primarily a barrier to wives and mothers, but the carry-over of attitudes can affect women with no ties, and the practical effects can also make it difficult for a man who chooses or has to take his family responsibilities seriously, as the film *Kramer vs. Kramer* brought home to millions, when the dad caring for his son alone lost his job because he was no longer willing to be an 8 a.m. to 8 p.m. company man.

What is rarely questioned is whether the demands made of workers wanting to climb the promotional ladder are either necessary or even beneficial. Do we want all consultants in obstetrics and gynaecology to be men? Men who, if they have children, have had time to see precious little of them while they were little? Wouldn't domestic architects benefit more from time spent experiencing the needs of the home environment – during the day, when the kids are up and about – than by attending national and international conferences to talk to other architects who also see precious little of their homes?

Few companies (about seventy at the last count) offer crèche facilities for employees. Few companies have formal equal-opportunities policies. Even among those that do, it is not always clear exactly what the policy is intended to achieve. One company who claimed to have a formal monitored policy of equal opportunity for its female staff said later that they didn't employ female sales reps because they would be worried about the effects on other companies she may visit! So old attitudes die hard, and many firms will still be reluctant to take on a woman trainee, particularly in traditionally male jobs, because 'she will eventually leave to have a family'.

An Equal Opportunities Commission Survey of 500 companies found that only 25 per cent had formal equal-opportunity policies and that only 15 per cent had carried out job-evaluation studies. Among management there was massive ignorance of opportunities and initiatives open to them under both the Equal Pay and Sex Discrimination Acts. Women, too, are staggeringly ignorant of what rights they do have. A recent EEC Survey[2] found that 42 per cent of working women in Britain either think there are no laws to demand equality of treatment with men at work, or don't know about them; 68 per cent either don't know whether trade unions are concerned with problems of equality between men and women at work, or think they are either not concerned or ineffective.

What *are* the unions doing to help? Women make up around a third of the total membership of unions affiliated to the TUC and between 1968 and 1978 the number of women in trade unions nearly doubled. However, there are very few women full-time officers and very few women serve on executive councils. Even at a local level, although there are a higher number of women representatives, only a small proportion serve as shop stewards or branch secretaries. Why is this? The answer is very complicated. Traditionally women workers have tended not to organize in the way that men have. Also, in the past trade-union bargaining has concentrated on the man, as the main breadwinner, and therefore the women have been marginal to the main union activity.

There is, of course, also the problem women face in attending union meetings. Unless they are held in working hours it can be almost impossible for women with domestic responsibilities to get to them. Even if they are held at the work-place during lunch breaks many women have to shop then and therefore can't attend. In addition, as one active woman trade-unionist said, union meetings are very boring, so why should people bother to go?

Another factor may be that many working women, if they are looking after a family as well, literally do not have the time or energy to devote to union matters. Many union officials work extremely long hours and carry heavy responsibilities. This, for many women on top of an extremely long working week (paid and unpaid), would be an impossible burden.

Then again, as we have already seen, many women are part-timers, and until recently many unions have fought against firms employing part-time workers because they fear they will undermine the jobs of their full-time members.

So it is probably fair to say that in the main unions haven't done much for women workers. Collective bargaining has concentrated on pay and conditions at work and priority has been given to the needs of the male 'breadwinner'. Consequently little attention has been given to the needs of women – in terms of hours, crèche facilities, shopping arrangements, time off, etc. As far as part-time work is concerned, the unions haven't wanted to know.

Times are changing slowly. More unions have active women's committees who are concentrating on issues particularly affecting women. Some unions, most notably the NUJ, are pressing for child-care schemes to be part of their arrangements and in some cases have negotiated crèche facilities successfully. Others are pushing for improved maternity benefits over and above the statutory minima and in some cases are seeking paternity leave, too. The TUC has recommended that all its affiliated unions include an equality clause – including pay and opportunity – in their agreements. However, without *active* grass-roots commitment to support such a clause, little action is taken to improve women's pay or conditions at work.

With this in mind the TUC is now moving towards 'positive action' for women. At a special conference called by the General Council in November 1980, various methods of strengthening the existing legislation in order to improve women's job opportunities were considered.

The conference was attended by 200 delegates from forty-eight unions representing eleven million workers of whom four million are women. Overwhelmingly the delegates argued in favour of some form of positive action either through collective bargaining or with legal enforcement. This means that there is a growing support within certain areas of the union movement actually to *do* something to improve pay and working conditions for women rather than merely sit back and talk about it, though there must be a question mark over what chance this has as the dole queues lengthen.

The TUC has brought out a 'Charter for Under-Fives' which outlines proposals for a comprehensive policy for government and employers to ensure that there are adequate child-care facilities for children under five and also that their parents – mothers and fathers – can have time off when the child is very young. The Charter also advocates consideration of part-time work or job-sharing schemes for either parent and urges unions to recruit part-time workers and improve their pay and conditions so that they are at least pro-rata with the full-time workers with whom they work.

Undoubtedly in the past ten years unions have begun to move forward and concern themselves with the needs of their women workers. This has coincided with a dramatic growth in the number of women trade-unionists. The unions are being urged by the TUC to negotiate far more effectively on behalf of their women members to improve pay and conditions and to press for positive action to improve women's employment opportunities.

Nevertheless, there is a long way to go. The main obstacles to progress lie not in TUC policies, which on the whole are egalitarian, but at the grass-roots, where changes to help women still tend to be the first clauses thrown out of a conditions and wages agreement in the bargaining process, and where many male trade-unionists are far from in favour of women working at all or at best hold very ambivalent attitudes. A man may know his own wife *has* to work for their family to have food and clothes, but inside he still feels that he *should be* the total breadwinner, so he battles to get men's wages up, not for equality in the work-place.

The extent to which trade unions have developed tunnel vision about which workers' interests they will really fight to protect – rather than pay mere lip-service to – is shown by the plight of home-workers, sometimes called out-workers.

This hidden army of about a quarter of a million, mostly women, who work at home, is generally agreed to be the most exploited sector of the British work-force.

They suffer in an extreme form the penalties suffered by women who want part-time work to fit in with domestic responsibilities. Home-workers are usually barred from finding normal work outside the home because they have children too small to leave and cannot find reliable substitute care for them, have a dependant such as an infirm parent they cannot leave, have a language problem, live in a very rural area, or are themselves disabled, or a combination of these. Anxious to earn just something to eke out a very low income – most are living at or below supplementary benefit level – they work for as little as 5p an hour knitting, like Iris (page 119), 50p for addressing envelopes or 70p to 75p an hour for manufacturing work. By comparison the poorest 10 per cent of female manual workers in 1980 earned £1.22 an hour in factories. Examples sent to Frank White, Labour MP for Bury and Radcliffe, leading a battle to get legislation introduced to protect home-workers, or uncovered by researchers, included one woman, using her kitchen as a workshop, filling 4,000 tins of baby powder a week and packing them in 240 tin cartons, for which she was paid 30p a box, or £5 weekly. And she paid her own bus fare to the factory to deliver the finished goods. Another sewed together umbrella panels, eight lines of stitching for each, at 75p per dozen completed umbrellas.

As well as abysmal rates of pay, home-workers often run health hazards from paint fumes, airborne dust and unprotected machinery. So do their children.

Home-workers often do not know who else is working for their employers and are often desperate to keep their jobs. They dare not press individually for improved pay and conditions, in case their job is simply given to someone else, and they cannot get together with other workers for a strong bargaining position.

Until very recently unions have been unwilling to help home-workers. They saw them as a threat to full-time employment in factories and offices, which they held to be the desirable work pattern. The fact that it is a work pattern effectively barred to some very needy members of society – mostly women – did not seem to bother them or their members.

*

Getting a picture of the pressures working against women being able comfortably to hold down decent jobs, we talked to a hospital consultant in London and a home-worker on a Bradford council estate, to a group of bright-eyed schoolgirls and a divorcee less than ten years older who had tried to kill her baby and herself.

Mothers aren't divided like sheep and goats into those who stay at home full-time and those who look for paid employment. Not only do most working mothers work part-time, perhaps only a few hours a week, they also tend to drift in and out of work. They have a job for a while, then the shortcomings of that arrangement get too much, or they have another child. A spell at home runs down family finances, so then they seek another job. The drawback is that it is very difficult for them either to push for decent rates of pay or to get any consistent job experience which might help them to get work when the family needs the money and jobs are in short supply, and to move on to more interesting and responsible work should they want it some time in the future. They usually have a series of rather poorly paid dead-end jobs.

Janice (East London)

Before I had my first child I was an audio-typist and telex operator. I was made redundant when I was four months pregnant. I could have done temporary work but didn't like the idea of the travelling. Although my husband was only bringing home £30 a week, I intended to stay at home about a year. I knew I wanted more than one child, but I wanted to be at home with that one for about a year so that I could give some time to him and then would think more of myself. As it happened, just before he was a year old I went back to work full-time as a typist in a hospital. My mum looked after Billy during the day.

I enjoyed it, but it was very hard work, and I gave it up after a month because I just couldn't keep up with it and cope with the baby. I didn't have a washing machine at the time, for example, and I found it very difficult working 9 to 5 and then coming back and looking after a baby and home.

Then I managed after the hospital to get a part-time typing job with a freight company, from 9 to 2, which paid £23 for five days, which wasn't bad for 1974. I'm sure that part-time rates of pay are lower than full-time, but even so I was getting almost as much for the part-time job with the freight company as I got at the hospital. I stayed there eight months, then I decided I'd had enough, and soon after got pregnant again.

It wasn't that I could afford to give up work, I just couldn't stand it any more, and there wasn't anything else that didn't involve a lot of travelling. Also I didn't want to leave it too long before another baby. Apart from the fact that a long gap isn't fair on the kids, I thought I'd get past the stage of wanting another.

I was at home for three years. We weren't exactly rich, but we managed. If we went out once in six months it was something to shout about. I didn't go out myself at all, neither did the kids, really. Billy was at nursery, and I'd take James to my mother, and that sort of thing, but evenings we'd just sit in and watch television.

Then the chance of a job at the hospital came up, helping to do the evening meal from 5.30 to 8. The money was good, £27 a week just for that, but the problem was I had to work Saturday and Sunday, just one day off a week. I did it for eleven months. I gave it up mainly because my husband got a bit cheesed off with cooking the evening meal for himself and the kids, and putting them to bed before I got home.

He's always agreed that I should work if I wanted to, but obviously he wasn't keen on evening work because it affected him. He wanted me to find somebody to look after the youngest during the day and do it that way. As for housework, he'll do certain things without batting an eyelid – he'll Hoover and make beds – but he absolutely hates to wash up and now he hates to look after Diane, our third and youngest. She's very much a mummy's girl and doesn't like me to leave her, so she gets upset and he gets upset because he really can't cope with her. The boys are fine, he's very good with them. Before Diane was born, he wasn't very keen; he thought two was enough, but I did want one more. I hoped it would be a girl. She was born nearly a year after I left the hospital job.

I was a childminder for a while. I looked after a little girl from 7 till 5, and then I took on a little boy from 8.30 till 5, so I had the two of them and James at home. It was nice in the summer, going down to the park with them. Then the girl left – her mother was laid off work – and the boy left in March, because his mother was finding it hard to cope.

Money was tight, but it seemed easier expecting Diane than it was after I'd had Billy and was expecting James. My husband was earning more, but still not a lot – about £60 a week. Out of that the rent for our council flat was £9.20, about £6 or £7 a week in the slot meter, and electricity bills around £50 a quarter, not a lot to play with.

Diane was born in August and I started this job in October.

But I didn't really intend to go back to work so soon after Diane was born. What happened was we had a speaker at our mothers and toddlers group about setting up a child-care project in our area for mums, mainly those with under-fives, who wanted to work but were finding it hard. I found it very interesting, and when she came back a couple of weeks after, she said the project needed a part-time administrative worker, three or four hours for five days a week. I applied, even though I didn't really expect to get the job.

It was a harrowing experience to be interviewed by a panel of four women – they wanted to know not just how many words a minute could I type but fired all sorts of questions – why did I want the job? did I think child care was important? why did I believe kids were just as well off with their mums working? I was trying to get my brain to work fast enough to answer them without making a fool of myself. But to my surprise I got the job.

The way it works now, Billy's at school, James is at nursery, and my friend who lives opposite has Diane for the few hours that I'm here. I take home about £130 a month, and give my friend £5 a week for looking after Diane. She's not a registered childminder though by rights she should be. I've told her all about it.

I'm still registered myself. When I started here, the health visitor at the clinic said there was a woman who wanted someone to take her little girl to and from school and keep her until 7 p.m., so I do that now. She pays me £6, which pays for Diane going to my friend. It's an amazing sort of patchwork, isn't it, the children and the mothers?

As for the job here, I'm finding it difficult to accept the responsibility – I've never had to do it before, I've just been a typist and someone's come along and said 'do this'. But it's good, because if someone's always telling you what to do, you're just a machine, whereas if you've got to think about things and make decisions, whether you make the right ones or not, it makes you realize you're not such an idiot after all, not just a stupid cabbage fit only to sit in a corner or bring up kids. I've proved that I can do more, and I think a lot more women could do the same.

I know a lot of my friends would dearly love to go out to work, for example, but it's impossible because they have young children, they haven't got friends who can look after them, there aren't enough nurseries. There's no one they can turn to.

*

Louise never saw herself as a career girl. She thought her dreams of happiness had come true when she was married at nineteen and expecting a few months later. But by the time the baby was six months old she was a single-parent family. Not having the training needed to land a job paying enough to support a family, the grim loneliness of her life in a dismal flat on supplementary benefit led to tragedy.

Louise (Essex)

I left school when I was sixteen. I didn't really want to leave but I didn't have enough qualifications to go to music college, which I would have liked, so I had several jobs but couldn't stick with them. I wasn't trained for anything. It was a very traumatic life at home. My mum and dad were always arguing. I left home soon after I was sixteen. I met Tracy's dad when I was eighteen and we started to live together. We got married when I was nineteen and he was twenty-five and seven months later I was pregnant.

I really wanted a child, someone I could give the love and affection that I missed out on, or at least that I felt I had, being one of six. But within months of Tracy being born I left her dad. We did have love and affection for each other, but he was a drinker and smacked me about.

At first we were homeless and living in a reception centre. I wasn't sleeping and what with Tracy not sleeping and what was going on between her dad and me, it was too much to handle. I had a pretty traumatic time leading up to divorce and custody and I was allotted a social worker.

I didn't have a job – I felt I couldn't work because I had a child.

Even now I feel very divided. I wanted to work and I wanted to be available to my child. I didn't want to give anyone else the responsibility of looking after her. I wanted to be the one to see her grow. At the same time I wanted to provide, which I couldn't do. The real difficulty was that because I'm not qualified I couldn't make enough money to really provide for us. I might earn say £35, but I'd have been worse off than on supplementary benefit. Mentally though, I'd have been better off. Mentally I needed a job.

So I had to go on to supplementary benefit. I was lucky in that I knew what I was entitled to, having worked for a while in a social security office. But it was pretty tight to manage with a six-month-old child, having to provide clothes, toys, food, everything, all out of supplementary. It was quite a struggle.

Jerry did make regular payments for a while, but then social security took it all over. He did have a good job when we were married which often got thrown up in my face. The fact that he worked and I didn't. But at the same time he believed my place was in the home, so I couldn't win. I wasn't allowed out unless I needed to buy something.

Soon after the divorce I moved into a council flat, but it was very sub-standard accommodation. I didn't realize what it was like until I moved in. It's old, in a bad area. You'd go out in the afternoon and get mugged by the kids. I mean, a couple of three-year-olds nicked some sweets out of my hand, that's how rough it was. You'd complain to their mums and they didn't want to know, they'd slam the door.

Once or twice a week the social worker used to come round. Sometimes I thought it was just being nosy, but there were times when I welcomed it. One day I just told my social worker how bad I was feeling and Tracy was given a nursery place.

I did try to get a job while she was at nursery but there wasn't anything available, not with the right hours. And again, because I'm not qualified, I couldn't have made enough money if I'd gone to work, after stoppages, fares and nursery fees, because you pay more fees according to what you earn. In the end I had a breakdown, which was quite bad, after all the trouble with divorce, maintenance and rehousing. Tracy at this time was fifteen months. I enjoyed bringing her up but there were problems. I mean, having to look after her and everything, it was just a lot. It's difficult being a single parent.

You feel so down when you're stuck in the house all the time and you don't really get a break. You've never enough money to go anywhere. Even when she was at nursery there was not much I could do, only a bit of shopping. I guess it's just the loneliness. It's nice seeing the baby grow, but there's no company.

I was very depressed and wanted to kill myself, but at the same time I had a young child. I didn't want her to be left to anybody and the chances were she would have gone to her father or my family, which I didn't want. So I thought, if I leave this world my child comes with me. But I couldn't do anything to myself until I had done it on her first. In fact what I tried to do was smother her with a pillow, but I got so far and couldn't do it any more. Then I tried to drown her in the bath, but I couldn't carry that through either.

I told the health visitor I couldn't cope any more. I didn't tell her more than that and I went into hospital that day. Tracy was fostered out. After three weeks I told them what had happened. I stayed in for four months and Tracy joined me the day I came out.

Tracy was on the at-risk register a long time. I don't know if she still is now – she's seven. I have never hit her. I've smacked her, but never hit.

I had one more breakdown, about two years ago. Tracy was put in a children's home for eight months. I went to see her every day, which was a journey of two hours. When she was taken I was told I had to sign on for employment. I said I couldn't do a full-time job because of going to see Tracy but they said you'll still have to sign on.

I tried for a few morning jobs, but there were no part-time jobs. I wanted something from 7 to 11, in order to be able to see Tracy before she went to bed. There was nothing going at all except for one miles away paying £10. It would have cost me that in fares, so I ended up on the dole.

There should be more part-time jobs with a decent wage. One thing I've noticed is that you'll get shops with two part-timers instead of one full-time, and they don't divide it so each gets half the full wage. It'll be £15 each, say, instead of the full-timer's £50.

I think they should give more consideration to women, especially women with children. The jobs there are for women are often for women as women, not women as mothers. And whether women are married or not, they still have the problem of children. If anything happens to your child you feel it's your responsibility. If your child is sick you don't know in advance, and you can't be in two places at once. It happened to me once, I took Tracy down to the doctor's and lost the job I had. You're put in a position where you really don't know what to do. Then there's the problem of school holidays.

I'm now in a hostel with Tracy, waiting to be rehoused. I've still got the old flat, but even the courts said I shouldn't go back there. It's just the borough housing authority holding everything up. The worst of it is that the longer I'm here the longer it'll take for me to prove that I can cope outside of this environment, on my own again.

I'd like to get a job, but everything I would earn over £6 has to be handed over while I'm on supplementary benefit. It's near impossible for me to earn enough for it to be worth it.

I do think things wouldn't have been so bad if I'd been more encouraged to get some qualifications at school. Schools should be a bit harder with girls than they seem to be, more encouraging. Not every woman is a natural mother. While there are more career girls than there were, there should be more.

Still, although I have gone through a lot, I think I've come out of it right side up. At least it all happened at an early stage in Tracy's life and mine too – I know I've got a life ahead of me.

In ten years' time I'll still be only thirty-five – young enough to start something.

*

A group of sixteen-year-olds, attending a school proud of its academic record, talk about current attitudes among this generation brought up to equality. Some things have changed – two have learnt metal work – but the career craze of the moment? Working with children, training to be a nanny!

Ruth, Michelle, Joanne and Lucy (Essex)

R: My mother's an artist. She works at home.
M: My mother and stepfather run their own business.
J: My mother works in the laundry at a mental hospital. It's hard work.

Q: *You're used to seeing your mothers working. Do you think you'll want to work all your lives?*

R: I will, I'd get bored at home.
M: I think I would.
J: Me too, except for a short period when you have children.
L: I'm not even sure about having kids. You have to give up so much of your life for them. It may sound rotten, but it's true. They're so dependent. I don't know if I'm prepared to give up that time for them.
M: Lots of people do say – women that is – they wish they'd never given up work for children.
J: Perhaps if you find the right man and the right circumstances.
R: Someone I know is a marketing director, living with a man, and she doesn't want children at all. She loves her work and wouldn't give it up for anything. I'm definitely not getting married before I'm twenty-two. Well, I don't think so.

Q: *Do you have much to do with computers at school?*

L: Not much chance because we don't do computer studies. If someone doing computer studies wants to come in at dinner-time they can. There's a group of them that hog the computers and the others doing the course don't have a chance.
J: I don't think I've ever touched a computer. They say soon

you'll be able to speak into a computer and you won't need typists.

L: All the boys at school are going in for computers or staying on.

Q: *Do your families expect you to work or do they think that once you get married that's it?*

R: My grandmother always says don't worry about school, don't worry about work. My mother's completely different, but she still wouldn't *push* me into anything. It's always me talking about what *I* want to do.

M: My grandmother says the reason my mum and dad split up was because my mum went out to work. I don't agree with her. She's old-fashioned and never worked in her life.

J: Grandmothers are like that. They didn't need an education as much as we do now.

L: My parents have never pushed me into anything, and they've never done with my brothers. They give advice and back up our decisions, but they never make our decisions for us.

M: I've always made up my own mind that I want to be with animals. They've just encouraged me to go for the highest level of being a vet. They say if I don't make it I can always be an animal nurse.

J: Some of the girls at school just want to get married. They say, 'Oh well, I don't need to work. I'll just get married.' I know one girl who's completely changed; she used to work really hard but now she couldn't care less. She doesn't even know if she's going to take her exams.

L: It's a wrong attitude. If you've got your qualifications nobody can take them away from you. They're always useful if you have kids.

M: Now divorce is easier, more families are splitting up, and if you're left with children and no education you're going to find it really difficult to get back to work.

L: Even with qualifications it's difficult. A couple of my brother's friends have degrees, but they can't get a job.

They've lowered their sights, ready to take anything. It's terrible. It makes you think what chance have you got?

R: Somebody I know left school at sixteen and went straight in as a bank clerk and started earning £70 per week take-home money. It's terrible if you think of all those people with degrees who are now ending up as bank clerks.

M: It's like my cousin, he gets a lot of money, but he works in a sewage farm, and I don't think he gets any job satisfaction.

Q: *Do the boys you know expect girls to have careers or stay at home?*

J: I think they realize now that girls want to go out to work. I don't think they like the idea of girls being engineers though. A couple of girls at school went into engineering and the boys treated them with amazement and contempt. They didn't like it.

Q: *Do many girls do things like metalwork, woodwork and technical drawing?*

M: I don't like needlework. I can do that at home. So I did metalwork and woodwork. At a different school, I didn't have the choice. Boys had to do needlework and girls had to do metalwork. I really enjoyed woodwork. I used to go home and make all these things.

L: In my third year I did cookery and metalwork. I enjoyed metalwork, apart from having to clean the grease off your hands afterwards.

M: When I came here I wasn't given the chance to do woodwork. I wish I could have done it. Too many people were already doing it.

R: You have to choose. Nobody could do domestic science and metalwork together, as they were the favourites. I ended up with domestic science and needlework. I didn't want to do needlework.

Q: *Are you typical of the girls in your class?*

L: I think the majority are like us. People in the D and E streams aren't interested, they accuse you of being a snob and a creep, but you don't really associate with the ones down below. It's hard to tell what they want to do. I think it was good when they mixed all the streams up in the fourth and fifth years. Now we've got to know whichever streams we're all in, but not them. Sometimes they're a bit wary. You're just talking normally and they say, 'Oh I don't know what the hell you're talking about.'

Q: *Have you had much in the way of career advice?*

L: Most of us have had half an hour with the careers teacher, and those that haven't have had a group interview. So in a way they've been helpful.

J: We haven't had much advice as we're staying on into the sixth form. There were films, which were no help to most of us, and we haven't had any interview or form-filling practice. Nobody watches the films. They're irrelevant.

M: There haven't been many for girls. It's all been factory work. There hasn't even been one about being a nurse. It's all on the boys' side.

R: Catering and being a hotel receptionist is quite popular among the girls.

L: What a lot of girls want to do now is to be a nanny, work with children; that's the craze at the moment.

*

At school, girls, especially the less academic, are pushed towards cooking and typing, while the boys do metalwork and woodwork, which can lead to well-paid jobs. The day-release course Mandy was sent to do was 'community care', while the boys learned bricklaying. When she left school, all Mandy knew was that she didn't want to work in a factory. Her mother wanted her to be a mother's help.

Mandy (Cambridgeshire)

The careers advice I got wasn't all that good. We just went for one appointment with the careers officer in the fourth or fifth year and that was it. You had to go in with a specific idea of what you wanted to do, so you could choose the books and they'd give you the information on it.

When I went in I just didn't know what I wanted to do. He didn't know what to say to me and I didn't know what to say to him. I just knew I didn't want to work in a factory.

All the boys wanted to go into the army. They were all right – there was tons of stuff on that, and on nursing. But if you only had a vague idea they didn't have the information to help.

I don't know whether things would have turned out better if they'd given me more information. It was a really big school I went to, more than a thousand kids. The bright ones were all right, but the ones who didn't have the ability weren't. If you got a bright kid in the C band, the lower one, the teachers weren't going to notice because they're busy dealing with all the rest. I would have liked more attention from the teachers.

They didn't push us to do anything. If they had, I would have worked a lot harder than I did. I just didn't take any notice of them. I didn't do my school work and that was it, and they didn't bother with me.

One subject I did love was English. Looking back, the only teacher who took an interest in me was the English teacher. He was always moaning at us if we didn't get our work done. Even though he wouldn't let me take O level, which I think I might have got, he was a good teacher. But all our teachers were changing all the time. They never stayed long at the school. I had four or five English teachers and just as many maths teachers too.

Some of them tried to make us work, but none of our class ever used to. We had students. One English teacher was only about twenty-three and we used to mess around all the time. Even though I liked the subject, I never did anything in her lessons. I don't know how I managed to get a CSE grade 2, especially since I didn't do more than a few pages on the big CSE project we had. If I'd tried, I'd perhaps have got a grade 1, or O-level pass, but I never did, because I wasn't told to. The teachers didn't mind whether we did or not.

I never discussed school or work with mum and dad. They never pushed or encouraged me. I used to go home with my report and show it to dad and he'd just say pull your socks up and that was it.

They weren't the sort of parents to check and make sure I'd done my homework. They weren't to know if I'd done it or not. If I said I had, they'd just believe me.

One good thing that I went on was a day-release course to college doing community care. Quite a few of my schoolmates went on that. The boys used to do bricklaying and woodwork and so on. If I could have gone on to college full-time for another two years, I would have done a course leading to the Nursery Nurses Examining Board Certificate. The only trouble was it would have cost £700 a year for tuition and living-in fees. It was too far to get a coach every day to and from home. But I couldn't get a grant – mum did go and ask – because my dad was earning too much. I say he was earning too much, but he was building our house, he had four other children to pay for, and he was buying building materials for his business, so he never would have had the money. I wouldn't ask him for it. He never had much.

My mum's a washer-up. She goes down every night to wash up at the local study centre. She used to be a cleaner at the school.

I liked it at college. They treated you differently there, like adults instead of kids. I wish I could have done all my lessons there. At school they didn't teach us anything about what it was going to be like when we left. Nothing about filling in forms or how to get a flat or anything. We did learn to type, but I didn't like it – the girls were always pushed into doing typing. None of the boys were made to type or cook or sew or anything. I liked cooking, learning how to do a basic meal, but I'd really have loved to do metalwork or something that only the boys could do. If you were a girl you were going to be either a secretary or a cook or a nurse. There was no crossing over.

Most of my classmates went into factories, repetitive jobs or became typists. Sometimes now I do wish I was still at school, because we had a good laugh there. I don't any more. Life did get worse when I left, but you get used to it.

On the day I left school, I wasn't worried. I went with my mum to an agency and signed up as a mother's help. I like children. I got a job straight away. My mum wanted me to be a mother's help. She liked the idea of me being under supervision and I suppose it did mean that I'd leave home – we'd had our ups and downs.

I was very happy in my first job and stayed for over a year, until their little girl went to nursery school. I still keep in touch.

The next job never really worked out well. The boy was very difficult to handle. His parents used to threaten him. 'If you don't get a star at school this week, you won't be allowed to ride your bike at the weekend,' so he had his problems. But they wouldn't tell him off if he was really rude to me. The little girl, who was three, was no bother, but I just couldn't take to her. I had held back from the offer of another job which I would have loved, because I didn't want to leave them in the lurch – it was just before their holiday – when they sacked me, giving me a week's notice. They said it wasn't my fault, but I just couldn't handle the boy.

The trouble with being a mother's help is that the pay isn't very good, so it's difficult to save, and if you lose your job you lose your place to live. I realized I didn't want to be a mother's help any more. I'd had enough of looking after other people's children and other people's homes. I wanted to get my own home together, and the next children I looked after I wanted to be mine.

I was lucky and managed to get a job as a cashier in a dress shop. I know if I left it now there'd be nothing else. Jobs have dried up. I'm very pleased. I feel as though I have a proper job at last. I've got a flat, well, a bedsit, but at least it's a place of my own. I had to borrow the money for the month's rent in advance, but I'm slowly paying that back.

The manageress of the shop said that she can see I have it in me to go on and manage a shop myself. I'd really like to do that. I feel as though my ambitions are within reach, so I don't really feel bad that more wasn't done for me at school.

My mum doesn't like the job I'm doing now, though I think

she's jealous because I'm doing what I want to. She got married at sixteen and never had the chance. I nearly got married last year when I was seventeen, but I'm very glad now that I didn't.

(Postscript: At the time Mandy got her job as cashier – and recorded this interview – she was pregnant. For months she was too scared to tell anyone. At the time of writing, she and her six-week-old baby are living at her parents' home on supplementary benefit. Mandy and her mother are hoping that she will soon find a mother's help job to provide her and the baby with a home.)

*

There are still many barriers facing women with excellent qualifications. Anne, a consultant anaesthetist and mother of three, calls herself 'one that got away', so formidable are the obstacles to any woman – let alone one who wants to have a family – becoming a consultant.

Anne (London)

It was made easy for me in that my parents were keen that I should be a doctor and I did have a grant, though not a big one, so I didn't have to work nights to keep myself.

When I entered medical school in 1953, there was a quota system – although as many women applied for places as men, only 20 per cent of the intake were women. Even now, my medical school has the lowest proportion of women in the country – 28 per cent. Some schools have 50 per cent.

I can't say there was any difficulty facing the women medical students. The only discrimination there was that men students tried to persuade the women to do the work on women's wards rather than share it out.

It was only when I'd qualified that people started to talk to me about what sort of career in medicine I'd like to take up or whether I'd pursue a career at all. For some reason this is blissfully ignored until you qualify then they say, 'You can go into general practice, that's good for women.' I decided to go into general practice but thought beforehand I'd get experience in obstetrics. I wrote for two jobs and they had thirty applicants for each. At one interview they said it was a very busy job, up all night, so many hours a day, and one evening off a week. Perhaps foolishly, I was honest, I said I didn't mind working hard during the day but I liked to sleep at night if I was working the next day. That was that, of course.

So I went into anaesthetics, visited a hospital, spoke to the consultants, and got a job. Because the consultants who were my superiors were enthusiastic, they made me enthusiastic and I stayed in it. Then I went to Canada for a year – I knew this place had a good reputation for anaesthetics and I wanted to travel. It was good experience. I came back to England and got married.

My husband was at that stage a senior house officer in microbiology. Since then we've both lived and worked in London pursuing our different specialties. Our careers were almost parallel until I had my first child. At the time I was senior registrar in anaesthetics, the most senior of the training grades, the one before you become a consultant. It was very exhausting.

I took eleven weeks off before and seven weeks after the birth, then back to full-time work, which for a senior registrar isn't just forty hours a week, it's one night in three living in the hospital on call. We were fortunate in having a good nanny, but I didn't see as much of my child as I would have liked and found it hard. That was one of the reasons that I decided when I was expecting the second that I would like to work part-time as a senior registrar, and I managed to fix it up. This was in the days when funds weren't quite as short as they are now. This option isn't readily available to women doctors today.

When I was working three days a week, my income just about paid for the nanny. It was just keeping my career going. I preferred to have a family and practise medicine rather than just have a family.

When women are wondering whether or not to stop work, they don't always realize how hard it is after staying at home a few years, not only to find a job to return to, but to get your confidence back in order to work. Also there's lost time to make up. Medicine doesn't stand still. It's difficult to get back when you've been out of circulation: getting someone to take you seriously and also getting yourself back into the way of life.

After I'd done more time as a senior registrar I wanted to be a consultant. Up until the sixties there were lots of part-time consultants, but by this time nearly all the consultants' jobs advertised were full-time only. There were a lot of consultants doing a few sessions a month in one hospital and a few in another and travelling about. It was thought this was a waste of time and it was more sensible to have them working in one hospital full-time. Also it was partly a political thing. They considered that if consultants only worked seven or eight sessions in the NHS then they'd do more private practice, which would be detrimental to the NHS.

This, unintentionally, made it hard for women doctors. I was lucky enough to get one of the very few part-time jobs advertised. I wanted seven sessions a week, but it only had five, which is why I started working for the Medical Women's Federation. I had some free time.

Although a lot of women do want to work full-time, many would like the option of part-time work, and I've been trying hard to make it available. In theory, it is available, but not in practice.

My children are now ten, nine and six. At the beginning, when the first one was little, I suffered, but I don't think the child did. They didn't seem to feel it, as long as there is some stability in their lives, and that can come from unexpected sources, not just the parents. We had good nannies, and the children weathered the changes.

I've been lucky, I always think of myself as one who got away. I had the special opportunities I needed, they were available when I needed them, but it's not happening for women doctors now. My view of the circumstances of women doctors has been influenced by my own experience and that of the many women doctors I have met in connection with my work for the Medical Women's Federation. In the surgical specialties, and obstetrics and gynaecology to a certain extent, it's assumed that women don't want to pursue careers. My colleagues – women too – say, oh, she's quite good as a houseman, but she won't want to continue in surgery. Until recently 12 per cent of consultants in obstetrics and gynaecology have been women, which is a higher proportion than most specialties, but what's happening now is nearly all these women are nearing retirement and very few women senior registrars are coming up to take their place. It has been more competitive and that doesn't just mean it's harder to get a job, it makes the training process longer. You have to stay on longer as a senior registrar because there just aren't many consultant jobs.

Men doctors pursuing a career have problems, it's just that women have most of the same plus extras. The hours you have to work as a full-time senior registrar make it almost impossible to have children – if you're a woman. When you have to wait longer for your turn, it means that a woman would really have to wait until she's about thirty-five to have a first child, nowadays – that's old in child-bearing terms. All round the country I know of places where women consultants have retired and been replaced by men.

It's absurd that it should be a handicap in a career in obstetrics to have had a baby and to have been a mother. In fact, for every field of medical practice, contact with normal people and normal children in everyday life would be an asset.

The crazy thing is there are so few consultants now that in full-time posts they have to work really long hours. Not as many as senior registrars, but still leaving very little time for anything other than medicine.

There is an argument that more part-time consultants would mean patients would see more doctors. As it happens, the fewer consultants, the more the work gets fragmented. Patients under the one consultant see so many doctors. More part-time consultants would actually give many more the chance of seeing the same person. This is one reason why the Medical Women's Federation is pushing for more shorter-hour consultants.

In general practice, however, it's always assumed that women only want to do short hours – also senior partners are terrified of letting women come in on an equal share and then finding them getting pregnant. There's a terror of the maternity-leave period. At the moment they're allowed money only for an absence of thirteen weeks and only if her absence leaves her partners with 3,000 patients or more, which is a lot. Arrangements for replacements are very poor. That's one reason why they get the women to do shorter hours. It's cheaper, they don't have to worry about maternity leave, and they can tell the patients 'we have a woman in our practice now'. Patients like it – male doctors like to offer it. So women GPs are often working shorter hours than they would wish – and earning less.

Only 12 per cent of all consultants are women. There are less than 1 per cent in general surgery. In anaesthetics it's 18 per cent. But there are a lot of women doctors in hospital service who are neither in recognized training nor consultants. They are assistants, which are considered temporary jobs, but they may go on doing them all their lives. Some combine this with general practice, which is fine. Others just do that, because for some reason they haven't progressed up the ladder. It's unsatisfactory because they have little say in how patients in their department are dealt with.

The reason they are stuck there is because they didn't feel able to progress in full-time employment. Many more of them are women than men. There are very few men as well qualified as some of these women who aren't on the career structure.

Most of the older women consultants had to choose between their career, and marriage and children.

In 1979 we did a survey of all women senior registrars in the country and about 70-odd per cent were married, whereas more than 90 per cent of male doctors were. So the incidence of marriage is still lower among women doctors than for men.

(Dr Anne Gruneberg is a former Honorary Secretary of the Medical Women's Federation.)

*

You've got to be desperate for money to work all day for a net profit of £4, as Marion does. Like so many hard-up mothers she has found that employers pay less for jobs which fit in with family responsibilities, and the family responsibilities prevent her from looking further afield for better rates of pay. Completely reliant on the 'little job round the corner' to earn any money at all, these mums have no economic bargaining power because of lack of back-up care for children. They and their families can be trapped in a 'home' all of us would loathe.

Marion (East London)

At the moment I do one day a week in a shop, £9 for 9.30 till 6. Out of that the four kids have got to have their dinner in the cafe next door, so that's £2 gone. Then the old girl next door has them from 3.30 till 6, so that's another £3 gone. I'm working all day for £4. It's hardly worth it, but if it wasn't for that £4 I'd be even shorter than I am now.

I really don't like being at home – we've got a high-rise flat. When I was working every day, at least I could sleep at night. Now I can't. The doctor's had to give me sleeping tablets. When I was working I was so tired that when I came home, that was that. I was shattered. I had to go to sleep. At the moment, I'm up half the night. I keep getting these recurring dreams that someone's gone off the balcony. The other night, it was the little one. I got out on the balcony ledge . . . it was only a dream, but it seems so real, you know, if you've got your own kids.

My eldest is ten. There's my seven-year-old – she was assaulted in the lift a while ago – and a four-year-old and a three-year-old.

At the moment the little boy goes to nursery school in the morning and the girl in the afternoon. The two big ones started at nursery school at two and when they came to go to school they were smashing. The two little ones love nursery school. If I could get them in full-time, it would be handy, even if it just meant I could get a lunch-time job in a pub. But you just can't get them into a straight nursery, full-time – so you're never going to get away for work, especially if you've got to travel.

The nurseries are booked solid. The ones that get in full-time are maybe one-parent families where the mother *has* to work. If you're married and got kids, they think, well, you've got a husband working for you – why do you really want to go out to work?

At the moment the nursery school costs £2.50 for the morning one and 30p for the other. They're cheap enough, but you can't work. In fact, the morning one doesn't take children if the mother works. That's not why they're there. You've got to go on the dole for them. I used to have a wee cleaning job in the morning at one time, but luckily the girls sort of covered up for me. I was always there to pick up the children at lunch-time. So I'll have to wait until the two little ones go to school before I can get a full-time job. That's why most of the jobs I've been doing have been evening work, which is hard. You're too tired in the morning to get the big ones off to school.

I did try a year of straight night-shift work in a factory canteen from 10 at night to 6 in the morning. I had somebody minding the kids, which cost £15 a week. But that was when one got attacked in the lift, so I thought I'd make sure I was at home to look after them. I got a pub job, 7 to 11.30, but then I either had to walk home late at night by myself – too dangerous – or take a taxi for £1 a night. It wasn't worth it.

I do get very depressed at home. I mean, some days I'm all right and other days I just sit here and cry. There was a time I used to get really violent. I used to get migraine headaches and people say if you lie down it helps but it doesn't. My husband was left black and blue a couple of times because I just don't have anyone else to take it out on. I'd be afraid to smack the kids in case I'd go too far.

But unless I can get the kids into nursery school full-time, there's another two years of putting up with it. We can't get out of the flat because we're in arrears with the rent. I've sent them letters from the doctor and all that, but still I can't get out.

Actually I've got to go to court tomorrow and give them £184.

I've got to. I phoned up three times to find out exactly what I owed and she kept giving me the wrong amount. As I'm trying to clear it, it keeps getting higher. I really do need to work to get out of here and start again.

At the moment my husband's working, but he was off for a long time with an industrial accident. He hurt his foot at work. Before that we were having trouble with our marriage because I was working late hours, so he had a lot of time off trying to get things sorted out. That was when I got into arrears with the rent.

My husband's working overtime to pay off the rent arrears, but if he puts in for a rent rebate, they'll look at his wages and say no, you've got a good wage, because they put my family allowance on top as well.

I would like to go back to full-time but I want to get the kids somewhere where they'll be safe. You leave them with private childminders and you'll always find something wrong with them. Once upon a time, I was working, and had a childminder, and came home one night to find my girl's back really burnt because she'd been out in the sun all day and hadn't been covered up. My husband said that's that, you don't leave them with anybody. The doctor told me that if she'd been any longer in the sun my daughter would have had first-degree burns. So it's got to be somewhere there's a lot of kids, they're all happy, and there's someone capable looking after them.

*

While all pressure has been taken off efforts to give women at work more equal pay and opportunities, increasing hardship is forcing women out to work who do not want to be there. There are many willing to criticize working mothers, precious few willing to give them any real help to stay at home. Desperate for cash, they are vulnerable to poor rates of pay because they must have work that fits in with family commitments. This mother wrote to me at the *Sun*.

Linda (Hampshire)

I have two children, both boys. One is nearly six and one is eight and a half months old. My husband works sixty hours a week to bring home about £65. I work three evenings a week to earn .15.72. By Monday I have nothing left and rely on the child benefit of £9.50 to pay for two days' food.

Every working-class family has had to put up with enormous ises in the cost of living, not only on what we buy, but rent and heating costs have soared. At the same time we've had to cope with cuts in services. All through industry there have been short working weeks, closures and low wage increases. Every family I know with young children is living from hand to mouth. And to top that our Council are pressing for a 66½ per cent rent increase.

I have cut down all our expenses as far as I can and I still find it very hard to manage.

When I first went in for the baby we were comfortably off and saved up enough to keep us going for about a year. But by the time the baby was born in June the savings had almost dis-ppeared. We managed to struggle through until just before Christmas, then I had to go back out to work. The baby was only ive months old and I felt very guilty about leaving him with my husband at such a young age, but I had no alternative.

If the child benefit had been raised to compensate the rise in nflation we might have been able to last a bit longer.

As an example of how hard we are finding it to make ends meet, I couldn't even afford any medicine last week when we all were ill with flu, and somehow I've got to manage this week with my husband's wages being two days short.

*

hortage of good substitute care at reasonable cost forced this mother to resign her job. She lost all seniority at work, should she be able to return when the children are older. She and her husband have had to give up saving for a house of their own and the sort of schooling they want for their children. Instead they have to worry about where the money is coming from for the next pair of children's shoes. Annette feels that the children didn't seem to suffer from her working – as long as she was able to find good substitute care – and the quality of her marriage actually seems worse now that she is at home full-time.

Annette (South London)

I was a clerical officer in the Civil Service for four and a half years. I had to give up because of problems with childminders. The last one I had simply told me when I picked up the kids on a Friday night that she couldn't have them any more. No notice at all. They'd only been with her a couple of months.

It just wasn't all working out. I thought they'd been moved around too much, and I gave in my notice.

My girls are now three and a half years and eighteen months. I worked all the time, right through both pregnancies and birth, not intending to give up work. I wanted to be able to afford to send them to a better school and I wanted to get out of this flat. We were hoping to get a decent deposit and buy a house. My working doesn't seem to have done the children any harm, mentally or physically. If anything they've been a bit quicker and brighter because of going out and me working.

My husband hasn't exactly been behind me all the time about working, he thinks the wife should be at home, but he tolerated it. The same as me, he wants to move out of this flat, but now he can't save. I used to pay everything, including the childminders' fees, and expected him to save for a deposit. Now he has to give me housekeeping.

I have to watch every penny I spend. It's difficult. I've always worked, ever since I left college, and I'm not used to worrying whether I can afford to buy the kids some shoes. But I feel a lot happier about the children, now I know I'm looking after them. We had some nasty experiences with childminders.

I can't remember how many they had. Let's see – the original one who had Sally from eight weeks couldn't have her back after Sarah was born because she'd taken on more children. Then I had one who wasn't terribly reliable for a year – she kept going on holiday. A friend of mine who was a registered childminder took them when she just gave up.

In between I'd been looking for nannies and reliable minders. There are day nurseries round here, but not for me – I'm married!

I'd been to the social services but they don't seem to know what's going on. They give you lists without knowing if there are any real vacancies. Then you ring them back and they say they'll see what they can do and you never hear from them again. I asked my health visitor and she tried her best but couldn't find anyone, at least, not in the time I could take off from work – seven days' unpaid leave was all I was allowed.

Until I worked out my notice my husband had to take time off work to look after them. It was quite an upheaval for us. I was doing well at work and I was really upset about having to leave. I'm twenty-five now. I've still got some years left. But if I do go back to the Civil Service, I'll be starting back at the beginning. I'll have lost my seniority.

At the moment I've given up looking for a childminder. I'm waiting until Sarah is two, and then I'll be able to get them into a nursery. But it will have to be a private nursery, about £30 a week, so any job would have to pay well to be worthwhile. But I'd like to go back.

For the first couple of months after I left, things were all right, but now it seems a waste to be just sitting in the house. I read to them, I try to do things with them, I try to improve their manners, which just went out of the window when they were with other people, but the children get bored. Sally tells everyone how she likes me to be at home, but she'll be sitting reading and say she wants to go out to so-and-so's house. She thinks she should go to playschool every day. She likes to be out a lot.

My older girl has always been very outgoing – she was used to being with childminders and I think I was in better spirits when she was little because I like being independent. Since I've been at home I've noticed my pre-menstrual tension a lot more, and the little one's clinging and getting worse as the days go by.

I found it was better for me to be working – you feel as if you're on top of things. I'm sure I did more housework when I was working than I do now. I do get depressed at home. I pick on my husband. If you're at home all day and things get too much for you, you just start as soon as he walks through the door, for no reason at all. My husband quite likes me at home, because he does like having his meals on time, but he does shift work, so for part of the day he's here. I think I get on his nerves as much as he gets on mine. I think it keeps you both civil if you're at work. It gives you something to talk about. He doesn't want to hear my chit-chat about neighbours and kids. That's why, when they have evening parties where I used to work, I do drop in now and again, to talk about different things and have a drink. I do miss it. I wish I was still part of them, but I feel like an outsider now. The day will come when everyone I knew in that office will have left.

In the afternoons I sit and read. In fact my husband gets angry. He says I read too much.

I play my violin more now. I was trained to be a peripatetic violin teacher, but that needs a lot of practising which I didn't have time for when I was working.

I wanted to have my children now, while I am young, so that when I'm older I can further my career, and be able to afford to pay for their education. Education is very poor round here – you've got to work.

There are advantages to being at home. I'm not rushing around any more. I sit around talking to the children. But I've become lazy and put on a stone.

Now I'm at home I have friends which I never had before. Nobody knew me. They are the sort who always wanted to be at home with their children and can't understand me wanting to be back at work. They think I'm cruel or something. But I've seen the effects of staying at home on them. They take it out on their children, shouting. I'm not used to shouting.

*

Home-workers typically are prevented from seeking better-paid work outside the home because of some disability or responsibility for dependent relatives. Their lack of freedom in the market place makes them the worst-paid of all workers. Iris, who suffers from agoraphobia, knits for 5p an hour.

Iris (Bradford)

My husband is a locksmith. For what he does he isn't paid well – the difference between his regular £70 and the £79 he gets with overtime is crucial. We've got three boys, thirteen, fourteen and sixteen years old, all studying. We can just manage on £79 but if it's £70 we fall short. That's why I started home-working a couple of years ago. I needed the money. I don't like to ask my husband for more because I know he's giving me what he can. I couldn't go out to work because I suffer very badly from nerves, some form of agoraphobia. The only time I can go out is when I have no warning, when it's an emergency. Also I like to think I'm always here if the boys need me.

I saw an advert in the paper – Hand knitting, home-workers, please ring so-and-so. I do the work for a woman, but who she works for I don't know. She's very businesslike. She just gives me what she wants me to do, pays me, tells me of any complaints and then she's off.

Once she brought me four garments that weren't even mine and asked me to undo and reknit part of each of them. For this – about twenty hours' work – she gave me £1. I was insulted.

The basic deal is 20p per oz. ball of wool; mind you she started playing crafty, bringing 2 oz. balls and paying the same, which I didn't discover for a while. And she only pays £2 for knitting up one of these Icelandic sweaters, which take me a fortnight, knitting every evening, and you can feel there's a lot more than 10 oz. of wool in them.

I once made a mohair sweater for her for £2 and my husband was mad about it. He told me to ask how much she would sell me one for, so I did. She said they sold for £17 but I could have one for £15. I said how come there is only £2 off, she said it was expenses and so on, and in the end I felt guilty about asking her. My husband said it was slave labour.

But I can't bear not to be doing anything of an evening, I have to have my hands occupied. I like knitting, and the little bit of money does come in handy.

When I asked for more money I got no answer, but I suppose I'd still rather be doing it than not. But when I get Aran sweaters I feel like throwing them out of the window. I hate them.

You can never get a straight answer out of that woman. I always feel dissatisfied when I've finished. She always gives the impression that, of course, there's someone else she can turn to if I'm not happy. If I could get something else to do or even go somewhere else with the knitting, I would. This Icelandic jumper I'm doing now, it works out at 5p an hour.

The woman won't even stop for a drink and I can't pin her down. You can't seem to get beneath her skin. She's always pleasant but there's something about her.

I don't know any of the other ladies that knit for her, but she must have a lot. The back and boot of her car are always full of jumpers, and she always seems to have an advert in the paper and sometimes she brings me the wrong bag.

I've never met any of the other ladies. I just see her. There's no way I could get together with any of the other women knitting for her to put the rate up. Occasionally I see an odd name but I have no idea where they live. She is very tight-lipped about everything. I've got to keep on the right side of her. When my husband gets only £70, my money goes on essentials, like school dinner money. Two pounds may not sound like much to some people but you should have seen the panic in this house when once we lost £1 dinner money. I rang the boys' schools trying to find it. I divide the wages up into boxes for fuel, rent, dinner money and so on and my money can make all the difference between whether the money goes round or not.

When my husband got paid the full whack, £79 a week, for three months, it meant we could save all my money and it was enough to repaint the sitting room. It does come in handy even if it's not a lot.

There's high unemployment round here. The chap next door hasn't worked for three and a half years, and there are loads of men on the dole out in the square. We just keep our fingers crossed and count our blessings.

*

When we campaigned in 1979 for 'Fair care for children and a fair deal for Mum' at *Woman's Own*, thousands of women wrote to us giving flesh-and-blood reality to our survey findings which had triggered us into the campaign. Sonia, Polly, Barbara and Molly are a tiny sample.

Sonia found life on supplementary benefit with two small children so grim she was desperate to get a job to earn them a more decent standard of living. The total lack of back-up facilities for working mothers – even single parents – in the end drove her back on to living in poverty off the state, but not before she and her children had suffered.

Sonia (Manchester)

When my children were seven and four, I left my husband to go into a battered wives' home. I got my divorce and I was living on social security. I don't and did not like living off the government, so I decided to look for work in the hours my children were at school.

I got a job but it meant my children had to come home from school on their own. I arrived home about ten minutes later. Now at that time I was confident that my children were all right, and on part-time I wasn't earning enough to keep us in bread all week, so I started full-time work. This meant my girls had to have an alarm clock set each morning so they could go to school on time – I left at 7.30 – and my eldest had to have a key to let them in at night. I arrived two hours later.

Now at the time I did worry. I wasn't heartless, but everything seemed to be fine. Then came the summer holidays, and to this day I can still cry for what I did. This is one thing I can never make up to my children and I can't really explain on paper what heartbreak it caused me and my children.

I left them on their own all day. Oh yes, they had drinks and I left sandwiches for them. They had enough to eat and drink and they could go in and out of the back garden, but by the second week I had worried myself into taking time off. I knew it was wrong to leave them but at the same time I couldn't face going back on social security. I went to the social services for help. They said the only thing they could do was to have a woman pop round at dinner-time to make sure everything was all right.

By this time my nerves were so bad at the thought of leaving them alone again I was being physically sick. I went to the personnel officer at work and explained my problem. He was very nice and tried to help. He realized that I didn't want to leave my children but at the same time couldn't face going back on to social security. He suggested going back on part-time for the time being. At least it would get me home earlier.

So I did that. Also, just around this time I heard of a lady who would have my children for £10 a week (I had tried advertising in the paper before but with no success). I went to see her and she said she would look after them. The only thing was that with being on part-time and paying her, I fell behind with my rent.

In the end, my nerves got so bad my children ended up in care for a month. I stopped work and went back on social security. I got my children back and everything went back to normal.

I say that, but to this day I have nightmares of what might have happened. I have to live with guilt for the rest of my life. Even telling you doesn't help. As I'm writing this I'm shaking.

If only someone could have helped me to find some way of looking after my children, everything would have been fine. As it is my heart still cries for how I left my children at four years and seven years to look after themselves.

In my way, I was trying to help us get a better standard of living. I made it into a nightmare for the three of us. If there was some way I could go to work again but knew my children were *well looked after*, I would, but till that day comes my children will never be latch-key kids again.

It's about time something was done to help mothers go out to work, and not have small children worrying and waiting for mummy to come home. My story is just one. I wonder how many more mums went through and are still going through what I did.

*

Employers' attitudes towards part-time work waste valuable experience and personal resources, as well as under-rewarding the workers. It can act as an inducement for mothers to work full-time who would otherwise far rather spend more time with their children.

Polly (Leeds)

I have two children, a girl of five and a half years at school and a boy four and a half years old due to start school next term. For the past four and a half years I have worked two nights per week (Friday and Saturday) as an SRN Staff Nurse on an open-heart intensive care unit. This is a very rewarding job most of the time. It requires an awful lot of experience. It is not a job you can adjust to in just a couple of months, it takes years.

I am now on top Staff Nurse's pay and bring home with night rate, less expenses, £35 a week, which is hardly a monumental amount but it does help to afford holidays and run our own home and car. My objection is that there is no way I can ever have promotion to Sister because I only work two nights per week. I must work full-time (four nights) to achieve this promotion, but I am expected to train and teach Sisters brought in over my head who have no experience at all, or very little indeed.

When my little boy starts school it leaves me freer but I cannot get home in the morning early enough for my husband to go to work, and during the school holidays I would have no one to mind the two of them while I went to bed – that is, if I was prepared to work full-time just to achieve promotion. I really would like to work during the day because my husband is a bit fed up with my working night duty, especially at weekends, but the 'age-old' problem occurs again. Who minds the children –

before school, after school and during the holidays? I have no family living close enough to help, even if I would impose on them all the time anyway.

*

This mother found that being a mother is a 'dis'-qualification.

Barbara (Cambridgeshire)

I have one little boy aged three and a half years. I have had part-time jobs since he was eighteen months. I went to work partly for the money, but also as I enjoy working and I am a better mother with a break from looking after him. Before having my little boy I was employed as a clerical officer with the Department of Health and Social Security, but the only part-time jobs I could find were, first of all, working in a newsagent's shop at weekends for a year, and now I clean offices for an hour and a half each evening. I am trying to find a more interesting job.

My husband looks after my little boy while I work and puts him to bed.

My son goes to nursery school each morning but the school holidays are still a problem, also after school hours.

*

Lack of child care back-up means many mothers look after their children during the day and then work at night to help towards a decent income for the family. The strain must bring dangers.

Molly (Liverpool)

I'm a midwifery sister, hospital based, working two twelve-hour shifts per week, nights from 8 p.m. to 8 a.m. I work the nights apart so that if I have some difficulty with someone to mind my daughter I can cope by staying up the following day as I sleep the next night at home. Usually I take my daughter to nursery school the two days following my night shift and rely on my mother-in-law collecting her and giving her lunch. I call for her about 2 p.m. I've found the three–four hours sleep satisfactory as I'm in bed the following night. It's necessary for me to work because of the mortgage repayments and so on.

I returned to work when my daughter was eight months old. I chose part-time night duty as I found no facilities at local nurseries. My sister looked after my daughter one day per week from then until she was two. She then moved house and I ran into difficulties. I placed my daughter in a private nursery two mornings a week from 9.15 to 11.45 as this was all that was available (this was before we lived close to my mother-in-law). I used to sleep the one hour while she was at nursery, then collect her, stay up the rest of the day and have an early night that evening.

My husband looks after her during the night while I am on duty. He washes and feeds her early morning ready for when I come home. It is a great help. I then take her to the nursery before going to bed.

My daughter will be four soon and can start school the following term. We would like another child but, though I qualify for maternity leave, I will not be able to find facilities for the child when the time comes to return to work. Things are working well now but if I have another child it will be hard-going again.

3. Should Women Go Back Home?

Women often have a hard time to hold down any job, let alone a good one. The job shortage looks like being long-term. Successive governments have squeezed social services and the burden of care is falling increasingly on women. Microtechnology isn't going to go away.

Maybe this is the time to reappraise the position of women and perhaps agree that their proper place is at the kitchen sink (or 'by the hearth' or 'in the bosom of the family' as people who don't want it to sound too much of a hard option call it). Will that result in increased happiness for families, women and society in general?

Well, to start with, many women have no such choice. There are very large numbers of lone women doing low-paid 'women's work', lumped in with those assumed to be working for a secondary income, for so-called luxury extras. They have no husband to support them. They need an income to survive.

The 1978 General Household Survey showed that of the 3.8 million single women aged sixteen to sixty, 140,000 headed single-parent families and 300,000 were caring for elderly or infirm relatives.

There were half a million widows, 125,000 with dependent children.

There were half a million divorcees, 250,000 with dependent children.

There were 205,000 families headed by a woman separated from her husband.

Very few people argue that women who do not have another income should not be able to work to support themselves and their dependants, if they have any. The alternative is almost inevitably supplementary benefit.

However, even this minority, whose need to work one might think equals that of any male breadwinner, are often given so little assistance with providing care for their dependants while they earn their keep that they are forced out of employment into poverty and perhaps on to supplementary benefit against their will. Two thirds of lone mothers who aren't working, such as Jenny, whom we talked to in Sussex (page 140), would work if they could find and afford suitable care for their children.

The snag for these women, who have to pay for the back-up care they need to make sure their dependants are safe while they are away from home, is that as women they are generally paid less than men. Their wages are often simply not high enough for them to be able to afford the full cost of decent care – and of course the view of many in government is that, while their desire to work is understandable, they must not expect the state to help out with services like child-care.

It's a series of vicious circles.

Say Bill and Sue, both on low incomes, get a divorce. Sue can't get a job that pays enough to allow her to pay for child-care so that she can get a better job. Bill can't earn enough either to keep Sue and the children above the poverty line, or to pay for the child-care that will allow Sue to work to heave herself (and him) above the poverty line. There is supplementary benefit, but if Sue spends that on child-care so that she can get a job that pays decently, she loses the supplementary benefit. It's a state-aided poverty trap that seems to be saying: divorce at your peril, we the state will not help you. This book is not the place to argue whether the state should use its financial controls in this way, or whether those couples who stay together should subsidize those who don't. But while the government are metaphorically slapping the wrists of divorced couples they are actually condemning the children of many of these broken marriages to a life below the poverty line.

But the economics of the present low level of provision seem crazy. Surely it would cost far less to pay, say, half the costs of the necessary substitute care, or allow them against tax, instead of paying to support the entire family on supplementary benefit?

Gingerbread Corner in Croydon, for example, by caring for their children before and after school and during the holidays, has enabled eighty lone parents to work, for the cost of keeping six of those families on supplementary benefit.

In present circumstances, then, few people would argue that these women should be forced to stay at home. Their interests suffer because they are lumped in with that other group that an increasing number of people, it seems, would like to see at home – the working wife, she who brings a second income into the home.

The traditional stereotype – father at work, mother at home full-time looking after the children – is now actually in the minority. It is true of only two out of five families.

The Gallup survey done for *Woman's Own*[1] found that the picture at the end of 1978 was as follows:

Mothers with children under five years

6 per cent work full-time
18 per cent work part-time
27 per cent don't work but would like to
8 per cent aren't sure whether they would like a job or not
41 per cent don't work and don't want to

Mothers of children aged five to sixteen

15 per cent work full-time
37 per cent work part-time
20 per cent would like to work
7 per cent aren't sure
21 per cent don't work and don't want to

One in four of the mothers who worked did so because the family did not have enough money to survive otherwise. This is a separate category from the one mum in three who worked to provide extra comfort.

One fifth of working mothers would rather have been at home full-time. (Presumably, though this was not run through the computer, this one fifth constitutes the majority of the one quarter who say they work from absolute economic necessity.)

The earnings of one in three wives make up 30–50 per cent of family income. A 1977 study found that, in one in seven couples in which both husband and wife are working, the wife is providing as much of the family income as the man, or more.

An analysis in 1978 of General Household Survey data showed that, without the earnings of working mothers, the proportion of families *with a working father* who would have been below what is now taken as the poverty line – within 140 per cent of the supplementary benefit level – would have risen from 17 per cent to 39 per cent.

As the Study Commission on the Family has recently pointed out, if a woman's place was always in the home, an extra 2,500,000 children would live in poverty.

In their financial policy, governments seem to rely on mother's earnings to support 'the family' that politicians claim to revere so much, for state child support for all children is worth less today relative to average earnings than when family allowances were introduced after the war.

Over the last two decades, the tax burden on the childless couple has gone up 122 per cent; that of the two-child family 382 per cent.

Since 1978/9, the proportion of income paid in tax and national insurance by a couple on three quarters average earnings and with two children, one under and one over eleven, has increased by 11.6 per cent. For a childless couple it has increased 1.3 per cent.

Between 1948 and 1980 pensions and other main benefits were increased twenty-one times. In contrast family allowance/child benefits were increased only nine times.

There has been a transfer of wealth away from families with children to the childless. In the 1980 budget, child benefit was deliberately allowed to fall behind the rate of inflation, and so the gap was widened.

So it's clear that asking or forcing women to go back to the home would have a severe effect on the incomes of many families. However, that does still leave a majority of working mothers who are not working under such driving financial pressure. Suppose all these returned to the home full-time?

What many people who talk about the growth in the numbers of working mothers in this country don't realize is that the *full-time* employment rate for women with children has hardly changed in the last twenty years. It is the *part-time* rate that has nearly trebled. Feelings about just how welcome a woman's vacated part-time job will be to a man left unemployed by heavy industry, and about how harmful a mother's part-time working may be to her children, may well be very different from feelings about wives/mothers working full-time. Nonetheless, getting all those four million part-timers out of the work-force could be seen as a way to find two million full-time jobs.

The Gallup Poll survey for *Woman's Own* found that four out of five women who work or say they would like to work would still want to go out to work even in an ideal world with all financial pressure removed. Over half of both working mothers, and those who say they would like to work say they are bored or lonely at home, or need a break from the children. We have quoted from a few of the thousands of letters written to us by readers to whom the subsequent campaign, Fair care for children and a fair deal for Mum, gave a chance to share their feelings.

Studying women at home,[2] sociologist Ann Oakley found that 70 per cent of the women she interviewed came out as 'dissatisfied' with housework and the role of housewife in an overall assessment of feelings during a long in-depth interview. Three quarters found it monotonous.

Housewives actually reported more monotony (doing bitty unconnected tasks instead of whole sequences) and time pressures than factory or even assembly-line workers (Table 3).

Table 3: Work experiment

Workers	*Percentage experiencing*		
	Monotony	*Fragmentation*	*Speed*
Housewives	75	90	50
Factory workers	41	70	31
Assembly-line workers	67	86	36

The majority complain of loneliness. While 'being your own boss' was the most praised aspect of being a housewife, the majority felt that the housewife role had low status, implied in the phrase 'just a housewife'.

They worked long hours – averaging seventy-seven hours of housework a week. Dissatisfaction with housework was higher among those who had enjoyed a job previously held. Generally housework is compared unfavourably with employment work which, whatever the particular nature of the work, offers company, social recognition and financial reward.

While studying the origins of depression,[3] researchers George Brown and Tirril Harris found that depression among women might be sparked off by what they called a 'provoking agent' – such as death in the family or being deserted – but found that the likelihood of such an event resulting in depression was greatly increased by what they termed 'vulnerability factors'. The four main vulnerability factors they identified were:

loss of mother before eleven

having three or more children under fourteen at home

absence of a confiding relationship, particularly with a husband;

lack of a part-time or full-time job.

None of the few women who took up employment *after* the occurrence of a 'severe event' developed depression. After Shirley (page 147) had attempted suicide her psychiatrist told her: 'A job is what you need.'

So it would seem that if the women had a confiding relationship with a boyfriend or husband, then whether she had a job or not made little difference to whether she suffered depression.

But having a job was a protective factor for those who didn't have such a relationship. And with one in four marriages now leading towards divorce, it's clear that a lot of women haven't.

Again depression seems tied to feelings of failure and dissatisfaction as housewives and isolation. A working-class woman who had not worked before but got a job after a 'severe event' and did not suffer depression (though she might otherwise have been expected to do so), commented 'the money was not much' but it 'gave me a great boost' and 'greater self-esteem'.

There seems to be another pointer to the beneficial effect of work in National Society for the Prevention of Cruelty statistics. Only 17 per cent of mothers of children placed on their child abuse registers in 1976 (latest figure) were employed outside the home, compared with 51 per cent nationally.

And this need to work isn't a recent phenomenon. In *Lark Rise to Candleford* (1939), Flora Thompson describes women *a hundred years ago* choosing to work in the fields in all weathers for four shillings a week, declaring they would go 'stark, staring mad if they had to be shut up in a house all day'. However, these were women whose children had grown up enough to be off their hands.

Even if it does make women depressed and dissatisfied to be full-time housewives, is this a sacrifice they should be prepared to make for the sake of their children?

For now we will ignore the fact that it is not a short-term sacrifice we are talking about, since stopping work has been shown to depress earnings potential and achievement for the rest of the mother's working life, and even her pension. How much *proof* is there that working mothers are worse mothers – that having a working mother had a bad effect on a child?

John Bowlby was the witting or unwitting father of the belief current since the last war that very small children must never be separated from their mothers and a mother who goes out to work is causing her child lasting damage. Bowlby's study was very handy just after the war when it was convenient for all the mothers who did 'war work' in the factories while the men were away fighting to go back home, now that the service men were back demanding jobs.

But Bowlby's study was of deprived children – not only deprived but disturbed, orphaned and institutionalized children after a world war. He found that separation from a permanent mother *or mother substitute* was highly damaging to the child's mental and emotional health and could affect the rest of his life. However, this conclusion cannot be extended to mean that children from stable homes left in good care while the mother works will similarly suffer.

Dr Mia Kellmer Pringle, director of the National Children's Bureau, and Penelope Leach, Vice-President of the Pre-School Playgroups Association, author of *Babyhood* and *Baby and Child*, and eminent child expert, have both been widely quoted as being against working mothers, certainly of young children. Their views have been leapt on with ill-informed fervour by those who believe that all married women should be at home.

Penelope Leach[4] does say that babies and toddlers need one-to-one care, and she does argue for economic and social changes to improve the lot of mothers at home and so encourage more to stay at home rather than work. But she also says – and this is less widely quoted – that a young baby will almost always accept a second caretaker, whether father, grandmother or dayminder, alternating with the mother. What Dr Leach is against is *group care* for babies and toddlers. She also makes it clear that she does *not* believe that women who are unhappy at home full-time should be compelled to be there.

Unfortunately, inaccurate reporting of someone like Penelope Leach lessens the likelihood of action being taken to help mothers whether they work or not.

Dr Kellmer Pringle wrote[5] of women being 'brainwashed to seek as a desirable way of life the heavy burden of two jobs, paid employee and home-maker', adding that she is excepting women who work through economic necessity.

We would take issue with the word 'brainwashed'. For a hundred years at least women have been extolled the virtues of being a dutiful wife, a dedicated mother, a nest-builder. Even seven years ago women's magazines hesitated to run fiction stories about mothers who worked – *happy* mothers who worked. Always the career mum became emotionally low or physically worn out and as the proverbial sun set in the west she would run back to the bosom of her family, once more to bake bread and wash socks. Even today, although the major women's weeklies cover a wide range of modern life-styles, a woman's traditional domestic responsibilities remain largely unchallenged. This is because half the readers work, half don't, and the magazines have to try to please all of the people all of the time.

Dr Pringle stresses the importance of the one-to-one relationship during a child's early years, but as regards different styles of parenthood is very positive about shared parenting. Though she may be *quoted* as being against working mothers, she does specify that women who are actually happier working should be able to do so, but she feels the most important thing at the moment is to get a child benefit high enough to enable mothers to stay at home as long as they want to.

She blames the low status of 'housewife and mother' on the women's liberation movement which, she says, by ignoring the fact that only women can conceive and bear children, has made educated girls feel they are wasting their abilities if they are 'only a housewife and mother'. What she doesn't seem to get to grips with is the long-term effect a complete break has on women's earnings, and the fact that *society generally* has surely been devaluing the worth of a mother's work and *employers* have penalized her since long before women's lib.

The National Children's Bureau Research Highlight on working mothers leaves the question open, but certainly produces no proof of detriment to children from mothers working.

For children under five it says, 'There is virtually no research evidence on the effects of full day care on young children whose mothers are away at work, but it does seem that the risk of any detrimental effects would be greatest in the very early period of a child's life, when the need to form secure attachments to one or two people is most crucial. Further, work with socially disadvantaged children has shown the importance of parental interaction with their children and this may not be easy after a full working day.

'The position with older pre-school children (three upwards) is a little different and research findings suggest that a few hours away from mother may be of *positive benefit*, both to the child, who is able to gain some independence and yet maintain a close relationship with his mother, and to the mother herself.'

No indication of marked maladjustment among primary

school children was noted. 'The National Child Development Study found that children whose mothers had started work after the children had begun school were slightly less well adjusted at seven years of age than children whose mothers had started to work during the pre-school period . . .

'A follow-up study of children in one-parent families at the age of eleven found that amongst illegitimate children there was a tendency for those whose mothers worked full-time to be better adjusted.

'Most American studies' (the USA is way ahead of us in this sort of research) 'of adolescents have found that school performance, psychosomatic symptoms and affectional relationships are unrelated to maternal employment. The only adverse effects were to be found among working-class boys where it was thought that a father who could not support his family on his own was providing an ineffective model. However, it was found that part-time maternal work had a positive effect on adolescents.'

Evidence on delinquency is conflicting. One study found that 'boys whose mothers had full-time jobs included, unexpectedly, a smaller percentage of delinquents.' Another study found that 'boys whose mothers had never worked stole less than their peers, but he found little support for the view that there is a causal link between juvenile theft and boys getting home while mother was still at work.' (It seems possible that this result could be because mothers who never work are in comfortably-off families whose sons are less likely to steal anyway.)

'In general research studies show only slight difference in educational attainment at either primary or secondary stage between children of working and non-working mothers. The NCDS showed that children whose mothers had worked before they started school showed some delay in reading, but that where the mother had started working after the child started school, there was little difference. When the same children were studied at eleven, no difference was found between children whose mothers were employed part-time or not at all, but children of full-time working mothers read less well.' However, it is now admitted that it is not so much the mother working outside the home which is important, as the quality of the substitute care.

The NCB Highlight goes on to say, 'The same study revealed, however, that the situation varied according to family situation, for illegitimate children and children of widows scored higher when mother worked full-time. There is also some evidence that working-class children, and particularly boys, show higher achievement when their mothers work, while the reverse is true of middle-class children.'

Recent studies have increasingly tended to argue that it is attitude, how the mother feels about work and her family, that is the most important factor – in other words, choice. 'A mother who likes working will react positively with her child, while the mother who dislikes working may seem less involved with her child. A satisfied mother, whether working or not, will be more adequate as a mother than one who is dissatisfied.

'Some studies have pointed out that anxiety and guilt felt by working mothers, particularly of young children, may lead to over-compensation. Many mothers will suffer strain from combining two roles. There is evidence, though, that the father tends to take an increased part in child-care activities when the mother works, and this is likely to benefit both family life and the children's development.'

Rhona and Robert Rapoport, writing in *Work and the Family*,[6] state confidently that 'there is no direct or intrinsic relationship between mothers working and negative outcomes for other family members or indeed themselves'.

Looking at the hypothesis that dual-worker families will produce marital conflict, they say that most reviews of the literature on the subject are inconclusive, but there are some helpful studies. An American study by the National Opinion Research Center in Chicago[7] found that marital happiness depended less on whether or not both partners work than on whether the choice was freely entered into. A study of British graduate couples[8] indicated that while conventional families show a slightly higher proportion stating that their marriage is 'very happy' the proportions are not significantly less for working couples. Moreover the latter are less likely to give stereotyped 'happiness' responses. The sub-groups which are markedly low on marital satisfaction are those in which the husband is *extremely* career-oriented.

It is true that the divorce rate and the numbers of wives at work are rising concurrently. The economic benefits of marriage are less decisive for wives who are independent earners. However, greater economic freedom to divorce might bring greater happiness rather than the reverse, and the Rapoports say that research to date has provided more questions than answers.

On the other side of the coin, there are case studies of dual-worker families in which wives who hold satisfying jobs by choice express the view that they are more fulfilled, while husbands view them as more interesting marital partners. They emphasize the idea that it is quality rather than quantity that counts, and that, though the pattern is stressful, they prefer it to the alternatives that they see for themselves – operating the conventional pattern and feeling bored and resentful.

In an earlier study,[9] the Rapoports point out that some people[10] argued that maternalism 'is instinctual to females, not only in this species but in mammals generally' . . . 'one cannot repudiate the whole gamut of innate masculine-feminine traits without endangering the species' . . . risking that 'male mothering' may bring about harm to all concerned including 'the sexual relationship between the spouses'. To repudiate the last emotive statement, a Norwegian study[11] of the lives of couples who were sharing both going out to work and child-care responsibilities found that 'the couples reported improved sexual relationships'.

Those who believe in equal opportunities would take it as read that women should have the same chance as men to land jobs even in times of contracting employment. However, on just a purely practical level the argument that women should go back to the home to free jobs for men is dubious. Most working mothers are concentrated in a narrow range of jobs, traditionally considered women's work. Because of their low pay, poor conditions and prospects and the qualifications required, these jobs have little or no appeal to men. The wholesale transfer of redundant steel workers or ship builders to jobs as cleaners or cooks is, to say the least, unlikely at present, though there are signs that men are moving into some new areas previously held by women.

It is not only mothers who risk being driven back home by present policies. The other major category of caring women is those who care for elderly or infirm relatives. There are at least 300,000 single women caring for parents plus many more married women caring for parents, disabled husbands, grown but handicapped offspring. They are being forced out of jobs, since home helps and other support services which help to look after the old and infirm are being halted or reduced.

The Equal Opportunities Commission report, *The Experience of Caring for Elderly and Handicapped Dependants*,[12] studied their problems. The dependants consisted of mentally and physically handicapped children; adults suffering from a whole range of handicaps; and adults aged over sixty-five, most of whom suffered from something as well as 'old age', half of whom lived with the carer and were largely housebound. About three quarters of the carers were women.

In general dependants, whether old, sick or handicapped, are not expected to require domiciliary care when there is a female relative at hand. On the other hand, many of the women who are caring for a dependent relative do not get the back-up support they need.

Of the carers of working age, some had had to give up work or thoughts of work altogether, as many had had to cut down their hours, and others had had to forgo promotion or training opportunities. Most of the carers for the sake of convenience could only work in the immediate vicinity of the home, which often meant taking jobs which were low-paid or unsatisfactory in some other way. (Married women caring for dependants, and so unable to work even though they would like to, are not eligible for attendance allowance, which is available to men and single women.) These carers often want and need to work for financial and emotional reasons. They need a break, as is clear from the cases we have quoted (page 160).

Many people who look after sick, elderly or handicapped dependants (and remember the majority are women) suffer considerable financial difficulty. Not only are they themselves less able to earn a decent wage if anything at all, but there are additional household costs – transport, fuel, special food, extra wear and tear on clothing, bedding and so on; even furniture may get worn out more quickly because of wheelchairs and calipers. A phone may well be essential.

Occasionally the effect of caring for such relatives is positive, but more often it puts a great strain on the family, leading even to the risk of divorce. 'At times it has been disastrous,' said one man. 'My wife and I enjoy a close, tranquil relationship but with the inevitable pressures that arise we have tended to withdraw a lot from each other. Tensions are very high at times.' And that is without counting the cost to the women who sacrifice even the thought of marriage to looking after their parents.

Because caring is such a full-time job, few people responsible for looking after infirm dependants are able to lead a normal social life. Moreover, just at the time when outside support is most needed, carers often lose the friends they had previously and become progressively isolated and lonely: 'If my mother is here and friends come, they won't stay.' 'I can't go out into the garden even. She needs you there all the time.' 'It's very hard but you lose friends. They offer to do things but now they avoid us. Even my best friend – we were inseparable – he just rings up now occasionally.'

Few of the carers ever get a holiday. Some would have been prepared to take a holiday if their dependant could have gone into a home while they were away, but this had never proved possible.

Given the pressure of care fifty-two weeks a year, the carers' own health suffers. Bad backs, constant depression, 'nerves' were all very common. 'Before long I shall be in a mental home.'

That's what lies behind the cosy talk of returning to 'caring families' rather than increasing 'bureaucratic care'.

*

There is a whole variety of reasons why sending women back home is not the easy answer it at first glance appears to some people – quite apart from any consideration of women's rights. What is too seldom understood is that reality is very different from the idea that all families consist of happily married couples who would both be suited by a pattern of the husband working and the wife at home full-time. Even couples who have set out along that path happily have found that it can lead to unexpected misery. To start with, many women are working or want to work because they are their family's breadwinner, or their family desperately needs their wage.

Jenny (Sussex)

Five years ago my husband, who is a landscape contractor, met a social worker and moved in with her, leaving me with the two boys. They are now eleven and eight. I got divorced. Neither of us got the house – it was sold at a loss of £300. I was left with nothing but the furniture, which is falling apart, as you see.

He pays £30 a week maintenance and £5 for school meals. I get £12.50 family allowance, a rent rebate, and that's all. When I went on rent rebate, the electricity board said I'd be better off with a slot meter than trying to pay the bills, so they disconnected my only heating – the storage heater. So I'm left with an electric fire. You can't have a slot meter and a white meter – so because you're hard up, you're penalized. I'm paying twice as much now. My last quarter cost over £120, and we're freezing cold.

It's very difficult to make the money stretch. I would like to get a job, to get us off the breadline. I would like to pay my own way, to feel independent, but how can I when there's no help with looking after the children after school and during the holidays? Paying for care for the children would mean that the first £30 of my wages would go on the expenses of just holding down a job.

But the bosses just don't want to know about single parents – the mothers, anyway. I've given up, really, trying to get one.

The last interview I went for cost me £3 in fares – £3 out of £42.50.

There was an advert for lady van drivers wanted. I walked two and a half miles in the freezing cold and when I arrived there were 200 people for one job. They interviewed us four at a time. I've got to the point now where I hardly bother. I did even try advertising for work. Destitute divorced mother – I suppose it was badly worded – anything legal and moral considered. The phone didn't stop ringing for two weeks for modelling jobs, as they called it. That's all that was offered.

I used to walk two miles to the employment exchange every day. I was told the other day that I'm too old for a job. That just about finished me – I'm thirty in September.

About eighteen months ago I had a lunch-time job in a pub. I enjoyed it and did it well, with the kids at school. Then I started having to do a few nights, so a girl round the corner used to baby-sit. But I had to give that job up. It turned out she was only fifteen, so my husband or his wife rang up the NSPCC – apparently the law is they have to be sixteen. My husband believes I'm a terrible mother. He doesn't want to take the boys, though, just make life difficult.

Things are worse now with money. When my husband first left, if I was very careful, I could afford to buy one article of clothing a week. He paid £24 then. Now I just can't afford it. Everything I've got is three years old.

I've tried so many things, legal and illegal. I wasn't really making money. There was a delivery man who used to come round offering me goods cheaply. Great, I thought, and the next thing I had the CID on my door. So I had to stop that. I didn't get done for it, they were very good to me. They let me make my statement at home.

I've tried Citizens Advice and there doesn't seem to be anybody they can put me in touch with. I've just had the brainwave of trying to write a recipe book. I'll struggle on with that, but it'll take time. I tried making fluffy toys one Christmas, then the sewing machine had to go. I thought of doing knitting, but a machine is expensive, and you don't make much.

I went to find out about a TOPS course. When I left school I did card-punching so I thought why not try and get into computers, but because I have no GCEs there was an entrance exam. The same thing for accountancy.

The only part-time work round here is house cleaning, which I'd be sick to death of, or pub work, which my husband would put a stop to. I loved that work, and I felt like a person keeping myself. It's better than queuing up at the post office than at the social security. It makes you feel self-sufficient.

I hardly get out at all now. I won't go unless somebody asks me, so I don't have to pay. I'm lucky that the friends I have will excuse the fact that I very rarely buy a round of drinks. They tease me but they know it's not meanness. Last Friday was the first time out in over two months. I take the dog for a walk and that's usually the only time I get out of the house.

I've tried going to Gingerbread meetings. It's OK if you've got money in your pocket; if you haven't you can't attend their special dos. So I gave up. Most of them have boyfriends, mother in the background, or they go to work.

I've been desperate. I felt as if I must get someone somewhere to realize how we are living. You get very low on confidence. I'm still picking myself out of it now, but when my husband left me I just felt I was no good to anybody. Even now he's constantly harping on how badly the children are being looked after. The latest is that I'm starving them, for Heaven's sake. It just shatters your confidence.

I had a nice boyfriend once, an accountant, and my husband just walked in – in the end I had to send a solicitor's letter to stop him doing that – and he said, 'You look like an intelligent sort of bloke – can't you teach my wife something about hygiene?' No wonder my boyfriends don't last five minutes. The last decent relationship broke up because we both smoked and my husband insisted on putting a smoke alarm in the house. What bloke is going to put up with that? I don't know why he can't let me go, but he can't.

He's making things that bit worse. He's got a Range Rover, a Cortina and a trailer. He's absolutely rolling in it, but I don't get any more out of him. In court he showed his P45 – I said I wanted bank statements, because half his jobs aren't going through the books. Even then, he gets a lot of cash and that won't show at all. He spoils my jobs, gives me little money, and goes to Italy for Christmas. Very nice too.

I think the whole system needs changing. For a start there should be proper holiday and after-school care for the kids so you can then get work. Family income supplement would be very handy for me, but it's only paid if you're working over twenty-four hours a week if a single parent (thirty hours if you're not).

There should be some sort of training programme to give one-parent families their confidence back, make them feel like a person again. I've tried very hard to change my attitude, but I'm convinced I haven't got the job before I start. A fair living wage – I don't believe in state handouts willy-nilly but they're keeping us below the breadline now.

*

The following small sample of six out of the thousands of letters we received at *Woman's Own* supporting our 'Fair care for children and a fair deal for Mum' campaign illustrates how little help and support is available for women such as widows, with whose need to work no one could quarrel, and how essential – for financial, psychological or emotional reasons – work is to many, many women.

Audrey (Berkshire)

For the last six years I have been a widow with one child to bring up on my own. My son was two years old when my husband died. As my widow's pension was completely inadequate, I found that I had to work. I have never in all that time been able to find permanent help in looking after my son.

Although I have recently remarried, and am now in a better financial situation, I feel very strongly that the government do next to nothing to help either widows, one-parent families or low-income families to survive.

Pamela (Lancashire)

In 1970 when my little girl Sharon was born I was adamant that I would stay home and take care of her, but as inflation overtook wages I was forced to go back to work. While my husband's wages covered almost everything else, I could no longer stretch it to pay the gas and electricity bills.

The latter weeks I spent at home were utter misery, in so far as I didn't even have any bus fare in my pocket to get out. Consequently life was absolutely predictable daily, and when life is *so* predictable, life is ultimately very dull.

May I stress that neither my husband nor myself drinks nor smokes. We do not have a colour TV or a freezer, but after eight years of marriage we do have a nice, comfortable home.

Discussing all this with friends and neighbours helps, as there are many more people today with exactly the same problems brought about mainly by inflation and lack of help for working mums.

The main worry of my life is the security and welfare of my child. I have to rely on the goodwill of neighbours to collect her and keep her after school until I arrive home from work. The problems of working mums are insurmountable and I worry more because I really care for that little girl.

I am left feeling more than a little bitter and cheated by all this because we would have liked another child, but there is no way I could face the utter poverty and destitution that another child would bring upon us.

Agatha (Newcastle)

I have an invalid husband and a two-year-old son who came rather unexpectedly and belatedly. Before his arrival we managed quite well as I could work. I did go and see several childminders with a view to returning to work, but was not very satisfied that my child would be well looked after, in addition to which, although their charges were quite moderate, by the time I had taken their fees, as well as other working expenses such as fares and meals from what I could earn, I would have had precious little left.

Hopefully, by the time he is school age, I could possibly find some temporary job to fit in with school hours, but if I wanted a regular, well-paid, satisfying job there would be the problem of school holidays and the gap between the end of school and the end of a working day, which is often 5.30, plus travelling time, which might make it around 6.30 before he could be picked up.

As far as anyone in my position is concerned, child benefit is merely a farce, as any increase in child benefit is immediately all taken off my husband's invalidity benefit, and all I have to show for it are two benefit books instead of one. Unless they alter that rule there would be little point in raising Child Benefit as far as I am concerned. What is needed are good pre-school-age and after-school care facilities.

Janice (Cornwall)

I myself am a working mother with three school-age children. I have to work, as my husband is in the building trade and frequently, as now, unemployed. The only real security I know is that I bring home a regular income.

I have a good job as produce manageress for a supermarket, and I love working. The trouble is school holidays. I worry constantly about them. Fortunately, with my husband on the dole, he has been able to look after the children recently. But I am already worrying about the summer holidays, in case he has a job by then. He is going mad at home all day.

I would willingly go without to pay someone to look after my children, but who wants to take on three children? Old people don't want to, youngsters would rather have more regular summer jobs without any responsibility – so back to square one.

I love my children dearly, but to be practical you can't opt out of a good job you need for a few weeks every year to look after them.

In my opinion it is working mothers that keep this country together. All I know are hard-working and conscientious workers, because we are not working simply for material things but to give our children a better chance in life.

Alice (Leicestershire)

It's very hard for us farmworkers' wives to cope on our own. I have no neighbours except for the boss and his wife, and she's out most of the time as all her children are at school. I can't start a course because I know my husband will be working late in the summer and autumn, and couldn't baby-sit. Luckily, I can drive, but with two children, one three months old, it is a bit difficult to see my friends. I can't remember the last time I went out with my husband for an evening. Our parents don't want to come. One lot have a fair way to travel and the other is used to central heating, not a log fire with no other heat.

I do exactly the same things over and over again every day. If only I could do some part-time work I would feel better in myself, would look after myself better, put on make-up a lot more, etc. Perhaps you wouldn't believe this, but if you came and saw what it's like, you would understand better. I am a cabbage at home. Let us get out.

Yvonne (Wiltshire)

I'm divorced, with two children under ten. I have no relatives to help and have experienced nothing but problems trying to find someone to watch my children while I work.

I had a registered childminder who gave them a boiled egg to eat all day from half past seven in the morning until half past four when I came to collect them. The children said that her own children tucked into bacon and eggs and other meals during the day.

My children went to a voluntary playgroup during the summer holidays which meant I had to come home at dinner-time to take them there, and come back to work, then go and collect them after work. It was twenty minutes each way so that was eighty minutes' walking on top of a full-time job as a clerical officer, plus a house and garden to run.

One day I met my little boy walking home by himself. He had been bullied there by the older boys and refused to go back. The staff said there was nothing they could do.

The children are now eight and ten, but while I was working most of the time they had to come home to an empty house. Once I came home and my little girl was standing at the gate being teased by other children. She was in tears and couldn't get in because my little boy had lost the key. He did this several times and I had to leave work early to let them in.

I earned a good wage at my job. My net pay weekly was around £49 plus family allowances, and my firm paid my removal expenses when they moved, and other cash benefits. The job was highly satisfying with promotion prospects but my children had to come first. I tried a job with the same firm but with less responsibility, but that didn't alter anything, so I left after nearly four years. I now get £26 social security and family allowance. I'm no scrounger and would dearly love to work if my children were properly looked after.

I think the solution is for schools to do what they did when I was a child and my mother worked full-time, that is to open after school hours and provide a light tea, sandwiches, cake, tea or orange etc., and games or television, and a quiet room for homework. My mother used to collect me about 6 and I was quite happy there, especially if my friends were there, too.

*

This mother had rosy visions of being a housewife and mother. They ended as she became so depressed she attempted suicide. 'A job is what you need,' said the psychiatrist.

Shirley (Essex)

I met Alan just before my sixteenth birthday. We went to the same school and youth club. We got married in 1963 when I was twenty and he was twenty-one. I packed up work nearly two years later when I was four months pregnant. It was a terrible winter and I had a long journey to work.

In any case, I had this picture of what it was going to be like being at home with a baby. Our mothers didn't have much, but our generation could manage to buy our own house, have a nice kitchen, I thought life at home should be beautiful. I had this image of bathing the baby, putting him down in his pram, going indoors and doing the housework, then going down to the shops in the afternoon. It certainly didn't turn out like the dream.

It was a difficult birth. He was very big, and I needed a lot of stitches. I haemorrhaged and had to have a blood transfusion. I was left desperately tired. I had put on an enormous amount of weight when I was pregnant but by the time I went back for my post-natal I was 7½ stone.

No one told me what to expect. The one time the health visitor came to the house when he was eight weeks old I said that he cried a lot at night and I was going to put him in his big cot that night to see if he would sleep. She said, 'It won't make any difference, my dear,' but she didn't explain to me that not sleeping through the night is nothing to worry about at two months. You should just thank your lucky stars if they do.

I suppose what made it more difficult was that my husband wasn't the sort to get involved. The first night we were at home with Andrew, he woke up and I handed Alan the baby while I went down to make a bottle. He ended up screaming, 'If you don't come and get this bleeding kid I will sling it through the window.' My neighbour heard it and was laughing about it the next day, but from then on I kept them apart as much as I could. It would actually have been much easier if I could have kept Andrew by my bed.

Still, Andrew did sleep a lot during the day and I used to do home-working – machining – while he was in his cot. All the wives on the estate did. I suppose I used to do a lot of hours for the £5 a week, but with that I could buy Andrew some new clothes, and I bought a fridge on HP, and I felt proud that I had paid for that.

I had Graeme eighteen months later. He was a very sick baby.

They had discovered I was rhesus negative, he was induced a month early and he was only 4½ lb. when he was born. He had to have transfusions, and when I came out of hospital I had to take him back every other day for a blood test. Alan didn't even think of ever asking me how I managed to get to and from the hospital with a baby and a toddler.

When Graeme was only two weeks old they decided to keep him in for an operation. I was ready for him not to survive it, but even then Alan left me to take him in by myself, and went to work as usual. He came in from work, and was reading the paper and saying 'I might be out of work next week.' He is a lagger and they are always being laid off. They work themselves out of a job or there's a strike – we've had this all our working life. I remember thinking, 'He's been in all these hours and he's never even asked how the baby is, or how I got there.' It was only when I went to phone the hospital that he said, 'Oh, how is he, by the way?'

Anyway Graeme came out of hospital and actually did ever so well. He was crawling about by five months. But then we started having money worries. Alan was out of work for a spell and with two children I couldn't do the work I had before. We had moved to an older house which needed decorating, and Alan then had no talents as a do-it-yourself man. He wouldn't ask how to do a job or get a book about it. He would get annoyed that I should even want it done. He left me to do the garden, too. His idea was to go to the pub on Fridays and football on Saturdays. He came home one Friday night, as I was up to my arms in nappies, with the grass a foot high, and I burst into tears. He said, 'You always start a row just as I'm going out.' I didn't want to stop him going out but I needed help.

Andrew was a very grizzly child. We found when he was six that he had a partial hearing loss, but he was a very whiny baby. Later we discovered that that was what he heard – a whining sound – and he was imitating that. But unless I shouted at him he didn't listen or seem to understand, and it became a pattern that I shouted at him. I used to get so frustrated and I was so tired – and worried while Alan was out of a job. Once I came downstairs with the baby in my arms, and found the potty and Andrew on the stairs. I pushed him down the stairs, not hard, but kicking him out of the way. Years later he said to me, 'Why did you kick me down the stairs?' I probably used to hit him a lot harder on the legs than I should have done.

Again, I was so tired. People just don't seem to understand how tired you get with two small children. From when he was five months, Graeme never slept through the night. I thought that perhaps it was because he was cold – he used to wake up screaming as if in pain. The house was very damp, with flaking patches, and I wanted to have central heating put in, but Alan was very abrupt and aggressive – not 'We'll talk about it,' but 'No, we can't afford it.'

Alan used to get very annoyed if he was woken, and I used to be in and out of our bedroom and the other room – the baby crying would wake the other one. If I could have brought the baby into bed with me he would probably have been all right, but Alan wouldn't stand for that.

The doctor prescribed Valium but I used to walk round the shops in tears, I was that depressed. One day I went into the playgroup – they were just starting up then – and asked if they had a place for Andrew. They hadn't, but the woman must have realized how depressed I really was. She phoned a couple of months later and said, 'I've found a place for you. I could see how desperate you were.'

She was the only person who did offer any help. I used to meet friends down the shops and tell them how I was feeling but none of them offered to help. They didn't say, 'Oh, I'll take one of them for you for a few hours.' They just seemed to expect that you should cope.

Anyway, I said to the woman from the playgroup, 'It's all right.' By then I had taken an overdose and they found me a place in the council nursery.

Graeme was nearly two by then. Alan had found a job but then it had crashed again. I can remember taking this overdose and going and sitting in the garden. I can't think where the children were. I can't remember that much about it. I suppose

I've blocked it all out, it was so bad. My husband came in and I told him I had taken them. I must have just gone to sleep, I didn't take that many. I went over to the doctor's and said what I'd done, and that if I'd had any more I'd have taken more. They got a psychiatrist to come out to me that night. He said I was to come off the Pill, have no more Valium, get the children into nursery and get myself a job. 'That's what you need,' he said.

Once I had something to occupy my mind, I was all right. It was the quality of the time I had with them, rather than the quantity which mattered.

I like working, and I like working with someone – I've been with the same boss now for six years. Nowadays we are all so isolated: husband, wife and small children. Years ago, when people lived in larger families, there was always someone around to help entertain the children, play with them, take them up to the shops. Looking back on it, I was mad. I used to clean my house from top to bottom every day. I have a friend now with small children who says she often walks down to the play area by the shops and just sits there for a couple of hours, because at least other people will come and talk to her, other people with small children.

With Alan's job being so irregular, too, my working means that we can rely on a bit more stability, we can plan our lives better.

*

Harriet trained as a teacher but gave up work on the birth of her first child. Her husband's business flourished and there was never any financial pressure for her to return to work but, comfortable though their life-style was, she gradually deteriorated as a person in her own right, she fell apart. After her husband's death she was unable to run her life, and ended up having a nervous breakdown and electroconvulsive therapy (ECT). It is in just such a life crisis as losing a spouse, that having a job has been found to be a protective agent. I talked to her daughter.

Harriet (Lancashire)

My mother trained as a domestic science teacher, though I think she envied her sister who studied French. Still, she got a good job teaching in a well-known local girls' grammar school. She met my father in 1939.

She was twenty-four, he was twenty-five. They got married in 1942. During the war he was a captain in the army, abroad nearly all the time, but mummy had uncles and aunts close by, so she wasn't going it alone.

When daddy came out of the army he had nothing – no job, no money, no training. This was the only time when mummy ever dictated what they did. She had the job – she found them somewhere to live, she had the money so daddy could buy himself into a firm of estate agents. A low-grade job, so he decided to train, and started spending all day working and then all his spare time studying. He did well, passed his exams, and bought his way into a partnership.

Mummy gave up work as soon as she was pregnant. I think being a mother at home was what she really wanted, and she never went back to work apart from a few terms of relief teaching in the sixties, which she didn't like. I think being in a secondary modern, with all the talk of girls getting pregnant and so on, really appalled her.

Mummy and daddy never showed their feelings, looking back, but it all seemed very normal to me. I had a normal childhood, all the usual things – ballet and drama club and so on, mummy used to organize all that and take me and my sister. I remember there were always complaints from mummy that daddy was working too hard. He'd always bring work home as well as working on Saturdays. When mummy was pregnant with my sister he bought some land and had our house built on it, so he spent a lot of time supervising the builders and so on, and also being a keen gardener, he spent a lot of time on that.

From when I was three we had au pairs, always French or German, so she didn't have too much to do. I think she was fairly neurotic about being a mother – I once swallowed a plum stone, for example, and she was absolutely frantic about it for days.

We come to blows now because she thinks I'm so capable and efficient and it intimidates her, and I think my father had the same effect. I'm sure it got into a vicious circle, not giving her her due for what she could do. After daddy died I used to arrive home on a Friday evening, I'd go up from London, walk through the door and take over, start making lists and cleaning up. She'd let things slip, being basically lazy, knowing I would come home, and I think she used to do the same with daddy, knowing he'd take care of everything.

I remember when I was a teenager, daddy did all the washing on a Sunday afternoon, and because he had business connections in the trade, he used to bring all the shopping home. My sister says it was all his fault, he should have left everything and let mummy do it, let the shirts pile up, but he was one who'd do anything for an easy life. I remember after he'd cooked a meal the dishes would stand till the next day. Mummy would just go into the next room and watch television. He'd get his papers out on the table and I'd stay with him.

I used to be very resentful that mummy used to have her hair done every Saturday morning, leaving all of Friday night's mess. I used to clear it all up and put everything away, thinking she'd be so pleased, and she never said a word when she came back from the hairdressers. I suppose she felt guilty.

She was proud of having qualified as a teacher – she's still also a member of her school old girls' association – but she got demoralized. Although she was proud of me doing well at school, she was far closer to my sister, who was more slapdash. I think because she didn't have so much to be proud of her for, she found it easier to relate to her. Mummy always harps on about how efficient I was and am.

She used to do a lot of voluntary work, meals on wheels, hospital trolley and various other things, sort of career substitute stuff.

I must say she's become much more humble, though, since her recent nervous breakdown and depressive anxiety.

I could never understand why her cooking was so terrible for a domestic science teacher. She couldn't even boil a pan of potatoes. She'd put them on to boil on the Aga and then go and spend an hour and a half on the phone – she was always on the phone – and it would be a horrible dry mess. She would throw salt in a number of times. Good fillet steaks would turn into bricks. You could never eat the stuff. Finally she stopped cooking altogether.

I can remember my father and I peeling potatoes for Christmas dinner on Christmas Eve. I always thought that was wrong. I can remember when he was making a Christmas cake he'd ask me to ask mummy how much butter to put in. She'd be glued to the TV, but she always knew these things, which surprised me because she never did any of it.

We always used to have parties, which meant getting caterers in. I remember her spending three hours to make sure every chair was angled correctly, going into a frenzy over whether we had enough ice or not.

She did a lot for us in one way, running us around for our various classes and things. She was always meeting us and dropping us off. She was keen that we had a good social life, parties arranged and dressed correctly and take us there.

Daddy would just leave her money, she'd say that she needed some and he'd give it to her. There was no budgeting of any sort. They never needed to consider it. We used to eat out a lot. He would phone up from the office and as usual mummy would have nothing organized so he'd suggest we had a meal out.

Mummy used to drink at all times of the day, but not heavily, not so she was falling about, just enough to make her bad tempered and evil. She used to nag my father terribly about his smoking. Eventually the drinking did have a horrible effect. My sister always kept out of the way. I used to be up in my bedroom doing my homework and I'd hear the stiff cupboard door opening downstairs and get a sinking feeling. I'd try and stop it by hanging around which made her feel guilty, try and divert her with a coffee. Then I'd start defending daddy tremendously and I'd get on to her. We rubbed each other up the wrong way totally.

I used to tell her to stop nagging daddy, that she did nothing round the house – we had a cleaning lady who came twice a week, but all mummy did was keep cleaning the lounge, so we were hardly allowed to use it. She'd insist on putting a cover on the sofa before we sat down. My sister was always mucking around with horses and didn't pay any attention to her at all but it got my goat.

I'm sure mummy was jealous of me for having some of the qualities she didn't, and because of the things I did to help daddy. She didn't like the time I spent with him, but I couldn't bear to see him doing all the washing. When he was in the garden I used to sit on a rock and just chat to him and it was so silly because if only she'd done the same she could have spent far more time with him.

He died when I was twenty-three. He was just sixty.

Mummy was sort of shell-shocked when he was taken ill; she didn't even tell me he'd collapsed until the day after, because she didn't want to worry me. I drove up and ten minutes after I arrived, he died. Mummy didn't go to pieces, she didn't have hysterics or anything. My sister did. I didn't react because I had to get down to coping with it. I steered mummy into the living room and made her spend the next six hours phoning up all the people who needed to know. Finally we called a doctor and she got some sleeping pills.

One good thing to come out was that mummy has a lot of very dear friends who love and respect her, and they rallied round, so for once she was getting a lot of attention. Even her sister was sympathetic. I took her back to London and this cheered her up. But then it all began to tail off. She was always on the phone complaining how lonely she was and how every time she looked out of the window she could see daddy in the garden which I thought was a load of rubbish.

She never did any shopping, just eating whatever tin she laid her hands on, the cupboards were getting barer and barer. She didn't know about shopping, because we'd always got everything on account and through daddy's firm.

She never thought of going back to work, she was too old. The voluntary work was tailing off, but she did do a lot of keep-fit classes.

Then she started saying how the house was too big, it was getting her down; and she did the most stupid thing, bought a house even bigger. She wouldn't let us see it. She said it was closer to town so she'd save on petrol. It was a huge house with three flats and a basement, one of them let out. Moving in kept her occupied for a while, there was lots to sort out, but then she had nothing left to complain about and she started to really go downhill.

She said she was going to kill herself, she didn't want to live any more because she was so lonely. She did start going to church about the time my sister got married. I tried to encourage her, at least it made her get dressed in the morning and out of the house. Sundays were her worst days, long and empty. She used to slop around the house in her oldest dressing gown for hours. Then she wouldn't heat the house, she got neurotic about the cost, which was absolutely silly, so it was like a morgue.

At one point she started nagging my sister, going on and on at her, so I ended up having a big row with her about that. She got worse and worse and we all tried to get her to pull herself together, which wasn't working at all. Sometimes she would be quite decent about everything and said she would make the effort, but she never did. Finally I contacted her doctor who told me all she did was beg for more sleeping pills, which made me worry she'd have an accidental overdose.

She'd already seen a psychiatrist who said the only way he could help would be with ECT. Of course she was frightened about that. So we found another, who said he might be able to help. Mummy tried every trick in the book to get out of seeing him. We had a terrible time getting her dressed the morning he was coming. At one point when I was in the loo she made a bolt for it. I chased out of the front door and went to the garages, which luckily have very stiff heavy doors, and she was still in her nightie with the car half out and me blocking her way out. She looked so pathetic realizing that she'd lost everything, and I pretended that nothing was going on. I said why don't we go back and finish that cup of coffee. I led her back and she completely went to pieces, saying I was trying to kill her, begging me pathetically and hurling insults. She was still at it, a real evil look on her face, as the doctor came up the path. Then when he came in the transformation was unbelievable. She was so pleasant and polite to him.

After half an hour with her, he said it would have to be ECT. She wouldn't agree, so as next of kin I had to give consent. There was three days to wait, the worst days of my life. She went through stages of being very violent and screaming and then being like a pathetic dog. But I'm sure the treatment did help, at the time. This was three years ago.

It's difficult to talk about something that didn't happen, but I think that if she'd kept her teaching up it would have made her more of a person in her own right rather than just a wife and mother. She'd have had more of an idea of ordinary life. I'm sure she wouldn't have felt so guilty about not coping with the washing and so on if she'd had a job, it wouldn't have demoralized her so much. She never showed that she felt guilty, but she was. And then my sister and I wouldn't have become so annoyed, if only she could have done something to get it out.

*

It's difficult for men sometimes to understand what women may be complaining about – until they experience it. This father used to have a very traditional view of women's role – including that of his wife. Now, as a single parent looking after their four children himself, he's more understanding.

Brian (Nottinghamshire)

We were married eleven years before my wife left me. It was a normal marriage. We had our ups and downs just as I imagine many couples do, but we got over them.

We had four children – the oldest was ten and the littlest less than a year old when she left. I wasn't really closely involved with the family before. I didn't do hardly anything around the house. I was an engineering works supervisor and I was out long hours with overtime. I just used to have my meals and go to work.

One Saturday night, about six months before she left, she said, 'Put your arms around me.' I'd been married eleven years and I more or less ignored her. I wonder now if that had anything to do with it. She was a bit depressed I suppose.

My wife is a very capable sort of person. She ran the house well. If she'd told me she was having an affair I could have tried to do something about it. My mates knew, but of course I was the last one to hear about it.

The first I knew that anything was wrong was I came home from work and she said, 'I'm leaving you.' She didn't take the children with her because she said she hadn't anywhere to take them at first. I felt terrible, especially for the kiddies. They worshipped their mother and still do.

I didn't know whether I was on my head or my heels. I couldn't boil an egg or anything. I didn't know what to feed the baby on without choking her. The social services gave me advice, and they put me on the straight and narrow because I was getting into arrears with rent.

I'd been earning £120 then. Now I get £27.10 supplementary benefit and £8.50 child benefit. I'm suing my wife for maintenance but if she does pay it I shan't get a penny. It will go to social security. I can understand why some women go on the streets. You just can't cope on the money.

When I told my boss that I couldn't go to work because I had to care for the children, he said, 'I'll keep your job open as long as possible.' They kept it open a year, but I couldn't go back because of the children.

I wanted to keep the family together. I didn't want any risk that they would be taken into care and split up. After a few months she tried to get custody of the children – when she and the other man had got a home – but I went to court to keep them. The fact that I had been to social services and asked for advice on how to do things properly went with me in court.

Wives in general have my sympathy now, though they didn't

have before. I love the children but looking after them all is such hard work and can be so frustrating on my sort of money that I wouldn't wish it on my worst enemy. It's got to be done, though.

Tea-time is my black spot. They all want something different. It's like a transport cafe. I should issue tickets. I do what they each want, because I feel I've got to try and do my best for them, be mum and dad.

At least the little one is out of nappies now. My wife's twin tub is still here, but the spin drier is broken, and I can't afford to get it mended. I have to wring it all out by hand, which is hard work if it's raining and you can't put them on the clothes horse if they're still dripping.

It hurts when my wife visits once a week. The children dive on her. I've been there scraping potatoes all week, but I'm taken for granted. If she buys them an ice-cream it's 'Oh great, mum.' Poor dad's just sat there. I go into another room.

At one time I'd put on a show for everyone. I used to take the little one down to the nursery, smiling and laughing. I used to put a right good face on. Then I would go home and cry my heart out. I told them how I felt in the end. Now I have a coffee down at the nursery every morning with the girls and have a bit of a chat.

And at least I manage to get out a bit. I've got two good baby-sitters. Some days when the children are out at school and the nursery, and I've got my housework done, I can get up to the local and have a game of pool. My mates have been terrific. They've bought me a pint when I've been down.

If I didn't go out I'd go potty. But all women can do is sit in the house or talk to someone up the street. A woman can't go into the pub, at least, not round here she can't, not without being called a whore or something like that.

I believe now that it's a mistake for a wife to have children when she's very young. Our children weren't actually planned but we wanted them while we were young so that they would grow up with us. My wife wasn't twenty when she had the first. I don't think it was a good idea.

Women often realize later that they want to take on a bit of a challenge in life. They want to reach out for it but they can't because they've got the kiddies to look after.

I think the men should compromise a bit. A lot of my mates think more of their pay packets than of their families. They take their wives for granted. It's home for dinner and then down the pub. I now think that fathers should spend as much time with their children as mothers do.

*

The Equal Opportunities Commission survey report, *The Experience of Caring for Elderly and Handicapped Dependants*, contained many moving stories. These are just three of them.

All of them want to work, though only one is able to. It would take a hard heart to say that these carers should never have the excuse for a break – and the opportunity to improve their income – which work brings. Certainly it would demand a startling lack of sympathy and sensitivity to claim that they are or would be better off at home full-time.

Dorothy (Yorkshire)

Jill developed this complaint affecting all her muscles three years ago. She's nineteen now. She's very bad at walking. In fact, she can't move in the morning after she's been laid in bed. I have to bath her and carry her downstairs, usually on my back. I sprained my back carrying her downstairs. She's bigger than me now but she has slimmed down a lot from what she was. She eats a lot of chocolates – soft centres – and ice-cream. It's about all the pleasure she has.

The muscles of her throat are affected so I have to make her special food and cut it all up very fine. She's on drugs all the time and I have to make sure she has all her tablets. I have to take her to the toilet and we have no inside lavatory.

She has to be propped up all night because she has difficulty breathing and we have to take it in turns to watch over her. I have a lot of washing to do. I have five children at home and Jill wets the bed. I can't afford to go to the launderette. Looking after her is a full-time job for me. My husband says the only rest he gets is when he goes to work.

The doctor says I should be at home with her all the time, but I do work a little, the odd hour or two in a mill when I can fit it in – I have to work because I need the money.

I spend a lot on special food for her. I need a lot of hot water. I have to keep a fire on in the lounge all day. We have to get a taxi at least twice a week to the doctor.

If it weren't for looking after Jill, I would go back to working thirty hours a week like I used to.

I couldn't get any less help – nobody comes round. I do it all. The social services have never given any help. Jill doesn't go to a day centre. We've been given no aids. She gets free tablets, and mobility allowance – and we can use a pool car or ambulance for going to the two hospitals she has to attend. That's all. When I asked the doctor if I could get a night allowance, he said I hadn't been looking after her long enough.

It's affecting our home life a lot. At one time my husband and I used to go out together like any other couple. Now we have to go out separately, one at a time. We fall out in the family. The other children say, 'You'll do it for Jill but you won't do it for me, or you'll buy her this and you won't buy it for me.' They think we favour her because what they don't understand is that I have to do all those things. My husband isn't well at all. All the worry is getting on his nerves.

Jill gets very depressed because she's in the house all the time and can only go out when I take her. She gets very nasty, and says awful things, even to her sisters. We've only got the one room and kitchen downstairs, so she gets no privacy at all.

I have to take her with me whenever I go out but we can only go as far as the shops and back. I used to have a lot of friends who came round to the house but they don't come now.

I don't know what I'd do if I didn't have this little job to get me out, though if Jill gets worse I expect I'll have to give it up.

Maureen (London)

My father looked after himself for eighteen months after my mother died, but then this started. He's got acute chronic bronchitis. He coughs a lot and is short of breath if he walks anywhere. He can't walk far, and can't stand for long and has to be dressed and bathed. He can't do anything tiring. I only go out to do a little shopping and I leave everything ready for him for a cup of tea. Even then he worries if I don't come back on time. He can't go out of the house without someone's help.

He knows what caused it – his father and two brothers got it – the younger brother died from it. It was caused by the copper dust when he was working in engineering.

We had to move to a flat. He's much better now we don't have any stairs – it's a ground-floor flat. In the other house I used to have to rub his back until everything came out. He could cough for half an hour. But the rent here is three times as high, and we're supposed to keep the temperature at 68° all the time for him. My husband complains about the electricity bill.

I feel awful not earning anything. My husband doesn't earn much – he suffers from agoraphobia. If I hadn't got to care for my father I would be at work, earning my money.

The only help we have had is with this flat – and we waited three and a half years to get it. We have had no aids and no one comes to help me at home. It should be easier to find a place in a home – I'd pay for it – though I suppose if I had refused to care for him he would have *had* to have gone to a home. My husband can't understand why I want to do all this for my father. He never had as good a life as I did at home.

I've got this sort of upbringing: they give you a good life, you've got to give them a good life. It's the least I can do, though sometimes I could choke him.

He takes me for granted and there are times my husband feels that I'm looking after father more than him.

My husband and I don't get out half as much as we used to. If we do go out, my father gets envious, he wants to get out with us all the time. I make friends easily but I can't ask anyone to come now. My father gets jealous, and he likes to watch TV in the sitting-room. He begrudges going to watch it in the kitchen. I find myself smoking too much because it gets on my nerves. I do get down and irritable at times, more than I ever did before.

Ellen (Lancashire)

I met my husband at the day centre where I was working voluntarily. I used to work at the mill, cap spinning, and I liked that. I would like to go out to work but they will not hear of it. I have to make sure he takes his tablets. Sometimes when he has bad fits I drag him upstairs to bed. I have to wash him, shave him and put him on the toilet – he wets the bed. I can't get him to bed up the stairs when he is bad. I feel we should have a grant to help us.

I married Bill two years ago. I didn't know he was as bad as he is. He must have been born like that. I cook for him when I feel well enough. It's a full-time job night and day; we take sleeping tablets sometimes. No friends help us but they do come and see us sometimes. No one in the family helps. My mother is too ill. I have a son, but he won't come home because Bill is not his Dad.

We both get very depressed and they keep giving me the wrong tablets. I think that before long I shall be in a mental home.

It's the money that we just don't get enough of. We don't have enough money to buy enough food, and they're coming to turn the electric off if I don't give them some more money. When they cut off the electric we can't have a dinner. He tears his trousers when he falls down, and he wets himself.

I don't think they help us anything like enough. I could do with a home help but they won't let me have one. Social services come, but they do nothing. I have asked for a pay meter for the electric, but they won't give us one. It's about four years since we had some money for sheets from social services. They won't give us any help with the telephone. We could do with a wheelchair to push him out and a commode.

It will get worse – it can't get any worse, it's bad enough now. They don't want to know, we have tried to get more help.

4. A New and Improved Sink?

All the arguments we rehearsed in the last chapter are not necessarily proof that women, particularly mothers, should be able to work, or so some would contend.

There would be three times as many families below the poverty line if it were not for wives' earnings. As we have seen, one quarter of working mothers work because their family needs the money for essentials.

Single women, widows, divorcees, separated women and single mothers generally need to go out to work if they and any children are not to live in poverty. Two in five lone parents live on supplementary benefit, though a study of the minimum costs of raising a child in Britain concluded that 'supplementary benefit scale rates for children need to be increased by about one half if they are to provide genuinely for even the minimum requirements of a child'.[1]

However, we know that one fifth of working mothers say they would rather be at home full-time if finances permitted. Many people feel that what we should be pressing for is not so much increased facilities to provide better substitute care for the children of working mothers as a far more generous form of child benefit to enable mothers, especially those with pre-school children, to be able to afford to stay at home full-time.

A social worker in a borough which, before the cuts at least, provided an impressive range of child-care for working mothers, told me that she was increasingly conscious of the paradox that they would subsidize a hard-up mother to pay for someone else to look after her child so that she could work, but were not able to subsidize the mother to stay at home to look after her own child, be her own childminder.

Child-care experts such as Dr Pringle and Dr Leach argue that under-threes are not ready for group care, and while under-fives can benefit from two or three hours at a time with their peers, they are not ready for anything like six hours a day, five days a week in nursery classes.

What small children mainly need, they say, is one-to-one care. A substitute can alternate with the mother without harming the child's development, but since for most people paying for a nanny or even a mother's help is out of the question, the sensible answer is to enable the mother to be with her child full-time.

Both also want to see the status of mothering upgraded. 'No longer would women feel obliged to apologize for being "only a mother and housewife". No longer would full-time mothers need to "ask" for money to meet home-making costs. No longer would women be brainwashed into seeking the heavy burden of two jobs, worker and homemaker, as a desirable way of life,' says Dr Pringle.[2]

Dr Leach says, 'While I would never argue that mothers should be forced to give up scarce jobs so that unemployed men can have them, I would argue that those who are working reluctantly, and have something else useful to do with their time in the form of mothering, could sensibly be *helped* to free jobs. A mothering allowance, even where it was not balanced by saving in state day-care, would still leave the national budget balanced by the consequent saving in unemployment benefits.'[3]

Dr Pringle wants to see women's equal opportunities in the work-place after those years at home restored by: 'Child-rearing experience to be recognized as having enhanced – or at least not retarded – their career prospects; training opportunities or refresher courses; and shorter, more flexible working hours . . . as well as unpaid leave during (children's) holiday periods and sickness.'

Dr Leach acknowledges that 'one of the principal complaints mothers make is that they are "stuck at home all day" and that they have "nobody to talk to but the baby". The need is for easy, unembarrassing, uncommitting and inexpensive ways for mothers with babies and young children to meet each other.' She suggests various models – neighbourhood clubs, mothers and toddlers groups, pre-school playgroups.

In other words, what both argue is that a brighter, better kitchen sink will be less stressful and more rewarding for mothers – most of whom, after all, do not have high-flying careers as an alternative but routine, even boring jobs – and much better for their children.

Julie's home, after her husband had left her with three small children, had no bathroom, no hot water and a loo shared with the barber's shop next door (p. 180). Some families' home circumstances are so grim that every member is better off out of it for a good part of the day. Also, there are other experts, equally respected, who refute their views that group care is unsuitable for small children, even under-threes. Rudolph Schaffer says, 'There is nothing to indicate any biological need for an exclusive primary bond; nothing to suggest that mothering cannot be shared by several people . . . Clearly some minimum period of togetherness is required but there is nothing absolute about how much. Beyond the minimum, it is the personal qualities the adult brings to the interaction that matters most. Provided that these can be given full play there is no reason why mother and infant should not spend a portion of the day apart – the mother at work, the child at some form of day care, or in some other arrangement with which the family is comfortable.'[4]

In this country, because in the main only children from one-parent families, those with physically or mentally ill parents and those 'at risk' get nursery places, it is difficult to make fair comparisons between children attending nurseries and others. However, studies in the United States have been able to compare groups of nursery and non-nursery children with similar backgrounds. Almost all found that nursery children form normal attachments with their mothers, and studies at twelve to twenty-four months found that attending nursery can help children to become less fearful when meeting new people.[5]

However, given the long-term employment prospects, it seems utterly unrealistic even to dream that a network of high-quality nursery care, or a range of different types of good substitute care, will be encouraged let alone financed in the foreseeable future to enable more mothers to work with less anxiety about their children's well-being. In that case, is the polished-up kitchen sink the right answer for today's circumstances?

There can't be many, if any, people who would argue with the idea that motherhood is a worthwhile job – as long as they are not asked to put any money where their mouth is. The 'back to the kitchen sink' lobby leap upon the arguments of experts like Dr Pringle and Dr Leach to justify doing nothing to make life easier for working mothers, but they don't follow up their positive demands, those which would make life at home pleasanter and more possible.

The sort of 'realistic responsibility allowance' Dr Pringle has in mind is along the lines of those in France and Hungary, related to the pay of trained teachers, the highest being for infants under three years. That is what it would take to enable mothers in hard-up families and lone parents to stay at home. But can you imagine the popular and political will backing such a measure in this country? Husbands will resent being taxed more to put the money into their wives' purse instead of them having the power and kudos of giving it as housekeeping (and being able to withhold it, as some do).

Husbands will also resent Dr Pringle's other suggestion that they should have to share their income fairly with their wife as of right. Most will argue that they are more than fair of their own volition (as most are) and it would be an unpardonable intrusion of the state into their marriage. The trouble is that a substantial minority of husbands do seem to see their wives and children as troublesome and far from equal dependants. There are still husbands who give their wives virtually no money on which to feed and clothe the family. Roughly one in five husbands has been found not to increase housekeeping to allow for rising prices, so wives and children suffer.[6]

Even supposing these suggestions were voted in, how truly effective could they be? There are still husbands beating their wives up and throwing them and the children into the streets, in spite of all the legislation to protect them and their right to their home. And it is not only husbands who would object to paying mothers substantial child benefit. Many single people and pensioners object even to the tiny child benefit at present paid in this country. In general they feel that couples shouldn't have children unless they can afford to support them themselves, so they would be outraged by the idea that wives should be paid anything like a wage by the state while they care for their children. But these days, supporting the children, as we keep stressing, often needs *two* wages – the husband's alone is not enough.

This is the double bind, the Catch-22 for mothers. They are knocked for working, but the knockers aren't prepared to do anything realistic to help them stay at home.

So, while in some ways we would love to see a new deal for Mums along the lines envisaged by Dr Pringle and Dr Leach, we get the feeling that a lot of lip-service will be paid to it, but precious little cash or action.

There are also reasons why, in the present circumstances and even because of them, we do not see their way as the best way forward, *bearing in mind the interests of fathers and children as well as women.*

There could well be a very real difficulty in making a mothering allowance generous enough to enable hard-up wives to stay at home. With high unemployment it has already been found that teenagers will leave school before sitting their examinations in order to start collecting supplementary benefit earlier. In many cases, their parents were urging them to leave early in order to relieve some of the strain on the family budget. Neither generation could see much point in staying on to sit CSEs when young people with far higher qualifications couldn't get jobs.

If there are few jobs for girls to go to when they leave school, a mothering allowance is going to encourage the idea that early motherhood is an appropriate career choice. This would be discouraged if the allowance was kept below the level of the supplementary benefit paid to teenagers living at home – £16.85 a week from November 1981 – but that would not be enough to help the older working mothers to stay at home. There could hardly be a differentiation that mothers under a certain age could not collect the allowance, since very young mothers are often those whose children are the most at risk. We should not underestimate the danger that sixteen- and seventeen-year-olds will choose motherhood in these circumstances. I talked to Chris, a youth counsellor in an area of high unemployment, who has already noticed that girls with no hope of work are very prone to have a baby to give themselves a role in life, something to do. She felt that pressure herself when out of work.

Generally, establishing even more firmly that for a section of their lives the norm is for women to stay at home while men go out to work will exacerbate all the problems already outlined that women face at work. Expectations of that crucial phase of their life will affect what both they and others expect of and for them throughout their lives. And it's worth stressing that for fathers to lead one life while mothers and children share another is not something basic to man. Until the factories of the industrial revolution, men worked mainly in or near the home and were often accompanied by their children.

Most women are mothers of pre-school children for only eight years or so. What about the decades before and after? Carol, a highly trained sociologist (page 188), gave up her career just while her two children were small, or so she thought. Now she finds she seems to have lost her place on the career ladder for ever.

As long as employers believe that they will lose a skilled woman for several years, usually just as she has gained sufficient experience to be really useful but has not been with them so long she has lost her edge, they are likely to be wary of giving women true equality of opportunity. Re-training and refresher courses are far from a full answer. In eight years away you can lose contacts, confidence, and a really detailed knowledge of developments and research that cannot easily be rebuilt. In any case, with more people than jobs to give them, what incentive is there for employers to set up all these refresher courses and training schemes?

The more women stop work for several years while their children are young, the most women's prospects will be depressed by employers' expectations that they will do so, and the more the women will find that they can never make up the ground lost while they were out of the work-force.

That argument may apply mainly to women with qualifications, training and expectations of worth-while careers, but in effect 'paying' women to stay at home for a few years as full-time home-makers will if anything reinforce the sexual stereotyping that leads women to do certain jobs and men others, and for 'women's work' to be poorly paid.

When Dr Leach says she believes that the cost of a mothering allowance could be balanced by the saving in unemployment pay, she is under-estimating the extent to which men will not take on women's jobs. For example, a letter writer to *Any Answers?* on BBC's Radio 4 pointed out how useless were efforts to bring new jobs to South Wales after steel closures: 'Making candy floss provided work for women,' he said, 'but not for unemployed steel workers.' Presumably those men sat at home while their wives worked, rather than take on 'women's work' at women's rates of pay.

Nor should we underestimate the difficulty of moving the population. If women did move out of the work-force in significant numbers you might have a shortfall of labour in parts of the country where there is work and industry has some life in it, while too few jobs would be vacated in areas of high unemployment. The politicians' answer has been that people should move to where there is work. That is one thing if you are middle-class, make friends in middle-class ways, have a home to sell, are used to travel. But it is hardly supportive of 'family life' to ask those people to move from one end of the country to another to whom family links are still of paramount importance, who have never lived or known anywhere else except their home town – or even part of town. A Liverpool social worker pointed out to me that many of the young people she helped had only rarely been to the centre of Liverpool from their home estate. Council-house exchanges are not that easy to arrange, especially if you are trying to leave a run-down area, and nearly half the population still lives in rented accommodation.

If it is even more the norm that the mother stays at home with the children when small, it is going to carry on being the mother who seeks the part-time work to fit in with school hours when the children are older, and part-time work will carry on being 'women's work', and badly paid.

Only 15 per cent of husbands are 'highly participant' in housework.[7] If a couple know during their early years of marriage that the wife will almost certainly stay at home full-time for the best part of a decade, there is little chance that the husband will feel much incentive to shoulder an equal share.

After getting used to a pattern of his wife doing most of the housework, it will be difficult for her to persuade him to do a fair share once her children are older, she loses her mothering allowance and now must go back to work. Women having two jobs – being left to do virtually all the home-making as well as their paid job – is known to increase their problems, from keeping them away from union meetings, so that their interests may be poorly served, to giving them less leisure than their menfolk throughout their lives.

After all, it's not as if husbands are often very keen to shoulder much more housework if their wives go out to work. While some husbands and fathers do now tackle jobs they would have totally avoided at one time, and spend more time on child-care and housework, the extent of change is limited. In the United States Katherine Walker found that in ten years of more and more wives going out to work, husbands had increased the time spent in meal preparation by an average six minutes a day, while their wives spent one and a half hours on this task if they did not have a paid job, and one hour twelve minutes if they did.[8]

While a minority of working mothers, we know, would feel that their worries were solved by a cash allowance generous enough to allow them to stay at home full-time (one fifth of working mothers say they would prefer to be at home full-time) it may not be anything like the answer for the majority: those who say they work for company, stimulation, because they get bored and lonely at home and who would still want to work even if all financial pressure were removed.

Many of these – like Rosalind and Valerie, whom I interviewed – may feel or have found that, while mothers and toddlers groups, playgroups and neighbourhood drop-in centres are of benefit to both children and their mothers, they are not any real replacement for the company, stimulation and sense of independence they can obtain through work.

Most mothers of young children talk about their children and themselves as mothers. They are very interesting, important topics, but discussing little else can eventually limit your views. At work there is a fair chance of a mix of the sexes and generations, of different interests and ideas with which you can interact. You can have more opportunity to make friends with people with whom you have more in common than that you happened to give birth around the same time, and so your conversation is more likely to progress from the day-to-day practical to deeper subjects.

It has been suggested that women could get the same stimulation from voluntary work as they do from paid work. Cynics say women are being encouraged to do for nothing the jobs they should have been paid to do if the social service budget was given proper priority.

For most working women, that is a very real objection. It is one thing to do voluntary work if it involves sitting behind a desk advising the less-informed and articulate. It is one thing to do mucky and unpleasant jobs if your general life-style is comfortable and such that you know deep down you only do these tasks for your own inner well-being. It is quite another thing to be asked to do voluntary work if you are almost inevitably going to have to do the more menial tasks, and you have had to do boring repetitive jobs for all your working life, but at least you got paid for it.

Even for those who may do the more obviously interesting work, the acid test of how real a replacement voluntary work is for a paid job is to suggest to a group of men that they should go and work for charitable organizations. There are men, just as there are women, who are highly motivated to work for others in this way, but many men would find all sorts of reasons why they should not, other than that their family simply could not keep a roof over their heads. While doing voluntary work is regarded as worthy, it does not bring with it the same status in the world and political power within the family as a paid job. The wife's voluntary work would always have to come second to any demands of the husband's job. It would not bring her any feeling of financial independence, as Gillian found (page 199), and a mothering allowance would bring only short-lived independence since it would end when the children reached school age.

That is all assuming that the 'voluntary work' is voluntary. There are also the women who are finding themselves forced out of paid work and into caring for the sick and helpless – a member of their own family. These women may be very isolated. They may have the satisfaction of feeling they are doing their duty, but the task can be grindingly hard and depressing. While the invalid care allowance has been extended so that it can be paid to friends of the disabled person, it still cannot be paid to a married or cohabiting woman. The assumption is that she has no need to earn a living, even though there is so much evidence to the contrary. It would help these married women caring for elderly parents and sick spouses if they were paid a decent home responsibilities allowance, in line with that suggested for mothers of young children, but they also desperately need a break from the home and its demands. Being able to do a job perhaps only part-time, is what many feel saves their sanity once they cannot, it is as if a trap has shut.

Now, because if women are contented, stimulated and well paid they are likely to interact more happily with their husband and children, all these points about the welfare of women are also very relevant to the happiness and well-being of men and children – to the health of society in general.

It may be difficult to prove through research whether a wife's working is in general good or bad for marriage, beyond conclud ing that what is most important is whether she is doing what she has chosen to do. However, given our jobs, reading hundreds of personal problem letters from men and women each week, it would be difficult for us not to have formed some impression of our own.

It seems to us that, even when a wife has chosen, with her husband's agreement, to stay at home full-time, this choice dictates such completely different life-styles for them that it often acts as a divisive influence.

Every day brings in problem letters from wives whose marriages have never recovered from the birth of the first child, when they gave up work. Their husbands have never helped to look after the baby (or babies) much, and have no idea at all how a person feels after a day at home with small children.

The men, like Richard, who wrote to me at the *Sun*, feel their wives have nothing on their minds but children and domestic chores, and have no sympathy for how a man feels after a hard day at work. They feel alienated from the life of the home. Because they see so little of it, it doesn't really interest them. Leading such completely different lives, it is awfully hard for the couple *not* to be forced apart. The man, perhaps, takes to having a drink on his way home from work, to put off going home. And so they steadily lose touch with one another.

Now, of course, couples running their marriages along traditional, he-full-time-breadwinner, she-mum-at-home lines, and perfectly happy about it, don't write to problem pages. On the other hand, while hundreds of women, like Jill (page 204) write because they are at home with the children and their husband seems to have lost interest in his family, a letter about a problem caused between husband and wife because of her working is extremely rare. Subjectively it seems to us that a wife's being able to do at least some work helps to cement the marriage. Far from working against traditional values, it reinforces 'the family' that we all want to see strong and healthy. Just giving a mother an increased mothering allowance will not mean that she and her husband will have any greater understanding of one another's feelings. And if a woman, like Miriam, unexpectedly finds that she just isn't a natural mother, money alone won't relieve the tensions.

Another important short-coming in our eyes of a policy of encouraging women to stay at home and leave the jobs for the men is that it does absolutely nothing to start repairing a truly serious and far too common gap in family life in this country – the gulf between fathers and their children, which causes heart-ache to parents and can scar children for life. Reinforcing the stereotyped roles might even make it worse. The Gallup Survey for *Woman's Own* found that one in six husbands had *never* looked after his child alone, one in four had *never* put them to bed, one in three had *never* read to their own children.[9]

While a considerable amount of research has failed to show that a mother's going out to work in itself has a bad effect on her children, inadequate fathering has been called the 'hidden wound' of children in this country.

Time after time we have heard working mothers and juvenile delinquency referred to in the same breath, implying or directly stating that one causes the other.

Yet a study in Britain by Robert Andry[10] found that delinquent boys (suffering neither from mental defects nor diseases nor from broken homes) tend to perceive greater defects in their fathers' roles than in their mothers' roles, whereas non-delinquents tend to perceive the roles of both parents as being adequate. 'Further, this seems confirmed in the main by both parents. Thus the prime differentiation between delinquents and non-delinquents, as far as parental role-playing is concerned, is the delinquents' perception of their fathers' role as being negative.' Chris and Peter, the two youth workers I talked to, felt that the father's role is crucial (page 206). One study found 98 per cent of a cross-section of juvenile offenders were without father or father substitute; only 17 per cent had no mother.

Though most studies of paternal, rather than maternal, de-privation have tended to concentrate on extreme situations, such as where there is a total absence of fathers either through occupational requirements or emergencies like wars or in single-parent families, this is beginning to be recognized as a problem more widespread and so more serious for society generally than maternal deprivation.

The assumption that if a man is a good provider he is a good father is taking a knocking.

Gaynor Cohen[11] studied a middle-class estate in south-west London. Most of the families interviewed had primary or pre-school children, most of the women were not in paid employment, and their commitments were mainly to care for their home and upbringing of their children. Their husbands were mostly in their mid to late thirties. 'Almost all of them felt they were at a crucial stage in the development of their careers, and were optimistic about their chances of future success provided they devoted their time and energy to their work. Their careers necessitated a great deal of mobility not merely residentially but within the job itself. *This meant prolonged absences from the home*. Only 9 per cent of those interviewed claimed that their hours were regular and involved little travelling. For most their jobs involved a considerable amount of travel. Some of them were away from home regularly for one or two nights a week, with long working days in between. Others were away from home for varying lengths of time, from two to ten weeks, sometimes as frequently as three or four times a year.'

Even men not employed by large organizations were often absent during weekends and evenings at meetings, courses and other activities. Wives were left to face the heavy burden of bringing up the children alone. Apart from their financial security, they shared many of the problems faced by lone parents, and the children had to cope with the fact that their fathers were often unavailable to them.

While Cohen concentrated on the effect on middle-class middle-management families of the father being absent during the vital early years of their children's lives, educational psychologist Tom Crabtree[12] has commented on the wide range of children affected by paternal deprivation. 'There was no class distinction among the paternally deprived, one job's as effective as another: the children still don't see much of dad. The fathers I saw included a doctor, a farm labourer, a teacher, a waiter, a policeman and a bricklayer . . . I'd expected to see long-distance lorry drivers and sailors. What I saw were factory workers and salesmen, and one milkman . . . These children are not the 72,000 mentioned in the Finer Report whose fathers are not living with them. That's absence. I'm referring to intermittent presence, concealed desertion, paper fathers – call it what you will.'

Ann Oakley rated only 10 per cent of working-class fathers as having a high level of participation in child-care, against 40 per cent of middle-class fathers.

It is often overlooked that often a mother can remain at home full-time only at the expense of a father who is almost always absent from the children's lives. One study revealed that married men under thirty with children worked four times as much paid overtime as similarly aged but childless husbands.[13]

While working *mothers* will pin a smile on their face and drive themselves to cope with their children's needs, there seem to be many fathers who simply do not see that their role need extend beyond earning and providing the odd bit of firm discipline when called for. There are fathers who work long hours and regret that they do not see more of their family, but many simply do not seem to give it a thought. They put their all into their career. Their children rarely see them. Mike (page 208) realized that his children's last school reports might have belonged to two strangers.

Sadly, men who do see very little of their children when young regret it bitterly later. Paul Evans and Fernando Bartolome,[14] interviewing reasonably successful managers, found among the younger men, with small children, that they would consciously regret being short-tempered with the children after a frustrating day at the office, but typically the young manager was 'less sensitive to the positive aspects of his relationship with them; that he may be missing the opportunity to play with them or share pleasures with them. A troubled frown appears on his face when we confront him on this. But then he says, "Well, I'm at a particularly important stage of my career now, and that will have to wait."'

'That will have to wait. He makes what we call the "assumption of equivalent time": one day invested three years from now is equivalent to one day invested today. Maybe he is a financial analyst and recognizes that time has a discount factor: so he says, two days invested in three years' time is equivalent to one day invested now. "I'll make up for it later." This assumption is false. A son who was three years old becomes now six. If he learnt to swim during those years, his father will *never again* share with him the experience of teaching him how to swim. If a daughter learnt how to read, he will *never* have the opportunity to participate in teaching her. The opportunity is gone and never returns. This is one of the most painful realities of adulthood . . . Unless it is pointed out in black-and-white, this reality rarely penetrates the awareness threshold of the younger man. Yet it becomes a point of maximum sensitivity for the man in his forties and fifties. He is aware not only of the pain in bringing up a child, but also of the pleasure. Usually, his awareness is coloured by regret. His awareness comes too late.'

How much children see of their fathers has a crucial and long-lasting, probably ever-lasting, effect on them. Boys obviously model their behaviour on their father's, and how is a girl to know what sort of tenderness and affection to expect from men if she rarely gets a chance to see her father behaving tenderly and affectionately towards her mother? What experience of good and involved fathering can they bring to rearing their own offspring if their own father has too often been remote and unavailable? And fathering is important to children just as mothering is.

In *Fathering*,[15] Dr Ross D. Parke points out that fathers generally encourage independent exploratory behaviour more than mothers – both inside and outside the home. Fathers' availability affects children's academic performance. One study showed that fathers who spend more than two hours a day interacting with their children helped them to reach their intellectual potential and have academic performance superior to those whose fathers spent less time with them. Another study found that boys of fathers who were 'nurturant' (kind, praising, helpful) scored higher on intelligence and vocabulary tests than those whose fathers were 'non-nurturant' (cool, aloof).

Fathers are found often to have less positive effects on girls, but this is because of sex-stereotyped attitudes towards their daughters. When fathers expect similar levels of achievement from daughters as they do from sons, they have a similar positive effect, and the girls achieve similar results.

*

I talked to – or received letters from – a dozen people who all illuminate a different reason why trying to polish up the kitchen sink, to make it a better place for a woman to be, can never be anything like a satisfactory answer to our unemployment problems.

A generous allowance for full-time mothering would certainly help many lone mothers, of whom more than 300,000 live on supplementary benefit, but it leaves many of their major difficulties unsolved.

Julie (London)

My husband left me sixteen years ago, when I was pregnant with my third child. I was twenty-four. Five years before that I'd given up work – I was a trainee nurse – because my husband didn't want me to work and also because I wanted to be a full-time mum. I gave up willingly. I had wanted to go to university too, but I gave that idea up as well.

He was a student, and we lived on his grant, which I had to supplement with a couple of nights' nursing a week.

When he left me I suddenly realized what an idiot I'd been to turn down a university place and not take my SRN. I was left with three small children, no qualifications, and he wasn't going to support me at all, travelling around the world as a freelance photographer. I was devastated. But looking back, I'm glad – it pushed me into doing things for myself and being independent. I tried supplementary benefit for the first year, which was humiliating. I was cross-examined about my circumstances, and always on tenterhooks in case they found a boyfriend staying the night and cut it off. I took part-time jobs. I was a petrol-pump attendant, office cleaner, night nurse, secretary, all sorts. I was homeless for three years, going from friend to relative, to relative to friend, which was difficult with three kids. I was ten years in temporary accommodation next, in a place with no bathroom, no hot water and a loo at the end of the garden I shared with the barber's shop next door. But you manage; you just do what you have to. It wasn't the sort of place you want your kids to grow up in, but they loved it.

Living off the state was ghastly. Their questions are intrusive, they probe into everything. When I went to university at twenty-nine, I was getting benefit on top of my grant. It was only £2 per week. A friend asked me if I knew someone was following me. I couldn't believe it. I thought it just happened in books, and in fact there was this guy I became very conscious of who spent three weeks sitting on the car-park bench opposite my house doing the whole thing on me as if I was a top-flight crook, swindling the government out of thousands. All because I lived with another student for a year. The £2 was stopped.

This is ten years ago. I was getting £17 a week grant for me, my children and my books. I was broke all the time. In those days it was a choice – shall we have toilet rolls this week or toothpaste? We went vegetarian – I thought this was a good idea anyway, but though my daughter has stayed with it, my sons and I began to really miss meat. I made lots of nourishing soups. I did feel healthy, though. You can get corrupted when you have all the money you need. But you have to have time to cook that kind of diet properly.

As for working or staying at home, it's one thing if you have a nice house and can prune the roses, and another if you have a dark little scullery basement with a tiny window and you have to have the light on all day, only cold water and lino fraying at the edges. A lot of women who don't live in pleasant houses are as depressed as hell. Children too – when you're living in a high-rise block and they aren't allowed to make a lot of noise, it's far better for them to be in a nursery with other kids. I'm not saying all kids should be in nurseries; every situation is different, that's why the choice should be there.

I happen to be extremely maternal and would have been quite happy at one point to be at home with my children. It's just now in retrospect I thank my stars that I was forced not to. They're now teenagers and I'm forty. They have their own lives. I'd have devoted my life to my children and have nothing.

After-school care was very hard. The planning involved would have taxed a top executive. One friend might have the boys, another my daughter, and when they were at different schools I had to arrange for someone to pick them up and take them to friends' houses and I'd have to collect them from different places. It was awful, constant tension. The thing was I couldn't afford to pay and I was really putting on my friends.

People like Patrick Jenkin say you should help each other out, but they don't realize the difficulties finding a friend who's at home at the right time who likes children and has some of her own the same age. Sometimes it can be done. I had a very good arrangement for six months, but then the friend moved. We did a survey for Gingerbread and found that most parents let children look after themselves from the age of about seven. Some parents had to leave their children at home if they were ill.

It's not a question of the government saying, 'Ah, it's so difficult, right, back home you all go.' You don't say these things to men. To give women a real choice they should look at the situation and say we could have a little help here and a little there. For a start, primary schools should be kept open till six, with whoever – it doesn't have to be teachers. School holidays need to be covered too. If you take six weeks off, you tend to lose your job.

The state say they don't want to take over bringing up children, that's the family's job, but the provision of child-care isn't going to take away from families. It'll support families so they don't have their children running round the streets or put in care. Other countries like France and Sweden do.

You can't say in one breath 'We are a party that wants to

support families' and in the next breath say 'We are not going to give this particular thing any support at all.'

Is a generous mothering allowance so that mums can stay at home the answer? I should imagine that any large child benefit wouldn't exceed the minimum wage, so say it was £60 per week. It sounds like a lot, but it's not much if it's your total income. For a married woman, it might just mean that the husband would give his wife less. I think families would be better off but not mothers.

There's also the danger that as soon as your children come of age, the woman's left with no income, no earnings-related pension, no unemployment benefit. I don't know what one would do about that. Even if women are forced to work, it isn't just the money they're interested in. They want to get out of the house, and they must be allowed that choice as much as men. At the moment it's a very unbalanced division. The man must work every hour God made him and never see his family, just support them, and a woman must stay at home all the time whether the kids want her there or not. Even if they're at school she must keep polishing.

I just think it's very rigid. I discussed it with my children. My sons wanted football boots, they didn't want to borrow the school's; my daughter wanted piano lessons. Right, I said, there's only one way you're going to get them and that's by me working, which will mean sacrifices on your part. They went along with it happily.

A couple of years ago my son said he felt sorry for his friends who go home and their parents are there; the minute they come through the door it's take off your shoes, come in, what have you been doing at school. He said they don't want to answer questions like that, they envy him his bit of freedom for a couple of hours.

Obviously all women don't want the same kind of care, their circumstances differ, but I'm darn sure that if men had the responsibility for children tomorrow there'd be every conceivable type of day care you could think of. But we get nowhere. If you've got a woman Prime Minister who says, 'I'm a woman and

I've always made it, I don't understand why other women don't,' what can you expect? She had money and a nanny. Women in general just don't have any clout. In times of unemployment and recession women are the first to go. We must get away from this idea that women should be at home and not at work.

The whole focus of the argument should be that people should choose, including women. The trouble is that women feel guilty about everything. If they work they worry about the children. If they're at home they're guilty about not contributing.

I've got friends without children and in their thirties who are worried about having one because the child will now have an older mum! Women just feel guilty. I think I'm beginning to feel a little less so now. I'm just glad I've done a lot of things. It's another look at life.

(Julie Kaufman is general secretary of the one-parents' self-help organization Gingerbread.)

*

Being on the dole is tough on anyone. Boys tend to get into more trouble with the authorities, finding a role as rebel since they can't establish themselves as earning adults. For the girls without hope of a job, let alone a career, there is one obvious age-old way to attain an adult role . . . nature's tender trap.

Chris (Merseyside)

I've now got a twelve-month temporary job through the Manpower Services Commission counselling at a youth centre on a big, tough estate. But before that I was unemployed myself for twelve months.

I'd given in my notice from my previous job because my husband, who's a seaman, wanted me to go with him on his next voyage, which wives can do. But things got unexpectedly tough financially. He'd expected to be home for only two months but as it turned out he only worked four months out of twelve.

As time went by we were almost desperate. My husband

would get paid at the beginning of the month and we'd sit down and work it out that there was no way we could survive on that, to buy food and things. Then there was my dole money, £41.30 a fortnight.

We'd have a couple of months when we could just manage and then the bills would come in the third month and it was just ridiculous. We'd be without a penny or in debt. So by then we were living on my dole money, but it didn't go anywhere. I used to dread shopping. Even yesterday, though I don't have to worry about it, I still walked half a mile down the road because I knew that in Tesco I could get something cheaper than in the shop I was in. You feel what a stupid waste of time, you're wasting your life running from one shop to another just to save a few pence. It's pathetic.

My husband and I were always arguing, bickering. We couldn't even get a break from it, other than seeing his mum or mine, or sit and talk with friends. But to actually go out into town and have a meal, we just couldn't do it.

There were days when we couldn't afford a pint of milk. You know, searching the house for a few pennies, and not wanting anyone to know you're in that situation. When friends asked us out for the night, I'd just make an excuse, say, 'You come over here'.

It was all right for people to say that I ought to be able to get something with my five O levels but there was nothing going. I started thinking I was good for nothing.

I tried as a clerical officer in local government, but with the cut-backs there was obviously nothing there. I tried the Civil Service, the health authority, then I got to the stage where I would take anything at all. I wrote for factory jobs and never heard from them.

You don't accept it at first but then you start thinking, 'What am I good for?' Nothing.

OK, I could keep house. I'd get up at eight and the house was like a new pin by twelve. My husband would get up at nine, go out and get the paper and have a walk, and come back and say he couldn't move in the house. Because I would say I've spent all morning doing this and you come in and mess it up. I would talk to him as if he was a pig. He would say that he didn't feel as though he lived here, just a lodger. He was scared to sit in a chair in case I came round with a brush.

I have always felt that I didn't want children, though I may change my attitude. But when I was out of work I thought that if I had a baby at least I'd have something to do. I know it was stupid but nevertheless the thought was there. I was thinking it out of pure boredom, and of course there was no way we could afford it. I know people say you can make do but it creates other tensions.

The area where I work now used to be a booming place with the industrial estate, but over the last few years everything's closing down.

The kids I'm working with, they're thirteen, fourteen and fifteen, they haven't left school but they don't expect to get a job – it's just, 'Oh, when I get on the dole . . .' and that's that. When they're older, eighteen or nineteen, they're unemployed as a way of life. They've grown up with it in this area.

We get some kids truanting and they say they can't go home because their parents are in the house all day. That's the majority, not just one or two. There's no work here.

You meet a lot of girls of sixteen and seventeen who think that if they don't have a baby in a pram by eighteen there's something wrong with them. Not necessarily married. They just don't talk about going to work. People I meet, youth club leaders and so on, sometimes ask me why don't they see any girls? Where are they all? The answer is they are in the house. They stay in and do the housework, especially if the mother does have a job. Maybe the mum'll give them a few bob a week to buy some clothes, maybe supplementary benefit. Working mothers here are nearly all full-time workers, definitely, and their husbands are out of work.

So a lot of girls stay away from school to look after younger children, do the shopping and clean the house. The boys stay off because they think it's pointless, what are they going to get out of school?

I had a girl in the other day who'd been unemployed for two years. She wanted to work with children and was put in touch with us. We went round various places where she could be a volunteer, but where there were volunteers in the past, now it's young workers. She's twenty years old, too old to be young, so she's not had much luck.

She told me that she does the housework, her mum goes to work, her brother and sister are both unemployed. She gets fed up but it's one of those things she's learned to accept. She's very closed in because she hasn't any money to go out with. But her friends are all in the same position. They support each other and learn to survive, and they get pregnant. They don't think about it. It's a natural process.

A lot of them get six months on a STEP or a YOP. They're quite content with that, working with toddlers or old-age pensioners and so on, because they get slightly more than they would on social security, but that's only six months. After they've finished a lot try to get on another one. The fellers tend to do painting and decorating, that sort of thing. The reason why they don't turn up for that work a lot of the time is because they see themselves doing a man's heavy job for £23 a week, whereas the girls might do their type of work voluntarily.

Some of the girls get married, some have babies and live with their parents, a bit of both. Usually if a girl of sixteen has a boyfriend he's a steady boyfriend, maybe a couple of years older, both unemployed. The girl's had the baby and lived at home and maybe a few years later they've got married but not rushed into it.

But most of the girls I see think of marriage as the ideal thing. That's it. You're a woman and you get married and have a family. They might get married when both are unemployed, not thinking about the pressures that might create. They wonder what's happening when things get difficult – they don't know. I mean, it happened to me, but at least I sat down and thought it out.

Obviously when they have all these problems the marriages break up and they take it out on the children and each other.

Because they've never had the experience of working, they don't know any different way of things. My first working experience – I enjoyed the work, but it taught me a lot, that people can be nasty when there's no need to be, they can be offhand and you learn how to deal with those situations.

To me, it all depends how you were brought up. You get people now saying you don't have to be taught to be a mother, it's natural, but things change, it's not like that any more. People are influenced by the media. Thirty years ago, a girl with two kids wasn't sitting watching television and seeing fantastic clothes, and she'd have had her mother and grandmother there to learn from.

*

Carol is a highly qualified sociologist who decided to stay at home, or at the most do only part-time work, while her children were small. As a result she now finds that she has lost her place on the career ladder for ever.

Carol (London)

Doing VSO in Jamaica for a year was the start of my political education. There was no such thing as social security; lots of beggars and handicapped and destitute lying around on the streets. I visited a so-called charity home which was worse than a nineteenth-century work-house.

I was badly advised at school. I didn't want to do English, I wanted social science. When I asked about doing anthropology at school there was nobody who knew anything about it, so because I did well at English, got all the school prizes and that jazz, I just went on and did an English degree.

I thought I must get into social work. So I went to the London School of Economics. Because I'd got into something that I was interested in, I had a successful academic year, doing a diploma, and I decided to stay on and do the MSc. I enjoyed it very much, even though, without a grant, I had to work in the evenings to pay for it, teaching English to foreign students. Then I did some research on race relations and then got a research scholarship in Manchester in the department of youth work. It was small and very good, a combination of research and action. The project finished after four years, and I couldn't find any comparable work. Money for that sort of research was drying up, the whole race relations industry was getting very dicey. I couldn't find anything in Manchester so I worked in a kibbutz for four months, came back to London and got a job with the Nuffield Foundation doing research on legal advice and tribunals. It was investigating the relationships between access to power, the class structure and how the legal system actually works. Two of us wrote a book on it which was published in 1977 – a long time after. The project lasted two years, and before the end of it I met Chris.

We started living together, I got pregnant and we were very happy about it. I gave up work in December just before I had Andrew in February.

I did say before Andrew was born that I wanted to start by bringing him up myself. That was partly because I married and had him quite late – I was thirty – but it was also influenced by the fact that, through no fault of her own, my mother didn't have much time to spend with us. She was divorced when I was two and neither my brother nor I really had her at home much at all. She was a headmistress.

I stayed at home for seven months, then I went back to work. Mainly it was for the money, because Chris wasn't very well paid as a teacher, but at the same time it was dawning on me that there ought to be something more than just sitting at home with a baby. I loved it, but it was an incredible shock. It changed everything so totally. When you've had years of being completely selfish, doing what you want, going out, spending money on holidays – we were hard up, we couldn't do any of these things. Also I was lonely – I didn't know many local people.

I got a part-time job lecturing in sociology at a polytechnic. Chris used to come home early so I could do two or three hours in the early evening. It was only five hours a week, but it helped. It was then that we bought the house. Having a child was certainly holding me back in the sort of work I could get. Even then it seemed to be that you couldn't do an interesting research job unless you went full-time, forty-eight weeks a year, were prepared to go off to conferences and attend meetings in the evenings – just a very rigid idea of what work was all about with little consideration for women with children.

I did the lecturing for about ten months. It was good pay – about £4.50 an hour – but I never got paid for holidays, or if something got cancelled. That was the main drawback – five months in the summer when you don't get a penny.

Then I started home tuition – it seemed like something you could fit in with children. But the contrast between lecturing at the poly and teaching basic English to pregnant schoolgirls, to children who are sick and backward and truant, is phenomenal. In many ways it's harder, but once you get into the swing of it, it becomes easier to the point where it's not interesting any more. Well, it always has been a stop-gap, quite honestly.

They encourage you to do about ten hours a week, but because it's mostly pregnant schoolgirls, they come and go at a rate of knots. Sometimes I'm doing four hours and sometimes twelve. It varies.

It's good for mothers with children. It's one of the few services that are – they are dependent on graduate women at home with children who can use their skill. They don't exploit them. They're trying to do whatever they can to help mothers. If you have to take your children with you to the centre to get books or do lessons, it's all completely accepted. It's very easy-going, not bureaucratic at all. I can see why people stick with it for years and years. No pay during the holidays again, you only get paid if the child turns up – so if they're ill or don't turn up you get nothing. They do pay your stamp though.

I've done home tuition on and off for three years. I've done lots of other stuff in between – freelance things, pieces for magazines, editing a community health council newspaper, consumer research, and I've had a couple of part-time jobs at another polytechnic, teaching sociology to nursery nurses.

But it was work below my capabilities. It was social policy for nursery nurses, the development of sanitation in 1880 or something like that. It wasn't the sort of thing I'd have expected to do if I'd carried on a straightforward career. I did it for the money, to get out of the house, to meet other adults, variety – a whole combination of things. The money's quite good, but when you average it all out over the year, I think since I left my last full-time job I haven't earned more than about £1,500 a year at the very most.

If I hadn't stayed at home with the children – we've two now – I could expect to be in a good research job, have a senior fellowship in some institute, paying £10,000 a year. I'll never catch up now. I'll pay for my choice for the rest of my life maybe.

Since last Christmas I've been looking for a research job. I've tried for half a dozen part-time jobs and not got any. I've applied for everything I thought interesting. I mean, I haven't applied for a job looking at the economics of running the railways, I haven't looked at being a secretary – but I've tried for everything that could possibly be up my street, and that's half a dozen jobs in nine months.

I've been shortlisted for nearly every one, but I just haven't got any. The last one wrote me a letter saying that they knew things would be difficult for me because I found the interview so stressful when they asked me what I was going to do with my children, could I cope with them and the job, and so forth. A large part of the interview was about this.

In a whole year lecturing I was only off two days, probably less than people with no kids at all. I'm not worried about my commitment. School holidays are a problem but when I've got income from a job I can make arrangements, but I can't do that till I've got a job. It's Catch-22. I'm tempted to say something completely untrue like my mother lives round the corner, because if you're honest and say yes, there will be problems but I'll work it out, they don't like it.

A friend of mine in much the same position as me always wanted to go back to work after her two kids but she now knows there just aren't any teaching jobs where she is in Cornwall, so she's having another baby. She's quite honest about it. She says it's just something to do. I know others who've just gone for the total domestic role, and it seems to have taken them over.

I don't know how happy they're going to be when their children have grown up, when they'll inevitably have lost their chances. It's unlikely they're really going to be satisfied with being the sort of mum who's always there when the kids come home from school, even while the children are still small.

Perhaps they've made the really fruitful choice – there are always those two voices in your head aren't there? – but I don't think being at home, usually in a limited social group, just with the children and other women with children, is varied enough. You haven't got that much to say to each other and you're not sharing the things you would share as an individual. You're not sharing the fact that you're both interested in art, say, you're sharing the fact that they've got a sale on at so-and-so and you get kiddies' nighties there. It's not enough.

*

Rosalind felt she was 'looking at the four walls going bananas' after the birth of her little girl. She found a local mothers' group helpful, but not the answer to her feeling that her brain was stopping – to the extent that her mind would go blank in the middle of talking to someone. She has felt so much better since she found a job that her only fear is that it might end.

Rosalind (Bedfordshire)

I was pleased to have the baby, oh yes. It was a bit of an inconvenience, but we'd planned to have one the following year anyway. I was twenty-seven. We were happy about it.

I was a bit upset that I wasn't having her at home, in Australia, but mum came over for two weeks just after she was born. I'm very lucky with my mum – she would and does sacrifice anything for her children. But she had to get back to her job. I was absolutely besotted with my baby, not a moment's resentment that she was stopping me from working. But as soon as mum left I started to feel miserable. It was all right having the baby to look after when she was awake. She was an alert child. But when she was asleep there was nothing to do, just sitting in this two-up two-down place looking at the four walls going bananas, thinking I've got to get out, what am I going to do. I used to go down the road to see my friend and say I just have to get a job, I can't stand it any more. I've since heard that she was quite worried about me. I always thought she was being friendly. I didn't realize she was trying to get me out of myself. I didn't know what the matter was. Then I started to realize what was happening – I'd felt like this before. It was when I was in a flat all one summer with nothing to do after taking my exams, waiting to start articles – I'm a solicitor by profession – my brain stopped. I couldn't be bothered to do anything, not even watch television. I knew it was starting again and I got very frightened. It was awful.

All I could see was that I was going to be stuck at home, not knowing anybody and Tony out at work all day. I missed my mum, not for the mothering but because she was good to talk to. So I used to think, 'My God, what am I going to do?'

I started looking in the paper for jobs but there was never anything advertised, because I wanted a part-time job. It wasn't actually feasible for me to get a job anyway; how I ever thought I was to continue breast-feeding I don't know. When she was four or five weeks old I went down to the office where I'd been working while I was pregnant and asked about doing some part-time. I went to a health visitor asking if she knew of a childminder who'd have Daisy for a few weeks here and there. There was nobody in my village but she gave me the name of someone in the town where the job was. I thought it would be nice if I could leave Daisy with her and just get out of the house, but there was no work.

When Daisy was six weeks old Tony was offered a job which meant going to Italy for a few weeks. I was down in the dumps, really despairing, my brain slowing down. I said I wasn't happy for him to go if he couldn't be home every weekend. He was concerned about all the travelling, so I said what I would really like would be to come with you. Then I was worried about all the mail and the bills to be paid, which was ridiculous. I'm not usually like that.

Even when we got to Italy I was paranoid about my milk drying up and not being able to get the formula. But it was the best thing we ever did. After the emotional upheaval of having a baby, having mum come and go and this sudden obsession of getting a job, we were in a really nice hotel and then a service apartment so all I had to do was cook meals. I hadn't realized how depressed I'd been. When I came back from Italy I felt much better.

Then Tony's parents came for a month. They are very old and difficult. No sooner had we got rid of them, when my mum and dad arrived. When we met them at Heathrow I remember saying right, before we start, there are a few rules. They looked at me like I'd dropped a ton of bricks. I told them all the things they were and weren't to do. I was all het up – it was ridiculous.

A couple of days later I was hysterical and crying. Mum was very understanding. Although I was really much better I was still in a state. Then when they went home everything fell apart again. That was when I found out about NCT. I was put in touch with a postnatal support group through the National Childbirth Trust. I can't speak too highly of the group. It's ongoing and marvellous. The co-ordinator, for instance, has a boy of five and a girl of three. We've all got to know each other, and I know there's always someone there if I need them. It's a pity I wasn't put in touch with them earlier when I really needed it.

I started playing tennis. I thought it was stupid, but I got friendly with the girls and we played all summer, then squash in the winter. It's difficult to get off your bum, but I had to do something to get out of the house, also to try and lose some weight. I'd put on a lot, even before I was pregnant. That was getting me down.

So again I started looking for a job. I was offered one as a part-time typist but that didn't turn me on. I didn't want to work for money, I wanted something so that my brain would be stimulated.

There was a definite tension in our marriage because I was so uptight and so often in a bad mood. Tony wasn't very happy with his job. All I could think of was that we had better go back home. I was miserable all the time.

I'd be talking to people and suddenly my mind would go blank, I just couldn't think of the right thing to say. When I was at university I got used to just sitting talking for hours, chat about just anything. But when we had people to dinner we would sit there and talk about babies. Even with the NCT, it's still not really stimulating your mind. You need to get away and have contact with people outside your world. I think all women need a break.

There's voluntary work, but I don't have the right sort of motivation to sit and talk to an old lady for an hour a day. I often wonder about people who do voluntary work, whether they do it because they get something out of it or for appearances' sake, because it looks nice. What good is it going to do the recipient if you aren't doing it happily? And a real problem about voluntary work is that you have to volunteer yourself. It's hard after you've been at home by yourself to go anywhere – it's always a bit intimidating. When you're depressed you think that you're inadequate and that nobody wants you, and to actually go along and offer your services is very difficult. Once you have a paid job you just have to turn up, you're not putting yourself forward in the same way.

When I finally got a job, I was terrified that it might not last, because having the job made me feel so much better. I was so desperate to have it and so happy to get it. Once I found my feet and got interested in it I thought how awful it would be if it went. I was so scared.

It's all well and good for people like Penelope Leach to say the answer for mothers at home is drop-in centres or other groups, but it's so hard when you're at home actually to get motivated to be up and out. You get so used to doing nothing. Even to go round to the shops is an effort. The people who most need to get to a drop-in centre are the ones that won't, who can't be bothered.

It's the same with NCT. It's the people on the council estate who really need it, but they're the ones who won't go. But once you've got a job you get so used to getting up and doing things that things aren't such an effort.

I remember I was sitting at home day after day and couldn't be bothered walking down the street to get a loaf of bread. Now if that happens to me, who's supposed to have a fairly active brain and should be able to motivate myself and find something to do, what happens to the women who've never been encouraged to have any other interests anyway?

*

This young mother happily planned to stay at home full-time until all her children were five, but even though she had no serious money problems, is a very sociable type and started a mother and toddler group, in the end she took a job to save herself from cracking up. She reckons it has saved her marriage too.

Valerie (London)

I'm twenty-four and my husband's twenty-seven. We've been married for eight years. We've three children – Sally's five in November, Mary's four in December and Ruth who's two.

I'd always wanted more than one child. I had Sally and then fell for Mary while I was on the Pill – breast-feeding as well! I wanted four children then, so we decided that as we had two that close together we might as well go for another. I wanted to be at home for the first five years of their life, so in a way the closer they were the better.

Being at home was easier than I expected. When I was carrying Mary I was very upset; one baby took up all my time and I really didn't think I could cope with two. I was panic-stricken at the thought, but when she actually came along – well, you haven't got any more time, so you just do more, you cope. I didn't have that many problems – with them growing up together it's been a lot better than I thought.

I found it easy, really, to let the house go to pot! I just did the dusting when they'd gone to bed and during the day my life was full of playdoh and paint. They were fed on time, clean when they went out, and I didn't worry apart from that. Luckily my husband isn't the sort to come home screaming that he wants his dinner on the table immediately. He's a postman now but when we married he was a paint-sprayer.

When Sally and Mary started at nursery, my main problem was time on my hands. They went at three years old. With just me and Ruth at home I didn't know what to do with myself. I thought I'd be able to cope but I found the company of children for that long was too much. I was finding that I had no conversation and my mind – I felt like I was turning into a vegetable literally, I really did. I was longing for my husband to walk through the door. I wasn't really depressed, just there was something lacking.

I took it out on Bill. I was miserable when he came home and I picked holes in everything he did. He couldn't do anything right. Because I felt as if I wasn't doing much, I was on the defensive.

The crunch came this June when we decided that I would have to get a job. It was getting me down, I would have cracked up. I was ratty with the kids. Well, I can't really take my frustration out on them, so I'd save it all up until Bill walked in the door and blast away at him. I did actually say I'd divorce him.

I was being totally irrational, but we go out very rarely because of the difficulty of getting a baby-sitter for three kids, so I was at home all day and we couldn't get out at night either. We never went to the pictures, we were never alone together. In the morning the kids all came crawling into bed, so it was a twenty-four-hour job. It got to the stage where it was a year since we'd been out together.

We decided the best thing would be for me to get a part-time job and Bill would go on to night work, because I didn't want them to go to a childminder. When he went on to nights it was as if a door opened for me. He said he'd stay up to take the two to the nursery and look after the little one until I got home. I was initially working in a biscuit factory – anything to get out of the house – and then I got my present job – accounts and wages clerk at a local charity that runs youth clubs and has an old people's visiting scheme. I've only been there a few weeks. I work from nine till one, at £2.15 an hour.

It's a bit of a strain for Bill. We still don't see each other all that often, but I can cope with that now because I'm going out in the morning. He's happier; he's backed me up right from the start. He gave me the money for my fares, he bought me a new ring, a new coat and a new jumper. He could actually make the money I'm making quite easily by doing overtime, but then I'd feel even more isolated than before.

Before I was working I started a mother and toddler club, but it was still a lot of mums all at home with their children so you all have the same frustrations and you can't help each other. It's nice for the children and it's OK in that it gets you out of the house, but you're still in four walls, you've still got kids playing round you, you've still got nothing different to discuss. It's fine as far as it goes but it's no real alternative.

It's good for my ego, working and getting about. Bill's a bit nervous about it. He worries if I'm ten minutes late, because I've got a bit of freedom, in case I stray from the straight and narrow. Actually my marriage is safer than ever.

It's had a good effect on Ruth, too. She's better behaved, and she used to be spiteful – that's stopped now.

I'm not so sure about the older ones. Bill's taking them to nursery, and it's choc-a-block with women so he feels uneasy and drops them at the door, whereas I used to go in with them and give the school their dinner money and watch them do the first painting. Mary says she prefers it when I take her to school, but Sally, I think, likes the responsibility. She'd be upset if I took her in and didn't give her her own dinner money.

They like bragging. They told the nursery teacher that I'm earning a small fortune and Father Christmas is going to bring them such a lot this year.

I think it has a good effect on the girls to see me working. It's a sexist thing. Sally will say when she grows up she's going to be a nurse and I say, 'No, you're going to be a doctor.' She says, 'But mum, ladies can't be doctors,' and I say, 'Yes, they can. There's a lady doctor at the clinic. Women can be doctors and men can be nurses.' But she wouldn't quite accept that. And you get things like 'When I grow up and have children,' and I say, 'Yes, but before you have children you're going to get a job, so you'd better find a nice job.' Now Sally says, 'When I grow up and go to work,' and that to me is a great relief. I say thank God. Mary says she's going to be a clown. She says she's going to have a red nose and make people laugh. I think that's great.

*

This mother found voluntary work very satisfying but still has a deep-seated urge to earn some independence.

Gillian (Middlesex)

My mother was just a housewife and mother. She was married at twenty so she didn't work for long. She didn't have a chance to decide whether she wanted to work as a married woman; I'm not sure that it was something she figured her generation did anyway. Unless they became a JP or some other voluntary job with status to it. When I told her I wanted to become a marriage guidance counsellor she was shocked rigid.

As a girl it never occurred to me that some mothers worked outside the home. I even went home to lunch; she could have got rid of me during the day – both my sister and brother went to boarding school for one reason or another and I didn't. I stayed at home, went to a local public school. Left at sixteen after O levels. I didn't have any idea what I wanted to do; other than that I wanted to go to agriculture college; but I think they figured that wasn't the thing for a girl to do. I still wish I had, though.

So I left and went to a finishing school. Actually I was rather pleased because it meant skiing a lot. I could have gone and done all the arty things in Paris, but I chose Switzerland. So I came back after a marvellous year having done wonderful things, speaking fluent French and having met a lot of nice people – not the toffee-nosed lot who were going on to be presented or whatever – and I arrived back and was sent to secretarial college.

I don't think I regret leaving early and not doing A's. The only thing I regret is not having an interesting job to go back to part-time. This probably is every woman's dream – something interesting you can combine with a home and a family and not working nine to five every day of the week.

My parents weren't pleased when I got engaged to James because he's Jewish and my mother kept saying we wouldn't be allowed into the golf club. I was twenty-one. They became resigned – now of course he can do no wrong. He's done so well in the firm.

I can't remember at any stage reckoning that I would go on working after I was married, children or not. After five months, I was pregnant. I think I just thought, well, this is the next thing. One starts a family and that was it. First there was Christopher and a year late the twins – a girl and a boy. Three children under two. It was very hard work. James was a great help taking turns with night feeds for the twins. But by the time they were nine months it was really hectic and we decided we could afford a mother's help. We had a series of helps and then we went on to au pairs who have more studying time and free time, and in fact we had au pairs until just over a year ago – the twins are sixteen now. Was I bloody idle? Probably; but we do quite a lot of entertaining in and outside the home and getting baby-sitters at a moment's notice wasn't possible. Anyway I didn't like leaving the children with someone I didn't know from an agency. My mother has never ever baby-sat – and she lives a mile away. It was always a bit of a trouble for her. So by the time you've paid a full rate for a baby-sitter, it almost worked out the same as an au pair.

When the children were all at school there always seemed too much to do to worry about what I was going to do with my life. And I was very happy doing it, may I say. It really wasn't until one started to read so much in magazines and papers that being at home – well you weren't pulling your weight. Actually, up until the last three or four years I think I'd have been perfectly happy just running the home. And even now I think I wouldn't mind, but if that's all you do you really do become a bit of a bore and it's not fair to James. You see there's this big house to run – yes, I know I have help – and there's all the entertaining.

Anyway I decided I wanted to do something; it was listening to a good friend who kept saying, come on you'd be good at marriage guidance. I think it was having someone think I'd be good at anything – it's rather nice. I was very surprised when they took me. I don't know why they did, though I suppose I'd always been a shoulder to cry on.

James was very pleased and keen for me to get out and do something. It didn't have to be earning money. I think he felt looking after home and kids for ever must be boring – I don't think he was finding me a cabbage. He doesn't want to know about marriage guidance but I think there are hidden reasons for this. He discusses his job with me, but I think he's frightened I might find out some of his deeper feelings if I discuss cases. He was very keen and supportive though. But if he'd felt my work was coming before his job, the home and the children he would have put his point of view – and I would have stopped. I reckon my first priority is James and the family full stop. There wouldn't have been any aggro. They are the most important people to me. Looking after them is more than a job. It's a vocation. But I can see it isn't for every woman.

I have clients who want to go out to work and their husbands won't let them, and others who have to go out to work to help with the finances and don't want to. You can't resolve it easily. With the first group it's a question of age. The younger husbands seem to think it's a duty for their wives to go back to work as soon as she has free time on her hands otherwise they're being carried. The older ones want their wives at home – it's a reflection on their capacity to earn enough to support their wives, I think.

I don't get many women clients feeling guilty about going out to work and leaving the children. Not outwardly. They go to great lengths to justify how well the children are being looked after, how happy they are, how they feel they are better parents. I feel there is a fair amount of justification going on; I've never got anyone to admit they are doing it for themselves. This is what they need and that they may feel subconsciously the children are suffering because they are brought up by someone else.

If I'm honest, I do feel that women should subjugate their own needs if they decide to have children until the children are say ten. The most important thing for a child is to have a mother there. Well I suppose it needn't actually be a mother.

I do feel terribly dependent on James though. I suppose this is one of the reasons I'm trying to set up my own catering business. I wanted to find something to earn me some money of my own. James thinks it's a thoroughly stupid reason, but when I buy him presents I want to buy it with money I've earned. I ask for money for my parents for birthdays and Christmas, and I use it to buy presents for James or the children. Whatever I want I can have – James is very generous. But I just want my own money to be there. It's a deep-seated feeling. James flogs his guts out and works far too hard; it isn't to relieve that – he'd work anyway. It isn't for the future – if he died I'd be a wealthy woman. I'd like to be as generous to him as he is to me.

I save money out of the housekeeping or pay cash so that he doesn't see in the cheque book what I'm paying for. I've been doing that for nineteen years.

The catering business doesn't make as much as I pay my daily. But it's a thrill to make £1.50 profit. It's too early to say that I've achieved anything, but there is satisfaction in someone saying they like what I'm doing.

Although I've had nineteen fabulous years of marriage, I'm telling Julie that she should try to find something that she can go back to when she's had a family. I wish I had something interesting to go back to – not just pounding a typewriter.

I heard Mrs Thatcher said married women want little part-time jobs to keep their hand in. Rubbish. What is the little job? Serve behind the sweet counter, school meals? Little jobs tend to be the boring, badly paid jobs.

I have a few friends who have gone back to work full-time and now they are all divorced. I don't know which came first – the unhappy marriage or the return to work.

I don't think the children will have the same problems really.

Although I don't understand them. They are fatalists. They say, enjoy yourself now before the third world war. Working, not working . . . it's all the same to them. I'd like them to have the stability of a traditional family life, mother at home, father working. But of course in the future it doesn't have to be that way round. So long as it's someone constant, long-term. In the future parenting could just as easily be shared by father and mother equally.

*

Three letters to my problem page at the *Sun* show the unhappiness that can lie behind traditional role-playing.

When the husband is out at work all day and the wife at home, their completely divorced life-styles can lead to a breakdown in understanding.

Richard (Skegness)

Since the birth of our second child two years ago, I've been driven to total despair by my wife's attitudes to our family life. At that time I was beginning to make an impact in my career and promotion was within reach. Since then, although we have often talked of our difficulties, it seems to me my wife can only see her own problems within the home. I can appreciate that she will have a busy time with the children but I wish she would try and occasionally see my point of view instead of just off-handedly dismissing any ideas I present to her.

You can't begin to appreciate what impact a casual comment such as 'I've had a hard day today' can create when the only reply it receives is 'What about me then?' Even the most distant of any loving contact is now non-existent.

The whole thing has led me to seeing a psychiatrist, who can only advise me to see a counsellor. On consideration of the whole thing I still love my wife. I know she would have a hard time of coping without me and want to sort this thing out with her, but if it goes on I feel it best to leave. What alternative have I?

*

Fathers who leave all responsibility for their children and home to their wives can put an intolerable strain on their marriage.

Jill (Aberdeen)

I really feel depressed. I've been married nearly ten years and have three children, ages five and a half, three and fifteen months.

We moved 300 miles eighteen months ago with my husband's job and although I wasn't keen, I've made the best of it and settled down. The problem is, I do everything for the children myself, look after the house myself, do meals etc. My husband's hours are long – often he leaves the house at 8 a.m. and doesn't get home before 9 p.m.

Now he often goes for a drink after work on the late night and isn't home before midnight. It's getting where he wants to pop out for an hour or so on his early night.

I just feel as if I've had enough. I spend so much time alone it's as if I'm going mad. I don't know whether to leave or what to do.

If I try to say anything he tells me he'll do what he likes, so I just feel as if it's not worth bothering. If it wasn't for the children I wouldn't stay.

*

Some women find quite unexpectedly that motherhood just doesn't agree with them. Home feels like a prison, the baby a gaoler, and if the husband objects to them getting a job it's as if he has thrown away the key.

Miriam (Scunthorpe)

I am thirty, been married for six and a half years and have a son of eleven months. The problem is that I should never have had him. He was planned, not an accident, but now he's here I realize that I have no maternal instinct. Maybe I left it too late. The baby himself is a lovely boy, everybody says so.

But I have no friends or neighbours to talk to. Both my and my husband's relatives live in another town, so no help or advice there. I feel so inadequate, no confidence. I've never had a break from the boy, even for a couple of hours – we know of no one to take him.

My husband wasn't a bit interested in the baby when he was born, never fed or changed or even watched him in the bath, just wasn't interested. I had to do it all, so I came to resent the baby but later on realized it was my husband I resented. It's not getting any better. My husband still does what he wants to do, when he wants to do it. We never go out, nowhere to go. The house is like a prison. I can't do what I like because I'm tied with the baby.

I gave up a good job and money to have him, I had lots of friends and colleagues at work, but now I don't see anyone from one week to the next. My husband is anti-social. He'd rather spend the time at home. I keep asking myself where it's all going to end. I've contemplated suicide – but I'm a coward – or leaving my husband with the baby but have nowhere to go. You don't have to tell me it's all selfish. I know it is but I can't stop myself. I just wish he'd never been born. I've had these thoughts ever since the baby was born but I thought it was getting better, but it's going the opposite way. The doctor gave me depression tablets, but they made me fall asleep all the time. We never do anything as a family. I want to get a job but he won't let me – just to get away from the boy – I feel as if I've lost my identity.

I feel like a zombie. I'm sure I could hit the baby. I am desperate. I wanted to see a psychiatrist but my husband won't let me.

*

Chris and Peter both work with young people and have seen for themselves that the father's influence is a crucial deciding factor in whether a youth becomes 'delinquent'.

Chris (Merseyside)

I work in a youth club in a run-down area. We've been talking to boys who have been classed as delinquents about their home life and one thing that does show up is that in general their fathers are the sort who do a lot of drinking, going to the betting shop, and don't work. More often than not the mothers are working, but not for luxuries. They are working to pay the rent, to hold the family together.

The lads stay out – it may not be an easy atmosphere at home – and they're likely to be stopped by the police even if they're not doing anything. They think that if they're going to be stopped anyway, they might as well make a few bob; break into places, cause a few fights.

When they do get into trouble, it's their mother they are frightened of. I often hear the lads say, 'As long as me mam doesn't get to hear about it.' She's the one with some discipline. While if they are truanting and the school knocks at the door, their dad will cover up for them, it's mum who's the heavy hand in the family. The mother may not know anything about it, because she's at work or at the shops, but if she gets to hear about it, the lads know they are in for trouble.

Peter (Bedfordshire)

From my experience running youth clubs, I'm sure that what the dad does is just as important an influence on the kids' behaviour as the mother.

There was one lad I had trouble with here for a year. I got on all right with him one to one. In a tough situation I could say to him, 'Do this or do that,' and it was all right. But as soon as his mates came in, it started. It wasn't physical aggro, it was verbal aggro. You knew very well that as soon as you turned your back you were getting some sly remarks from him, and it would just snowball. He didn't have the sense to see when he went too far and he started swearing, and so it went on.

When it goes on for a long time, that sort of thing is very bad for the atmosphere, so one night I went to his home to have a chat with his parents. From the moment I went down there I realized why he had been like he had all year.

His father had been picked up not long before for being drunk and disorderly. All he could say was, 'Sorry, your Lordship, but it was the booze. Let me off and I'll be a good boy.' Apparently he has a reputation for it.

When I told his father what was happening down at the club, his father's first reaction was to cover up and say he didn't swear, knowing full well he did. Then, when the boy turned round and swore at his father in front of me, what did his father do but beat the hell out of him, while I was there. I had to separate them.

As soon as that lad opened his mouth at home he was shouted down, so no wonder he tried to throw his weight around outside. The mother seemed to be forced into a dual role. She is doing a good job when father is out but when father's in she daren't say too much.

If a father is a tearaway, that can cause a hell of a problem. One family I know have lived here all their lives. There are seven kids, all boys. I have had four of them through the club and not one can manage to get through adolescence without being in trouble. Right from the first it has been the case that if one steps over the line people recognize the name, and slam down on them hard and ask questions later. Also, the older boys model themselves on dad. Now if one of the younger boys gets into an argument with another lad, they'll wade into the thick of it and make the whole situation worse, so he gets a name for trouble and violence, too.

Some of the boys and girls down here look on me as a father figure because their own father shows such little interest and will accept so little responsibility for them.

A fourteen-year-old girl walked into here one night recently and asked me to change a £10 note. During the course of the evening I found that she had got £25 on her. From where? – that was the question I wanted an answer for.

Next day I managed to have a word with her father, since I bumped into him in the street. I said, 'If I say anything to hurt your feelings just walk away,' but I explained to him about his daughter having all this money on her and how concerned I was.

He just asked me to go and tell her mother! He basically didn't want to be bothered to do anything for his own daughter. He just wanted to shrug off any responsibility or effort. He provides for his family but he has nothing to do with the kids. He doesn't think that what they do or what happens to them is anything to do with him.

*

This father is a terrific provider for his family, a successful businessman and breadwinner, but his children's last school report-cards might have belonged to two strangers.

Mike (Cheshire)

The thing that makes me most unhappy is that all the pressures of my job, all the travelling and so on, means that I left the raising of our children entirely to my wife.

In the morning I have to leave home before they're up. The style in this company, which is American-owned, is to start work at 7.30 in the morning. So I have to leave at 6.45. The terrible thing is that during the day I keep thinking of my kids, missing them, and make all sorts of good resolutions, but by the time I get home again at seven, the hour I promised myself to cherish with them, I'm so tired that all I want to do is watch some TV and then go to bed. I just don't have the energy. Which leaves the weekend. By Friday I'm so punch-drunk that all I want to do is just lie around. But then there's the house and the garden to keep up, and I feel I have to play some sport just to take out the tensions and keep physically in shape.

Last night the kids had brought their report-cards home. They could have belonged to complete strangers. There were so many things that I just didn't know – that one was good at history, another at reading, all those things. I simply don't know my kids. I keep thinking that they're going to grow up and leave home and I'll never have known them. Meanwhile, all this trotting around the world, never being in one place long enough to put down roots, means that the pattern for all their relationships in life is going to be loose, shallow and superficial.

My wife is unhappy. She wanted a home and a family, and never had a career she wanted to continue with; but I think she'd have enjoyed life more if I'd been around to take some of the load of bringing up the children. As it is, I never even wash up. I'm not saying it's good, but that's how it is.

And tonight, my wife and I are going out to dinner. I'm exhausted after a week's work – and it's one of those jobs that are never finished, there's always more calling out to be done to make things more efficient – and so it's a business dinner. We're going out with one of our distributors and his wife. So once again I won't see the kids. It'll be in the house, change, and straight out again.

The awful thing is that I enjoy my job. It really satisfies me; but the treadmill can't keep up like this. I can't go on sacrificing half of my life for the other; soon they'll offer me promotion, but eventually I'll have to say enough. The reason why I'm so well paid, like other multinational executives, is obviously to compensate for the devastation in other areas of our lives.

I have a great admiration for my cousin who's in the States. He used to work for IBM, but had always wanted to be a doctor. So he and his wife decided on what the ideal town would be. They spent two years looking, and finally found the place, which had to satisfy all sorts of criteria. They worked it all out. So he gave up his executive job, enrolled at the local medical school while his wife worked, and finally got his qualifications, and joined a medical practice in the town. Now he has the job he wanted in the place he wanted with the family he wanted. He is a very happy man. But I never even talk to my own children.

*

In the eyes of the world, Tim's dad was an admirable father. He was successful, provided a very comfortable and prestigious life-style for his family, took them on marvellous holidays. The family's inner reality was very different. To his son this 'marvellous' father was a figure of complete mystery, whom he rarely saw during his most impressionable years, and whom he can never remember giving him a cuddle.

Tim (London)

By trade my dad was a diplomat. I have very few clear memories of him, when I was young, but plenty of my mother. I remember he always seemed to have a very long working day. He'd gone by the time I went to school and came home after I'd gone to bed. I don't think I had any sense of loss when I was young because we lived in a commuter village where it was the same with all the kids. I didn't feel as if I hadn't got a dad. That came later. My image of my dad from that time really comes as other people's image of him – because he was successful and powerful he was deferred to a lot, so it came from an area of his life that I didn't understand. I didn't feel close to him, except for one thing. He loved the sea and fishing, used to go out with the boats himself, and when I was young he started taking me freshwater fishing with him, maybe once a fortnight or so. That was his version of baby-sitting. That was the main point of contact we had and it's continued up till now.

It was very different from anything I did with my mother, and I enjoyed the sense of equality and being treated by him like a human being. At the same time, he didn't realize that I was often physically very uncomfortable – very cold in the winter and wanting to go home – so I used to get shouted at a lot. But I did value it, and was afraid that the fishing might be withdrawn.

I was much closer to mother. She didn't really have a job until I was thirteen. She made a decision to sacrifice a good career. I think before I was born she was earning more than my father; she was a civil servant and doing very high-level responsible work, but she abandoned it to have me. I've always been pretty close to her.

At a very early age I was aware of tensions between my parents and that I was partly the cause of them. My parents never made any alliance against me but regularly one would enlist my support against the other.

I don't think they could talk to each other clearly. Quite rightly my mother resented having to subjugate her adult life to his career. Presumably some bargain had not been honoured and she felt he wasn't giving her the credit for her contribution to his success. He was belittling her, though terribly polite and well-behaved in public. He has a violent temper and is also very big physically – I don't remember seeing him hit my mother, but he certainly terrified me. Once he threw a carpentry plane at my head when I was ten or eleven. I can't remember it, but my mother does. By my late teens I was in open conflict with him. I saw little of him and resented the way he treated my mother.

I can remember that my mother would give presents at Christmas and my father gave cash. All cash matters went through his hands. He ruled the family through the cheque book. When I was a student he would threaten that if I didn't toe the line over something or other he wouldn't give me any more money so I wouldn't be able to go back to university.

Apart from the money the question of raising me was left to my mother. It's one of my great regrets that I don't know him. Over the last few years I have consciously tried to get close to him before he dies. For years I've been obsessed by the way I don't know him – he was a figure of complete mystery and of great power. Now I can see more of him – little revealing things like he will only go into shops of certain sorts and normally those he's used before, where he's established a relationship with the people and impressed upon them that he's an ex-diplomat, where he doesn't feel himself at risk in any way. In certain circumstances he's enormously confident and blasts his way through and in others, though you'd never imagine it, he's desperately shy and nervous.

Because of his over-rigid attitudes I never wanted a straight job, though I've ended up with a reasonably straight career. It's only recently I've realized that what he did didn't satisfy him. It satisfied his need for power and security in a very superficial way but stopped him developing emotionally. All his friends were tied up with his work, which put an intolerable burden on my mother, who knew that people were sucking up to her. He was taken in by it. If ever we suggested that all his friends were seeking advantages from him he would be outraged. His judgement was no good, partly due to his lack of confidence. He always regarded people in terms of what they earned, very snobby.

He had a profound effect on my emotional and sexual relationships. I found myself in this constant double bind. On one hand he wanted me married because he thought it would get me settled in a steady job and living my life in terms he could understand. He was obviously terribly threatened by a way of life that didn't fit his preconceptions. In practice, on the few occasions he met a girl I was going out with, he was hostile. Very cool. The only ones he liked were ones I'd already decided were hopeless. He wanted someone to change me.

On the other hand, I think he felt there was something in marriage that he missed out on and I should be out there trying to get it for him. There was a tension in him that has been passed on to me in a more open form. Even in the three-piece pin-stripe suit was someone whose ambition was to go out to the desert and disappear off in a jeep. I often take time out alone and I've been able to do that because I'm not married.

I am thirty-four and I would like to be married now and have children. I have only gradually begun to realize that the other person involved is more important than the institution. Before I was reacting against my father's attitude that everything had to be done by the book.

I don't remember being myself cuddled by my father and I have found it enormously difficult to be physically demonstrative. The only time I ever saw my parents kiss was at airports. I've never seen them hold hands. When my father and I meet we make a formal handshake, more like 'shake hands and come out fighting' than an expression of warmth. We're very inhibited with each other.

I feel that his job brutalized him viciously, in return for giving him the strength he needed. He once told me that if anyone's aggressive to you, the best way to put them down is ignore them. In practice he would often flare up in a temper, but in more serious ways, in long-term relationships, he did just that. When the going got emotionally tough he just shut off, including to me and my mother.

5. The Way Forward: Share the Care

If what we truly care about is the welfare of children and parents, a healthy and happy society, then the evidence seems to suggest that, far from encouraging mothers to stay at home full-time, we should be encouraging fathers to work shorter hours and share more in family life and child-care. Both parents sharing the kitchen sink *and* swimming.

As with any major social shift, it is not easy to start plotting the practical steps which would have to be taken to get from present-day realities to some envisaged Nirvana in which both mother and father have the option to work twenty to thirty hours a week sharing the child-care between them. But let's at first just look at how worthwhile an objective this is.

What happens to a child in his first five years very much affects what he is like, what contribution he will make to society and his chances of happiness, for the rest of his life.

In general, children would be happier, more balanced, more healthily independent, fulfil their potential better and be less likely to become delinquent if they received more of their father's time and attention. (If they were being brought up in a social atmosphere which assumed that child-care was a shared task, then fathers would be less likely to make the stereotyped assumptions about what little girls should do and are like, assumptions which tend to cramp their potentially very positive effect on their daughters at this time in their lives.)

If fathers were generally involved in the care of their children from when they were tiny, this would encourage warmer, closer bonds between father and child. Some men might find it an effort to get involved in the very physical, tactile world of a small baby, but so do many women faced with their first baby. A friend of the authors, a teacher and now a very happy, competent mother of two, didn't bath her first daughter for ten days after she brought her home from hospital – she daren't. We are nearly all inexperienced in child-care until we produce our own. We are nearly all too divorced from our bodies and natural functions and sensations. Being put back in touch with them can only do men and women good, and help children grow up more comfortably than many of us have been able to. In *Fathering*,[1] Dr Ross D. Parke writes, 'In my studies of fathers and new borns I have consistently found that fathers are just as responsive as mothers to infant signals.'

With both parents spending half their 'working time' doing their paid job and half looking after their child or children, the quality of care the children would get from each parent would be improved. They wouldn't consistently see dad and mum either only at the end of eight or more hours at work or else irritable from the lack of contrast and outside stimulation that being house-bound can induce.

There should be much less pressure to place children in any unsuitable form of care, whether poor group care or bad child-minding, or to leave them alone at too young an age. It should be easier to ensure that children get one-to-one care for as long as they seem to need it. The parent at hand would alternate, but babies brought up to expect care from both parents from when they are tiny are pretty well equally happy in the care of either. The babies who cry when left with daddy are those whose daddy hasn't had the opportunity to establish close caring bonds with them. The daddies who are unhappy when left to care for small babies and children are those who haven't had or taken the opportunity to build up close ties with their offspring. This is not saying that the child's and parent's responses are identical in both cases, but that the care the child receives from each parent is of equal value.

Another bonus which comes from parents sharing care is that there is much less likelihood of small problems getting out of proportion – or even becoming problems at all. Mums can get locked into real battles with their children over behaviour, feeding or toilet training. If every meal, every 'accident', isn't their responsibility, there is far less chance of neurotic cycles starting up.

In *Fathering*, Dr Parke reports on several studies of the effects of fathers having got more closely involved than usual in child-care. Erik Grönseth studied couples who either shared a job or both worked part-time, mostly because they hoped for better relationships with their children. Most of them had children under five. Mother and father generally shared equally in child-care (though interestingly the wife usually still did most of the housework). The fathers felt that they had 'better and more open contact' with their children, felt closer to them and understood them better. Mothers said they enjoyed their children more. All agreed that the 'children are the ones whose interests are best served by the work-sharing pattern'.[2]

Graeme Russell[3] studied fifty Australian families in which fathers took major or equal responsibility for the full range of child-care, generally 55 per cent for mothers, 45 per cent for fathers. In comparison, traditional fathers perform the full range of tasks, including feeding, changing and bathing, only about 12 per cent of the time.

In these sharing families the children were played with more – mostly because fathers were spending more time with the children – and they were played with in less stereotyped ways. Dad might spend less time in rough and tumble and playing football, but devote more time to talking, singing and drawing. Mother was more likely to join in both indoor and outdoor activities.

Norma Radin[4] studied families in the United States in which the father was the primary care-giver, responsible for their pre-school child about 60 per cent of the time. Both boys and girls showed what is called 'greater internality' – belief in their own ability to control their fate and determine what happens to them, which is extremely important to a child's later achievements, development and happiness.

Both boys and girls from these families scored higher than those from conventional families in tests of verbal ability. Child-rearing fathers had higher educational and career expectations of their daughters as well as their sons, and worked harder at stimulating them, than traditional fathers.

The children's own sex-role identification was unaffected by the fact that dad mainly cared for them. Where they did differ from children from conventional families was in expectations about practical matters such as who generally uses the vacuum cleaner. Dr Parke points out that sharing or reversing roles is still very unusual. 'Such parents may be different in other ways from parents who maintain traditional roles, and might have influenced their children differently no matter which parent stayed home with the children. However, it is likely that parents who reverse roles are significantly affected by their choice, and that therefore the non-traditional environment in which their children develop is at least partially responsible for differences between children from traditional and non-traditional families.'

Certainly studies show time and time again that a father putting more than the usual amount of time into child-care is beneficial for the children.

What about the fathers? There are many who would now consciously welcome the opportunity to be able to spend more time with their children. There are many, like Frederick and Tony, whom I interviewed, who would welcome the opportunity for their wife to work outside the home more, knowing it would make her – and their marriage – happier.

Those fathers who at present feel it is necessary to invest the vast majority of their time and energy in building their career while their children are young, only to regret it a decade or so later, could be spared this dilemma and later unhappiness if society's expectation of an ambitious young father was that he would spend half his time and energy on his children.

A move to enable fathers to spend more time with their children would certainly seem to support what they are choosing to do already. While there are still men around who feel they did their bit on the day of conception, studies consistently show that, in general, fathers now spend more time on child-care than they did – though they remain resistant to taking on more housework. David Maklan[5] compared men who worked four ten-hour days a week with men working five eight-hour days. The men who worked four days a week spent nearly four hours a week more on child-care, but no more time on housework. There's a clear suggestion that choice and not just circumstances is at work. Fathers who spend more time taking care of their children get a great deal of pleasure from it. One father in Graeme Russell's study commented: 'We started out doing it because of the money . . . we wanted to buy a house. When we got the house, Barbara wanted to stop working . . . she wanted me to go back to a 9 to 5 job. I didn't want to because that would have meant that I wouldn't have seen the kids so much. I felt I had as much right to see the kids as she did. The way we were meant we both took care of them for about equal time. I want to stay like this.'

Other fathers said of their relationship with their children: 'I think it has increased the amount of pleasure I get from them.' 'Being with them all the time has helped cement my relationship with them.' 'I became a lot more involved, understood her a lot better, and got on a lot better with her.' Harry, whom I met in County Durham and who has been forced to spend more time at home with the children through unemployment, is thoroughly enjoying the greater involvement (page 235).

Remember we are making these suggestions because the present system is breaking down and there are already unacceptably high numbers of men, let alone women, out of work. Increasing the emphasis society gives to fathers caring for their children will provide them with a much needed alternative peg on which to hang their self-respect, apart from work. At present men out of work and their families suffer not only because of the shortage of cash but because the man feels demoralized and aimless. Without a job he feels less than a man. In *The Collapse of Work*,[6] Clive Jenkins and Barrie Sherman stress the need to educate young people not to see their lives as being given value only by the job they do. They say the shame and financial penalties must be taken away from unemployment and people educated to expect a life in which leisure is as important as work.

We are sure that Messrs Jenkins and Sherman would support women's equality as 'people', yet their book must cause many a wry smile among women. Their conclusions never really mention family responsibilities – all the work that lies outside the place of paid employment.

Following their suggestions there would be a real danger that men would be educated to expect a life of paid work and leisure, while women would be educated to see their life in terms of raising the family unaided except financially. Women rarely see their future only in terms of paid employment. More commonly they see their future only in terms of being a wife and mother. That has its dangers for them, but surely this is the time to be stressing to boys that they should see their future in terms of some paid work, *fatherhood* and leisure? If men had the aim of being good, active, involved parents as well as breadwinners, it would give them a valuable extra area in which to feel successful and find opportunities for personal growth.

It's also worth noting, from Norma Radin's study,[7] that the fathers who were the main carers for their children were just as masculine, assertive and forceful as men whose wives were mainly responsible for child-care. In Erik Grönseth's study, the couples who were either sharing a job or both working part-time and sharing child-care equally, said that their marital relationship improved. They experienced less conflict, improved solidarity and had more mutual understanding. The couples to whom I spoke would not choose to return to the traditional pattern.

A lot of strain is removed once parents are not forced to take on two extremely different and rather unbalanced life-styles. Men are saved working forty-plus hours a week, driving themselves either to endure boredom, physical discomfort or pressure, and taxing their physical health. The benefit to women of being able to do something like twenty hours' work a week, and of having a partner equally sharing the burden as well as the joys of child-care, are obvious in view of all we have already said about the toll exacted by their staying at home full-time.

Most women feel that the quality of their life in the home and interactions with their family are greatly improved if they have some regular but not overwhelming employment outside the home.

Three quarters of working mothers with children under five work part-time, as do one third of those with school-age children. According to the Gallup Poll survey done for *Woman's Own*,[8] part-time work would also be the choice of more than three quarters of the mothers now working full-time. The reason why they were working full-time would vary: they couldn't afford not to, particularly since part-time jobs tend to be so low-paid, even pro-rata; there wasn't a part-time job available and they felt the need to work full-time rather than not at all; and/or it wasn't possible to carry on with their particular type of work or career part-time.

Once an equal number of fathers were both seeking what we would now regard as part-time work and at home a good part of the day, there is a strong prospect that the whole picture would change for mothers. Men just wouldn't put up with things as they are.

At present most employers and trade-unionists see the work-force as consisting of men, women and mothers. Fathers don't exist. When journalists at a large publishing company conducted a survey to see how many employees would use a crèche if one were established, more male employees than female said that they would place their children in the crèche – women employees who had become mothers having already been forced to give up their jobs there because there *wasn't* a crèche. The men had been able to carry on working because their wives had been the ones to give up work for child-care, but these wives were now anxious to return to work. The response from fathers surprised the union representatives who conducted the survey and had seen it as a 'woman's problem'. A management representative had trouble at first grasping the results. 'I see,' he said in the end, 'you mean that our male employees' *wives*' children would use the crèche.'

Both unions and employers would wake up if fathers *en masse* were tailoring the hours they were prepared to work to their children's needs. Men just would not accept that this meant that they could only do less skilled work, or that they should do the same work as they did before but for less pay per hour.

Unions would talk fiercely and emotively about employers profiteering at the expense of little kiddies, and a 'father's shift' would be paid pro-rata with everyone else – or else!

The argument might not be all that fierce, because the management, nearly all male, would themselves be putting in their hours at home, and so would have every sympathy with the idea that being a parent should not devalue the paid work done. In fact, it could quite quickly become accepted that, at least among people whose paid work involved dealing with people, home experience would be an added qualification, not a disadvantage. This would rub off on women, too. With parents sharing problems like holidays and times when children are ill – and it being less likely that either would have to take time off work to cope – their role as a mother would be seen as the experience qualification it is, instead of a handicap.

Once employers became conscious that most of their male employees aged, say, twenty-five to forty-five were fathers with children at home, they would think twice about fixing conferences so far away that it meant days away from home. New technology will help them here. As video link-ups become more possible, it will not be so necessary to fly someone across the Atlantic for three hours' conversation. Again, working mothers would lose another handicap.

Once the expectation had gone that a keen employee should spend twelve hours a day on the job, it would be astonishing what could be fitted into half the time. Again, working mothers in creative work, for instance, would lose what is seen by many to be a handicap, in that they are not prepared to sit around the office 'throwing ideas about' until the mid-evening.

All sorts of things now fruitlessly demanded to restore *mothering* to its proper status would have a much better chance of becoming reality if fathers were going to benefit as well as mothers. We would be acknowledging in a very real way the value of *parenting*.

'It is not enough for children to be important, they have to be seen to be so,' says Dr Penelope Leach in *Who Cares?*[9] Well, they would be, virtually automatically, if fathers were making a personal commitment and spending as much time with them as mothers.

Bringing up children would be seen as being as prestigious and as major an undertaking as an architect's three-year project on a big building scheme, as Dr Leach claims it should be, if male architects as a matter of course, along with all men, were accepted and expected to be devoting a good part of their energies to bringing up children as well as to completing building projects.

Dr Leach has pleaded that roads, shops and parks should be organized with mothers and small children in mind. But if it was *parents* and small children who were regularly affected, so that all men who were designing and planning who have had children (which will be most of them) had had a great deal of personal experience of getting around with a pram plus toddler seat, or a baby in buggy plus fed-up four-year-old, it wouldn't be something you'd have to lobby for hopelessly. Once the men had all experienced it, it would be as stark staring obvious to them as it is to mums at present.

And just think how the neighbourhood drop-in clubs that Dr Leach says are needed in every area – and we do agree! – would be transformed if the usual mix of parents was fifty-fifty male and female. Any playgroup leader will tell you that they appreciate the occasional man who can spare the time to be a helper sometimes – he will bring an added dimension for the children and to their play.

Why should our children spend their most lively hours of their formative years exclusively in the company of women? It is quite unnatural. The stimulation given to children in playgroups is wonderful, but it would be even more valuable, have a wider range, if men were bringing their particular strengths and abilities to bear regularly. Playgroups I have been to are strong on painting, sticking, music, story-reading, but there hasn't been anyone developing the spatial skills that are supposed to be the masculine forte – because the women play-leaders either truly never had them or they were allowed to atrophy because of attitudes about what girls are good at when *they* were brought up. No one was ever urging the children to discover the full potential of the Lego – there in profusion but left for the children to make the best of under their own steam. No one was leading the girls and boys in a game of football or bat and ball to develop their hand, foot and eye co-ordination.

Drop-in clubs combined with the toddlers and playgroups would also be a very different stimulation for the parents if both mothers and fathers were there. The sharing of ideas about child-care would be far livelier. Men actually involved in the day-to-day routine have, in our personal experience, a refreshingly straightforward approach to details that bog mothers down.

When I used to visit a friend of mine nearby with a baby the same age, I went encumbered with all the equipment for changing a nappy, plus clean spare, and carried home a soggy and rapidly becoming smelly and germ-laden soiled nappy in a polythene bag. When my husband and my friend's husband were both looking after the babies for the day and got together, they spent the time we women would have spent in the kitchen in the garden of the local pub, since it was a sunny day, having a beer. My husband took nothing but the baby with him. When she needed changing, he used all our friend's gear, dropped her wet nappy straight into their sterilizing bucket, so it had no chance to become offensive, put on to her the clean one from their supply proffered by the other dad, and that was that. A small example, but it illustrates how we mums, in trying ever to prove our self-sufficiency and ability to cope unaided, actually make life far more difficult for ourselves than it need be. Men often do see a straight way through, so let's use their prowess more.

And of course, there would be a sexual element in the added interest there would be in meeting other parents. Great! Any man or woman at work usually has the opportunity to meet the opposite sex now and then. At present there is often a dangerous imbalance in that a husband can talk to women at work, not to flirt especially, but knowing that his conversation is welcomed by them. There is an incentive to look presentable. There is a quite proper and necessary added zest in spending time in mixed company. Often this is very hard for a wife to cope with, when she is at home with a baby being sick over her T-shirt at every feed, when there's little incentive to keep reasonably smart, when the only people she has any chance to socialize with during the day are other mums, when she has no men to chat to in order to reassure herself that she is still capable of interesting the opposite sex and to help her to keep the mental muscles in trim that enable her to hold an interesting conversation. At present, one mum commented to me the other day, you can walk down the street and know which mothers have got a job just by looking at them.

As things are, of course, even the fathers who are sometimes at home during the day with their children – perhaps because they work shifts – won't go near a mothers and toddlers group (no wonder, with a name like that!), a drop-in club or a playground. But that's because it is too unusual. What man is going to walk into what he sees as a hen party? But he wouldn't feel the same if he could count on seeing a few mates down there.

Generally the atmosphere surrounding the first few years of a child's life would be much brighter and breezier if dads were around quite a bit more and mums could comfortably be around a bit less.

Another point from the father's point of view is that, according to Dr Leach and Dr Mia Kellmer Pringle, child-rearing is more satisfying work than most, and done in better conditions. In that case, isn't it grossly unfair to allow fathers to have so small a share in it?

Dr Pringle[10] is actually very much in favour of shared parenting – though this tends to get less publicity than those of her views which can be used to fault working mothers. She sees benefits in shared parenting for children, for mothers who would be able to 'keep their hand in' by carrying on with work outside the home after a relatively short break rather than lose confidence by having left the labour market for ten or more years, and for fathers, since 'instead of feeling left out and even jealous – as is not infrequently the case in the conventional family – he would be contributing an equal share to the children's personality and character development, rather than being seen mainly as the provider of income and sometimes of discipline'.

The only disadvantages she sees are the possible embarrassment and discomfort while only a small minority of parents share child-care, and these would be overcome if a way can be found to encourage it to become a common pattern – because of all the very positive and lasting advantages we know follow on from shared parenting.

Dr Leach allows that fathers can play a valuable role in child-care, but at the time she wrote *Who Cares?* felt that, in these times of high unemployment, for a man in work to talk 'high falutin' nonsense about sharing that job with his partner so as to take an equal share in the care of their children would get him the push as soon as the laughter died down'.

Actually, in these particular times of high unemployment it makes a lot of sense. We are not dealing with just a short-term recession but a long-term, probably permanent reduction in the number of working hours available per head of the population who want to work, because of the growth of microtechnology.

In *The Collapse of Work*,[11] Clive Jenkins and Barrie Sherman forecast: 'Remain as we are, reject the new technologies and we face unemployment of up to 5.5 million by the end of the century. Embrace the new technologies, accept the challenge and we end up with unemployment of about 5 million. Whilst there is a world of difference between the two consequences and the possibilities that can be exploited inherent in these two strategies, the latter is by far the most favourable. What is clear is that whatever road we take work will collapse.' They see the answer as being to share out work more equally. 'The whole approach to working time must be treated on a working lifetime basis. To start with, a prime objective must be to reduce the number of weekly or monthly trips to work. A four-day week on an eight-hour day basis is more likely to require the taking on of more extra workers than a reduction of one hour per day, which can be covered more easily with shift and pattern changes . . . If our projections of unemployment are correct and this method of job-sharing adopted, then by the year 2000 the working week will have to become a three-times eight-hour day.'

In *The Mighty Micro*,[12] the late Dr Christopher Evans, who was one of the world's leading experts on microprocessors and the future of computing, prophesied, 'sixteen-hour working days have given way, in a century or so, to seven-hour days. In the next decade or two, the seven-hour day will become a five and perhaps even a four-hour day. As we hand over the job of providing wealth to the computers we have created to help us, it will be further reduced and eventually the nil-hour day will arrive. The trend may have its ups and downs, but its direction is inevitable, and the 1980s are the decade when mankind as a whole will at last realize this fact.

'But one of the main problems faced by the inhabitants of the medium-term future will not be understanding the truth, but learning how to cope with it . . . The Computer Revolution faces us with a choice between a world transformed either into a paradise or a disaster area. The transformation could take place within the mid-term but the most likely period would seem to be some time in the 1990s.' To see as the solution to problems of working mothers and their children, and to those of high unemployment the idea that mums should be subsidized to go back home full-time, while dads work full-time, not only denies what is really best for children, mothers and fathers now, but swims against the tidal wave of a future rapidly engulfing us.

Men need as soon as possible to be encouraged to value what home life has to offer, because they are inevitably going to see a lot more of it in the end. The fact that they have invested so little of their time and values, feelings of status and self-esteem in home life is one of the reasons why men at present out of work are so prone to severe depression and their marriages break up, as any marriage guidance counsellor in a hard-hit area, with weeks-long waiting lists, can tell you.

Also, with such turbulent times already upon us and certainly lying ahead in the world of work, *women who once leave the work-force for any length of time are finding it, and are going to find it, increasingly difficult if not impossible to get a foothold again.*

It may at present be highly qualified women such as doctors who do not feel able to take five to ten years out of their career because they lose touch with modern developments in their field. A woman out of the office or off the production line for a few years in future may try to return only to find that the work is transformed, and she no longer has any relevant experience. With labour so plentiful why should an employer bother with her? Also, suppose an employer decides to bring in new technology which will reduce the number of working hours needed. Workers on the spot can fight for them all to be kept on, working fewer hours per week. Mothers staying at home for a few years but hoping to return will not have any voice at the bargaining table, while decisions are made that may affect the pattern of working for the next century.

*

Talk of fathers taking something like a fifty-fifty share in child-care can sound like so much soft, liberal theorizing – pie in the sky. I talked to a few of the – admittedly uncommon – couples already practising it, or trying to, but also to an unemployed dad who used to be a firm traditionalist until redundancy forced him to be at home more – when he found he enjoyed it – and to two fathers who have successful careers but would consider sharing child-care more fully if career structures could be changed to allow for it.

Frederick is enjoying a successful career in the Civil Service. Perhaps his only regret is that his happy family life has been achieved in part at the expense of his wife's self-confidence. He would be willing to share more in the care of their two children, were it possible for him to work shorter hours – though the disparity between their earning power makes him wonder whether it would ever be feasible.

Frederick (Hertfordshire)

Working in London as a Civil Servant, I leave the house at 7.15 and get home at 7. I see more of the children now because Janet doesn't go to bed until 7.30 or 8. Mark is five and is usually in bed. When he was a baby he used to be just waking up as I left home. He'd wave to me out of the bedroom window as I walked down the street and I wouldn't see him again until I was walking down the street the next morning. For five days a week he had no idea whether I'd come home or not.

What makes it worse is that you don't have a normal life at the weekends because you spend all your time making up time with the kids. If you want to dig the garden, you do it with them, so it takes eight times as long. If I got home earlier in the evening I'd have time to play with them and do the other things. As it is, you've got to let them participate in the jobs you've got to do anyway. It's okay if you can bear it; I find it extremely difficult, which is bad from my point of view and from theirs.

I think I'd be a much easier person to live with if I was home earlier in the evening, with more time to devote to the kids, my wife, or just sitting down to go to sleep in the chair. I mean, I don't long to be at home so I can play with the kids, but I do long to be at home, and if I was home I would play with them more.

Selfishly speaking I wouldn't like to come home at lunch-times and take over any of my wife's burdens, doing the jobs she does in the house, but I think we would both have benefited if she had been able to go out to work, if I'd been able to look after the kids more.

The difference between our lives is that my job is mentally very demanding. For all my working life – I'm now thirty-five – I've been in an environment where my brain is being tested all the time and that's enabled me to retain the faculties I had when I was eighteen or nineteen. My wife's been at home for eight years, and her main companions have been kids. It's terribly difficult when you're surrounded by kids to form deep intellectual relationships, even if you have got friends – the children interrupt all the time.

It's not just her – blokes at work say their wives are going through the same thing. They get to the stage where they feel slightly inadequate. If I take her along to socialize with the guys I work with, it's on a different plane from our normal relationships. We spend our time arguing, talking and flexing our brains. It would have been good if she could have shared it. She'd certainly have been much happier intellectually, or at least she thinks she would. I don't think she lacks anything for not working, but she does.

Fathers in my position tend to be court jesters. If you only see your kids for a short time, you try to make them laugh and have a good time. If you go to the swimming pool on a Saturday morning, the fathers are larking about taking the kids swimming. You go on a Thursday afternoon and the mothers are actually teaching the kids to swim. That seems to sum up the difference. I think it's difficult to have an instructive role when you see your kids for a short time, unless you have the wait-till-daddy-comes-home syndrome, father as a threat, which I couldn't ever agree with. I do feel, though, that my relationship with Janet has got much better over the last two years. That's because I do take time in the evening to talk about what she's done at school. It's become a sort of ritual. One guy I work with gets home at five every night and actually teaches his kids, maths and so on. I don't think I'd like to get into that. I think really he's doing it for his own self-glorification, to make sure that his kids do well at school. I don't have any involvement in what Mark is doing at nursery school at all. When I get home he's in bed; sometimes I read a story to him. I get everything he's done at nursery from my wife. Mark doesn't get much encouragement from me.

What would make it very difficult for my wife and I both to work something like part-time and share child-care is the difference in earning power.

My wife used to be a teacher. I can't see any way, with the government putting such a low value on education, that she'll be able to earn as much as me. Even if they should start paying teachers a reasonable wage, then I suspect that more men will be attracted to teaching and more women teachers put out of work.

As a practicality, I can't ever see the point where I'd replace her in the home. I might in the future take it if I was offered say ten weeks' holiday without pay, though at the moment I couldn't possibly afford it. In the Civil Service at least we do get six weeks' holiday. And we do value time at home a great deal. While most of us talk about leaving, to go to BP or somewhere, while you might get more money, you only get four weeks' holiday. When it comes to it, that fortnight difference is enough to make people decide against moving – they put time with the family before the money.

*

Sarah and Chip share both a job and care of their daughter. It means their academic careers are slowed down temporarily but they feel the advantages for their child and their marriage far outweigh the disadvantages.

Sarah and Chip (Lancaster)

Chip: Our baby, Edith, is now fifteen months old. When we took this job we hadn't thought about children very concretely. Now everyone's saying how well we planned it all, how we have an added dimension to our family life, but it wasn't in our minds then. We simply wanted to get academic jobs that were combined.

Sarah: It's hard enough to get one job when you're an academic, let alone two in the same university. Couples we had known in the States who had two jobs usually ended up commuting from one town to another, with their marriage almost inevitably breaking up. We wanted to avoid this above all. When this job came up, both our specialities seemed to come under it, so we thought we'd have a try. I'd seen an article mentioning a couple in New Zealand who shared a job, and that sowed the seed in my mind. We applied separately, but at the end of our applications we said that what we'd really like to do would be to share the job between us. They accepted it.

Chip: We each have contracts paying us exactly half the salary, and with an extra clause at the end saying that, if one of us should go, then so will the other – a powerful cementing factor in our marriage! We were used to living on one salary before, while Sarah was doing her research, but this job is better paid than the full-time job I used to have, and because we are both now working we get more tax relief.

Sarah: Another social and economic factor is that, now there is so much unemployment, I think that people should live on only one salary, especially if they can both be working and getting job satisfaction. No doubt we could have eventually got two full jobs, but that would have meant another family wouldn't have got an income out of it.

We were lucky in that I had Edith in March so I only had to have a little bit of maternity leave at Easter. I didn't have to do any teaching in the summer term anyway – all I had to do was mark examinations at home in between feeding times and go to a few meetings. I started teaching again in October, which did require a little planning. I had to cancel one big course I was due to teach, but I did it the next year, which meant a heavy load of marking and seminars, taking two years in one.

You could say that people shouldn't have to work to make up for maternity leave, that it's a right, but that's a delicate thing. In our work, if you're not there it's a heavy burden falling on your colleagues. It's different with manual work or clerking, when you're giving someone overtime.

It wasn't particularly easy, but things worked out well. When I went back to work I felt much better than when I was just at home looking after Edith. I found it very difficult just being a mother with her child. Still, if I'd gone back to a full-time job I don't think I could have coped physically. This is where the half-time job has been crucial. I'm able to give my career its due without the pressure of full-time demands. Sometimes when I'm at the university I find myself thinking about how Edith is and there's a kind of physical pain. I wouldn't be happy myself for her to be brought up by a nanny, although I'm sure it can work and doesn't ultimately damage the child. But it's more pain for the mother.

Chip: I really started looking after Edith when she stopped being breast-fed at six months and Sarah went back to work. I'd always changed her nappies though, given her her daily bath and we've always shared getting up in the night.

Sarah: Often in the early days I'd put her in the bouncing cradle and say to Chip, 'You have her now,' and I'd go and have a lie-down. Edith was a poor sleeper and I was permanently exhausted. I can't remember him ever saying no.

Chip: When Sarah started work again, we split the five-day week into two and a half days each for a while; but the hand-over in the middle of that one day turned out to be too much of a pain so now we do three and two. Actually at the moment it's more like six to one. I do the six at home and one in the office because Sarah is trying to finish her doctoral thesis at the moment.

Sarah: We've negotiated a new regime just for this summer, which is very hard on Chip, so that I can get over this major hurdle in my career. But I'll do the same for him when he's doing his book. It's all flexible.

Chip: Normally we have a calendar up on the wall with two colours. Red for me in the office and black for Sarah. You have to be organized, there's no choice – because you have to fix appointments with students who want to see you about their work.

Sarah: Our department is very understanding. They know that we can never both be there at the same time. What's more difficult is when people from other departments ask you to serve on a particular committee. If I say sorry, that's my husband's day in the office and I have to be at home with the baby, they don't understand. Obviously we can't pretend we're one person. One of us doesn't know what the other's done, and we don't have the same opinions about some issues. We are separate individuals.

If people ask me to speak for Chip I sometimes have to say that I'm not my husband's keeper.

Chip: I feel I've gained a fantastic amount by not being a working father always out of the house. Edith seems very well adjusted, maybe more outgoing than other children of her age, but it's early days.

Sarah: Chip has a let-it-all-hang-out approach. He encourages her adventurous spirit, where I'm more protective. The house runs on different regimes on different days. I keep more of an eye on Edith and Chip does it more like an African woman; he lets Edith keep an eye on him.

Going to work for me is physically – though not mentally! – like going for a rest. It is for both of us. I can sometimes be having a lovely lunch with friends and have it almost spoilt by thinking guiltily of Chip besieged at home with Edith.

Chip: There is something delightful about watching your baby grow up and seeing it happen for yourself rather than come home at night and be told. She's closer to me than she would have been.

Sarah: My father was a rather distant figure. Even now I can't speak to him easily. We hope that won't happen with Edith. There are disadvantages – there are two books that Chip would like to write but at the moment just aren't getting done, while I'm doing mine. I think it's very hard on him. People are conditioned to assume that when a woman has a baby she's either going to give up her job or leave it in abeyance for five years. They don't expect a woman with a baby to write books. On the other hand nobody expects men to reduce their work because they're fathering children. It's usually at precisely the point when they do start fathering that men put their greatest push into work.

If I finish my thesis, then there'll be more chance for Chip to do his book, especially if I have another baby. No other men I know are willing to do as much as Chip. They're more career-minded, they're the ones with the job, and to do right by their family they have to work hard and get promoted. And also, most wouldn't like what Chip does. Let's not mince words – looking after a house and child can be boring, exhausting drudgery!

But Chip and I have decided that high-flying academic achievement is less important to us *at the moment* than being sure we're doing right by Edith, and of course our students. They come first. On the other hand, we do have to make sure our research is going well, otherwise we're not doing the job properly.

Chip: Luckily in theology, our subject, there's a tradition that you do your best work when you're quite old. This isn't true in other fields, like science for example. I wouldn't be so happy living this way if I was in that sort of discipline. But at the moment, we know I'm not suffering from the American phenomenon of executive burn-out.

Mind you, the big day will come when Edith actually leaves the house and starts going to school. That will be the millennium! We'll actually be able to sit down at our desks and work.

Sarah: One area of difficulty is when Edith has been ill. Even though it was my day at the university, I'd have to be home. Even though I know Chip would do the right things, I'd never forgive myself if I wasn't with her. It seems to imply that I don't trust him, though of course I do.

In small things, however, we do things differently. One of us might be more inclined to give her a Smartie than the other, one of us will react if she does something annoying, while the other just ignores it. Already we see her looking backwards and forwards between one and the other to see who's the better bet. But I suppose all children do that with their parents. Perhaps because we are both here so much it makes us discuss things more.

But you can't be smug about the way you bring up children. They always catch you out, don't they?

(Dr J. F. Coakley and his wife Sarah both lecture in the department of religious studies at Lancaster University.)

*

Harry was a traditional breadwinner dad who never even touched the washing-up – until unemployment forced him to stay at home. But while some have been unable to cope with this blow to their image of themselves as men, Harry has thoroughly enjoyed getting more involved with his home and children.

Harry and Jean (Co. Durham)

Harry: I worked as a labourer on a building site. When that finished there was a labourer's job twenty-five miles away. I used to leave at quarter to six in the morning and get back home at seven. I didn't see the children. When that stopped too, I just couldn't get any work. I must have written hundreds of letters, all over the country, but I can't find a job.

Our oldest is John, he's seventeen. He used to be in the merchant navy, but he left during the long strike, and now he's found a Work-Experience job. Then there's Jane, sixteen, Sally, fourteen, Heather, twelve, and Catherine, eight. They're all at school.

There are a lot out of work here. Half the marriages are breaking up. It seems to worry them being suddenly out of work and being at home. But it's no use worrying, there's no work. Young couples, they're used to buying take-aways after work and going to clubs. You just have to give some things up.

There have been quite a few suicides round here, they've been so depressed. One lad in his thirties just threw himself in front of a train. Another took a hose from his car exhaust. They're not the only ones. They just can't adapt, they don't know which way to turn. You've just got to shake yourself out of it, if you can. I talk to quite a few of them. What I've done is put a lot of attention in the home since I've been out of work. When I was working before I wouldn't even wash up. Now I do my bit.

It's important for me to see more of the children, and for them too. They are more for daddy now than they have ever been. We talk a lot, we argue, I help them with their homework, I sort out their quarrels. I felt fed up at first being without a job. At first the kids got on my nerves, but now we get on better every year.

Jean: If something happens to one of the children he makes a joke out of it and has them laughing in no time. It hasn't had any bad effect on them at all having Harry at home, just good – that they see more of him.

Some of the other children round here think it's terrible for their father not to be working. The only thing ours didn't like was getting free school meals – though for the last eighteen months nearly all the other children round here have been on free school meals, too. But that was the only time they asked why he hadn't got a job. We said that if he did have one, which he couldn't get anyway, he wouldn't be able to come out with them. We got over it that way.

Harry: There are more men out of work than women. In the marriages that are splitting up, it's the wives who need the jobs so that they can manage without the husbands.

Jean: He was never on a high wage. It was worse when the children were younger, but now they all have paper rounds, which gives them pocket money and helps pay for the clothes.

We cut down on everything – we only buy what we can afford. I don't buy many biscuits and cakes, we go for the cheaper things, but if we've got money we eat well, and that's it. It all depends what bills we have to pay that weekend. You get the gas bill in and you think you'll leave it a couple of weeks, then you'll have the rent money.

Harry: Once we owed £2 to the electricity. Like a fool I let him in and he cut us off, though I had the money in my pocket. Then they charged us £5 to put it on again. Luckily they're a bit more lenient now. I enjoy doing things about the house now, washing, making beds, doing the garden, all sorts of things. If I got a job I'd still want to be involved with the house and the children. I'm a lot closer to them now.

Jean: He's very soft with them. To hear them talk you'd think he was their brother instead of father. They think he's marvellous. You hear about marriages breaking up but we're stuck together like glue. We have arguments with the children, and they think it's just marvellous. We never keep rows up, no sulking. The children aren't allowed to sulk. I was allowed to sulk as a child – my childhood was unhappy, my parents were unhappy. We make them apologize if they're wrong, which takes a bit of doing; but we let them do it in a jokey way so they aren't embarrassed. You don't have to make them crawl. We sit down and sort it out.

Harry: That's where the happiness is, at home and in the family. Young ones now want a nice house with no children, that sort of thing. Then when they're out of work it causes all sorts of argument. He's got nothing to occupy himself, no money to go out. We've always been happier together. Being poor, we sorted out what we could buy. We've had to adapt to the situation. It would be a lot easier for some if men had always been brought up to be involved with the family. Some marry and don't look after their wife – she's just there and that's it. They don't treat them properly, they just go out and enjoy themselves. They get their nice house and they won't let the children do a thing, won't let their friends in. But everyone's different, I suppose. My parents died when I was five. My father was a Jarrow marcher; he'd steal food and clothes to keep us. But I didn't know him. In a way I think losing my parents helped make me stronger. I think our kids should adapt all right because they've had to do without. They also have the determination to do better than us and get good jobs. They want a higher standard of living, but I suppose it really doesn't bother me too much being out of work. I've looked upon it as early retirement. My spending more time at home has definitely drawn us closer as a family. We were close before but I feel it even more now.

*

One father who has found part-time work in order to share bringing up his child says, 'For me what we're doing is the only way.'

Robert (London)

We'd been together for about eight years when Olivia got pregnant, which is three years ago. It was planned, as she was getting on a bit – she was thirty-six.

We both wanted to bring up the kid for the first five years and be as involved as possible. It just seemed naturally important. Neither of us had been particularly fond of kids – we hadn't been around them, we didn't know too much about them, but we'd been leading a fairly selfish life. Having a kid seemed a sensible thing to do.

I did want to be involved right from the start. Some decisions were before the birth and some after, but it just seemed an awful thing to lumber anybody with just totally looking after this child.

Most of our problems turned out to be financial ones. To get a place with a garden – we were living in a flat – I had to stay in a job to get a mortgage, because I knew if I went freelance they wouldn't even look at me for a couple of years. The trouble with this is that if one works all day and the other not, it can be bad for the relationship. You come at each other on a different level at the end of the day and you miss. When we got the mortgage, the house and the central heating, I went freelance.

Olivia does proof-reading for publishers. It's difficult in that the choice of jobs is pretty negligible if you work at home. The number of jobs you *could* do, if it was properly organized, is immense. When I say organized, I mean linked up through VDUs and so on.

Olivia's doing research for a book now. A slightly annoying job in a way. She has to do jobs that she can pick up and put down, and although it can be interesting, it's underpaid and can be very boring sometimes. And you really have to put the hours in. We do still spend most evenings and weekends working. But we'll get there in the end.

Polly is three in August. We roughly share out the looking after her. Although having said that I wanted to get involved from the start, I did find it hard to *feel* involved at first. It seemed like something she had in *her* body, something *she* was breast-feeding. For six months, I couldn't feed her. I did change nappies, but it didn't seem part of me for a while. More of a routine than something done with love.

Our relationship has certainly got better now. Having Polly seemed to broaden it – I mean, what the hell were we going to do with our time after eight years? It's a chance to grow yourself.

I don't feel especially good or bad about a day with Polly, I just get on with it. I never had the feeling that we were doing it right, or trail-blazing, I just hoped that what we did was roughly OK. Polly is changing all the time. It's obviously important to be there and watch.

For me, I feel that what we're doing is the only way. If I'd had to carry on with a job I'd have gone bananas. It was partly luck and partly choice. As a journalist I was in a trade that didn't have a rigid structure, so that helped. I do think women can and should work. Job-sharing, four days a week, or something. It gets hard when you're the one who has to pull all the bread in, so Olivia working is a bonus for me. It takes off the strain.

She wouldn't have it any other way because psychologically she needs a bank account with her own money in it. What happens to the money doesn't matter, just that she has it.

But there have been a lot of career opportunities that I've had to pass up because of my home life. Maybe they'll come again, but it does seem probable that I won't get quite the opportunity I've had in the last few years. In journalism opportunities tend to come when you're young. When I had the full-time job in the first year, I took a day off and looked after Polly once when Olivia was ill. I said to one of the directors, if she'd been ill for three days, would you have accepted a sick note from me? He hummed and hahed. I was trying to get a crèche going at the time. I'm not saying they're the best things in the world, but you need something and they are practical.

When I'm at home I tend to give my time to Polly rather than the house. I used to do much more housework before Olivia had her. I don't think I've done the ironing in eighteen months. Olivia has got the house better organized now – it seems to fit in with the routine of looking after Polly – but we do both chip in.

We're not too house-proud really. We only do what needs to be done.

Before Polly, life was definitely going downhill. I was struggling at the job and coming home knackered. Life wasn't funny any more, she wasn't funny. Life was losing its edge and I was being very selfish. You need something to look forward to again. I think the parental mechanism must be to stop you going off your head.

We've got a good group going now, a baby-sitting circle. It works very well. The kids are shared in a way – everybody shouts at everybody else's kids. You're bringing up the neighbourhood as well as your own. It's nice that there are other parents around – fathers as well as mothers – to talk and share your experiences with. There's no doubt you do feel a bit freakish when you go down to the playgroups, being a man. There was one chap who went down and was asked was his wife all right? He was so affronted that he just walked out.

*

Sushila and Mick happily share care of their fifteen-month-old daughter, hoping to make the sharing out of the duties and pleasures of child-care even more equal in future.

Sushila and Mick (Leeds)

Mick: I work in a building collective, a general building contractor. We're now competent builders, we take on whatever we can get. The profits and losses are shared among us – that's the idea of it. Work-sharing works very well in it. We get paid by the hour, so you can do three or four days if you wish. I work four days at the moment, but I'd prefer three. The problem is that we have to put the hours in to keep the business going, and also that the hourly wage is quite small. We want to make it a work/child-care regime.

Our daughter goes to nursery one day a week and I look after her the other and we're both at home at the weekend. Sushila works two days a week, sharing a job for the International

Volunteer Service. It's not an absolutely fair split, but I have work about the house to do and in the allotment. It's just a matter of fitting in other things apart from my job.

As it happens, none of the women in our building collective have child commitments, so they're the ones who are at work on time. It's the blokes who have the children!

Sushila: I have to travel a lot in my job. Last Saturday I was in Rotherham. Sunday I was at meetings in Leeds. Monday and Tuesday I was in Leicester. Mick looked after Lelia all day Saturday. I had her with me on Sunday. Monday and Tuesday Mick took her with him.

I wish he could spend more time with her. At the moment when things go wrong she comes straight to me. I know some of it is because I'm her mother, but other children of parents who share child-care don't necessarily run to mum. I've seen it with our friends.

Mick: There's still an imbalance. I only have Lelia for one day, Sushila has her for three. This creates problems which would be worse if we were doing a five-day week. It would be better if it was more evenly split. We're aiming for half and half in the long term. Though I get an awful lot out of my work, it comes to the point that I get so involved in my job that I don't look forward to coming home. I've seen people doing a five-day week who end up disliking their kids. They don't see them, and when they do come home they're knackered.

Sushila: Having had Lelia, I realize that to be at home all the time with the father not there would drive me mad. On the days when I have her at home, I can't stay in all day. I can't stand it. It would be the same if I didn't have a job. I end up depressed if I stay in.

Money is still important, especially to women. I know I resented it when Mick earned more than me – I couldn't spend as much as he could. It took me a long time to get rid of that feeling.

When we decided to have a child, I came to resent that I always came second to his work. I still feel an element of that.

We split the cooking and housework. It's the other things like actually looking after Lelia's clothes, noticing when she needs new plastic pants, that I find I still do.

Mick: The things about the house are automatically done by me because of my building skills. She makes sure of the clothes and I make sure of the timber. As Lelia gets older I think I'll have more to do with her . . . I'll go down the park with her and kick a ball about.

Sushila: We know a lot of men who look after their kids. There's Martin, who job-shares with me. He works three days a week and his wife too. They only started this summer and he says he would never go back. There's another chap who's unemployed who spends a lot of time with his son. We're lucky because they often leave the kids here and we often leave Lelia with them. It does work. To some extent it doesn't matter who's in, the father or the mother.

When I'm working on building I have to learn how to use the tools, and Mick shows me. But he resented it if I showed him a different method of cooking or doing the washing. It took a long time before he would accept that off me. When we first had a home of our own, I wanted to do things my way. We spent a lot of our first year arguing, and we could have even split up. Just the pressure of two of you being around. I've found that when we're both around, and that relates to Lelia as well, I tend to interfere. It's very difficult not to poke my nose in when he's looking after her.

Mick: When it's my day looking after Lelia, and it's me doing housework and chores, I feel like 'get out of my kitchen'.

So far I haven't taken Lelia away by myself, but we've been together for odd weekends. The first weekend when Sushila was away at a conference I was dreading. Lelia was ten months old and we were weaning her off the breast. I was specially nice to her at bedtime, read her a book, gave her her cup, no problem. She went through the night, no trouble. In fact, it wouldn't have happened so easily if Sushila had been there. If Lelia falls over and bashes herself she comes to me and I comfort her, but if Sushila's around, especially if she's tired, she wants her and not me.

Sushila: That's bad. If we had more time with her it wouldn't matter who she went to. The other side of it is when I'm telling her off, she doesn't listen to me at all. But she does to Mick.

Mick: We have one rule which has evolved. We put her to bed together, the three of us.

Sushila: It's so easy when one of you is working that it can be like pass the parcel. Sometimes Mick gets into a job and carries on and on working; we just didn't think it was fair. She could go all day without seeing him. So we think it important for all three of us to do it together.

Mick: It's a drag sometimes to think that I have to go upstairs and put her to bed after a day's work. Sometimes I don't have to do anything, but I'm there. Sometimes it's the other way round, but the three of us are together. It's a good compromise. She really enjoys it.

*

Tony enjoys his full-time job as an engineer, but can see the potential in sharing both work and child-care more equally with his wife.

Tony (Bedfordshire)

I work thirty-seven hours a week as an engineer but on top of that I average four or five hours' travelling. Usually I leave home about 8 o'clock in the morning and get home at about quarter past six. But my job often involves overseeing contracts abroad or in this country. Sometimes I make day trips leaving at seven in the morning and not getting home till late at night. I may have to be away for a couple of days at a time.

I see Daisy, who's eighteen months, for half an hour in the

morning at breakfast and then an hour or so in the evenings. Not really very long. She notices this because she gives me a lot of attention over the weekend.

I would like to be with my child more. I wouldn't want to be a house-husband and swap my role completely, but I would feel comfortable about going 50:50 on working and looking after Daisy. We share out the housework anyway, about 60:40. Ros has always done all the cooking and I am supposed to do a certain amount of cleaning up. It doesn't seem to work so well now we have Daisy. I used to do the washing, vacuuming, but I'm not as good at being able to housework while Daisy's there. On some Saturday mornings Ros has gone off shopping and come back and not been altogether happy with the amount of housework that I've done!

For one thing I have always enjoyed getting off by myself. One of the important things about not having a full-time job would be being able to be at home by myself, doing the things that I want to do and not have the other one there.

What I find at the moment working full-time is that at the weekend when I've got time at home there's pressure on me to get on with all the jobs that have to be done, and therefore I can't relax at the weekends. If I had an extra two days at home, one of those days it would be really nice to do nothing, to do the things that I want to do and not have the pressures to do anything else. I know that when my wife was working three days a week she tended to have one day a week off – though she had Daisy with her she didn't really do anything. In that day I might do something else that was work but not paid work – not necessarily voluntary work but perhaps a hobby that you don't have a chance to get involved in while working five days a week. I would value having that one day to myself without Daisy. I would want to trade my two days' work for something of value to myself, because at the moment if I stopped working five days a week I would feel that I was giving something up. My feelings might be different if our life now was how it was a little while ago, when Ros was fed up at home all the time. Supposing we hadn't been able to get the terrific childminder we have found, then the idea of my staying at home a couple of days a week while Ros went out to work might be quite difficult to sell to me at first, but once it had been set up I think it could work quite well, because I could reorganize myself to cope with that new situation.

It would take something to push me into doing it – Ros would have to find a job and then there would have to be some additional pressure to make me cut down my working hours, but I think once I had done it, the arrangement could work out very nicely.

I have certainly noticed a change since Ros got a job. She doesn't rant and rave like she was doing while she was at home all the time, she's not bursting into tears all the time. There's no doubt that her job has benefited her – us, really – a great deal. It was a typical male problem. I could understand how a woman at home all the time could feel very frustrated, but understanding is different from actually being able to do something about it. She used to get very upset and uptight. Certainly since she's had a job she's much better. I don't think the money is so important – though she probably wouldn't do it if she wasn't paid reasonably – as having something to do out of the house, meeting other people, having other interests.

I think women would still want to work even if the government said, 'We will pay you this sum of money to stay at home and if you go out to work you will not get paid any more.' Even if they were told they could go out and do something stimulating but would not get paid for it, most women – most people – aren't going to go out just for the stimulation, even if that is the most important thing they get from a job – they need the feeling they are being paid for it, and I think the *initial* reason for going is usually financial even if that isn't so important in the long run.

I wouldn't worry too much about whether working fewer hours would be a detriment to my career. I'm not the sort of person who thinks I've got to work sixty hours a week because then I'll get promoted in three years, get more money, and this sort of thing. I anticipate that I'll be able to earn a reasonable standard of living without having to overextend myself.

I certainly think Daisy would benefit from seeing a lot of both parents. My father wasn't particularly hardworking but I never had much contact with him. Up until I left home I didn't have a very good relationship with him. He was so busy with other things that there was never much time to do much with his children. My father wasn't very involved in work but at the weekend would be busy in the garden, rather than being occupied with his children. We had a large piece of land at home in Australia and had a choice between a pool in the back garden or a holiday house. We had the pool in the back garden, and that suited him really because he didn't have to make the commitment to go down to the holiday house. I had other friends whose parents spent a lot more time with them, and Ros's family are very close, and I would like to do a lot more of that for our children.

But it's a bit difficult to theorize about all that at this stage, because I don't really know what being a parent is going to mean over the next ten or fifteen years. It's a bit early to tell.

But I realize that I was always rather afraid of my father. His discipline was really based on fear rather than the day-to-day can and can't do. I think a better situation is to have a more equal partnership in the day-to-day running of the children's upbringing. That does need a lot more communication in the marriage about what the attitudes are going to be about behaviour and that sort of thing. But I think this would be a good thing. I think one of the main problems with marriages that run into difficulties is that there isn't enough communication.

The basis for a lot of the problems mothers run into with children, when their relationship with their children gets very stressful, is the male not being able to understand and sympathize with the mother's feelings. I always remember the first day that Ros went out for the day while I looked after Daisy by myself – she was about ten months. That brought it home to me what she was having to go through every day.

The situation is improved for her now that she is working three or four days a week, but if you are looking after children seven days a week and don't get any break from it . . . Certainly the dividend is high of having a break from it – whether that is while the child goes to a childminder or the other parent looks after the child – which theoretically should be preferable.

I think that sometimes fathers don't have any inkling the pressures their wives are under. That day I had with Daisy made me realize. She wasn't being bad but you couldn't have five minutes peace all day. At the moment she has this thing that you've got to be reading to her all the time. It drives you up the wall. Ros gets a book shoved at her at five past eight in the morning. I get that at the weekend, and that could quite easily be extended to give Ros more of a break. It's good just from the point of view of the health of the marriage to bring it home to the other partner just what child-rearing is. In a lot of homes, the only time the man is at home is when his wife's there to do the job anyway.

Relating my kind of job to shorter working hours could be rather difficult. It probably wouldn't matter much if you were there fewer days each week but you would have to be there for the full day. I don't think for some types of jobs four or five hour days would be a very good idea because you don't necessarily think very efficiently in four or five hours. By the time you have thought of what you want to do, cleared all the other things that have to be done just to keep yourself going, you need a full day actually to get anything done. Another thing is that if people want to find you, if they know you are in today, then they know you are in all day, and not just for some core time or flexible time. But jobs like these on a production line, or more routine work, can more easily be organized into shorter shifts. Splitting a ten-hour day between two shifts on that type of job doesn't really cause any problems.

The thing I see as being difficult for my type of job is that if you are not there for a day, will the job wait for you to come back? Jobs could be shared out among more people but it would be a matter of reducing the amount of work people expect to do.

I am interested in how you could organize this sort of thing from the personal point of view. Even though I see the advantages of neither of you having to give up work entirely and both working shorter hours, once you have been embedded in a job for five years or so I think it would be extremely difficult for you to give up part of what that job has been – though, of course, women usually have to.

If you have been working forty hours a week then to cut down to twenty would require you to give up some of your duties. I think it would be difficult to say, right, that's what I am going to set aside. The sort of work I do people come up to you and say we have a problem here. It would be difficult to say, no I'm not going to do that work, I'm going to do this work. If you have one person three days and one person two days, the work theoretically should balance up between the two people, but whether that would in fact happen, I'm not sure. However, while I think it might be difficult to sort it out in the first place, once you had established a method of working then it should work quite easily.

The idea of husbands and wives sharing work and child-care more does need an urge from up on top somewhere really to get it going. This country seems to be quite a long way behind other European countries in dealing with the implications of unemployment. In Italy, which is a very similar country to this one in terms of its economy, you are allowed *x* amount of overtime and that's all. In Norway overtime is illegal. In this country you can work any overtime you can get hold of. People in this country still seem stuck on the idea of earning as much money as they can and the idea of cutting down on hours, sharing the work out, is a long way off. People think, 'I've got a job. I'm all right. I don't care about the other folk.' That's the attitude here at the moment. I'm all right Jack.

People can't see that they will have to pay anyway, through taxes to support the unemployed. And it is the same about women going to work – like when Ros got a job. It is difficult to see in advance what the benefits are, especially since they aren't very clearly defined, not cut and dried.

6. What Can We Set Our Sights On?

Any major change in society causes some grinding of gears. But at the moment society is running steeply downhill in fourth. Unless we do change gear, the chances are high that there will be a messy crash. We are heading straight for the five million-plus unemployment forecast by those who took microtechnology seriously before most of us had even begun to grasp it existed, and we are getting there faster than even the most alarmist predicted.

Unless there is a major shift away from the idea of the forty-hour or even thirty-five-hour working week, we are going to end up with a huge army of unemployed that those of us in work are going to have to try to support. The taxation levels such support will demand will eat into our incomes, even if we only provide them with subsistence level allowances – and there is a limit to how far unemployment pay and supplementary benefit can be cut without causing disastrous unrest. Already one in ten British citizens are supported directly or indirectly by the Supplementary Benefits Commission.

Where so many others have failed, it would be laughable if we pretended to have any original ideas about climbing out of this recession, but certainly in the longer-term we are with those who feel it is pointless to take a Luddite view of new technology. Trying to keep our industry labour-intensive when the developed world is moving into new technology would only make us inefficient and uncompetitive. We would end up with much the same number of people out of work, and poor profits from our industry with which to finance their welfare.

We would like to see investment in new technology to make industry as profitable as possible, and then a radical reappraisal of how the work and the profits are shared out. It is lunatic, surely, that we have so many unemployed and yet a shortage of services – from the old people who are left without care, to the headmistress we know who goes into school on Saturdays to weed the flower beds since the local authority can no longer supply gardeners.

Even assuming we can't as yet afford to fund improved services, if the number of hours being worked in the country in total at present (allowing for overtime and part-time workers) were shared out equally between all those now working and believed to want to work – registered and unregistered unemployment – they could each work roughly thirty-one and a half hours a week. The calculation is as follows (the figures are based on those for the beginning of 1981, rounded to the nearest 1,000):

10,100,000 men work full time, averaging approx. 43 hours a week	= 434,300,000 hours
588,000 men work part-time, averaging approx. 20 hours a week	= 11,760,000 hours
4,502,000 women work full-time, averaging approx. 37.5 hours a week	= 168,825,000 hours
3,219,000 women work part-time, averaging approx. 20 hours a week	= 64,380,000 hours
	679,265,000

2,404,000 were registered unemployed seeking full-time work.
36,000 were registered unemployed seeking part-time work.
Estimated 375,000 were unregistered unemployed seeking full-time work.
Estimated 375,000 were unregistered unemployed seeking part-time work.
Therefore 679,265,000 hours of work are now shared between 18,409,000 workers.
If shared *equally* between 18,409,000 workers and 3,190,000 registered and unregistered unemployed, they could each work 31½ hours each a week.

If you assume that all those at present working part-time averaging twenty hours a week do not want to work longer hours, and that those seeking part-time work want to work only twenty hours or so a week, then the working hours available could provide full employment if a 'full-time' week was just over thirty-four hours. This figure is close to the TUC's official objective of a thirty-five-hour week, but to result in full employment the working week would have to be strictly limited to thirty-four hours, which differs from an 'official' thirty-four-hour week with overtime (on time-and-a-half or double-time) for the lucky few.

This length of working week would only be a halfway house, however. The recession may further shrink the number of hours to be worked considerably. As microtechnology really gets under way, we should be thinking in terms of twenty-five-hour and probably twenty-hour working weeks for everyone.

The speed of desirable change could be very swift.

There might well be women at present not seeking employment who would do so if they could get a decently paid job without having to work a forty-hour week.

There would be a lot of women at present working part-time or seeking part-time work who would reconsider a full-time job, with its better hourly rates of pay and better opportunities, if only thirty hours had to be worked.

There would be even more wanting 'full-time' jobs if that involved a twenty-five-hour week. The more the work was shared out, the greater would be the pressure to share it out further.

The TUC, at their 1979 Congress, has already outlined some objectives which move towards this goal of sharing out what work there is more fairly.

'At every stage, technological change should be linked with a reduction in the working week, working year and working lifetime. This should be seen not just in the context of sharing out less work to avoid increasing unemployment, but in the more positive light of job-creating targets for enterprises. These should be accompanied by measures which enable existing workers to take some of the benefits in the form of increased leisure whilst providing more jobs.

'Priority should be given towards:

– the thirty-five-hour week

– a reduction in systematic overtime

– longer holidays

– better provision for time off and public and trade union duties

– sabbatical leave, and

– early retirement for older workers.'

Like Clive Jenkins and Barrie Sherman, authors of *The Collapse of Work*,[1] the TUC seems to have looked at the implications of microtechnology without once considering the fact that there is a whole other dimension in the lives of many people, men and women, apart from paid work and leisure. It's called being a parent. We would have thought that better provision for time for parenting should have at least been placed before longer holidays in their list of priorities.

However, if all those suggestions were actually put into practice at the grass-roots of the union movement, in individual agreements, it would certainly be a considerable move in the right direction. But, given the urgency of the present crisis, it doesn't seem to be happening very fast. Money, of course, is a major obstacle. While there have long been union leaders pressing for a shorter working week, the man on the shop floor has consistently shown that he would rather have the money. He would rather work long hours, do plenty of overtime, even if that means seeing little of his family, for the sake of a fat pay packet. The working week has barely changed since the last war.

Is there any way of changing it? Unless it is changed, any more sharing-out of available work is going to be very limited. The people in work, and so in the relevant union, are going to carry on making agreements which suit their interests and not the more pressing interests of the unemployed.

Perhaps if we do manage a very successful technological revolution employers will be able to pay something equivalent to current weekly wages to people working far shorter hours, but that is a long way off. In present conditions, working shorter hours is going to mean financial sacrifice, at least in the short term.

Yet deciding to sacrifice earning power to other considerations isn't that alien to human nature, in spite of what we've just said. Young couples choose almost inevitable financial sacrifice when they decide to start a family – they obviously think it's worth it. Women choose to put family commitments before earnings when they look only for part-time jobs. Many men choose to sacrifice earning power for the sake of an early retirement, and more do so when the Job Release early retirement scheme in part compensates for their loss of earnings. Under this scheme people approaching retirement age are encouraged to retire early – and so free a job for a younger person – by payment of a special allowance. Some couples, like those we spoke to in the last chapter, are already experimenting with job-sharing. The Equal Opportunities Commission published a booklet on the subject in August 1981, and the New Ways To Work group encourages such schemes.

When considering which other workers should be encouraged to spend more time at home, it does make sense to concentrate attention on parents with children under the age of five or ten, because there's little doubt that these are the people experiencing the most conflict between the demands of their home responsibilities and the need to earn a living. However, what we hope we've made clear is that this is not the woman's problem alone, even if the couple themselves at the time see it as only her problem. The whole family may suffer if she alone takes on the burden of providing physical care for the children.

Let's encourage those with things to do at home to spend time doing them, so that others who have little else to do (apart from getting depressed or into trouble) can work those hours in their place. But let's try to do it in a way that doesn't involve one staying at home full-time compulsorily.

Suppose a special home-responsibilities allowance were paid to any family with young children in which the major breadwinner works, say, twenty-five hours a week or less, and the second earner, if there is one, works no more hours. Fathers of young children work more overtime than any other group, and since this twenty-five-hour limit would specifically preclude overtime work, this would go a long way to achieve the second objective in the TUC list. However, we have called this allowance a home-responsibilities allowance rather than parenting allowance, because this would also be paid to those caring for infirm dependent relatives.

Obviously this allowance would have to be a worthwhile amount if it is going to persuade a man (or less frequently, a woman) to give up ten or fifteen hours' or more pay. The most effective arrangement in terms of persuading people to work fewer hours would seem to be to make it an earnings-related allowance with a built-in earnings ceiling.

Although other earnings-related supplements to benefits such as maternity, sickness and unemployment benefit were discontinued at the end of 1981 as an economy measure, unless the home-responsibilities allowance were earnings-related it seems very unlikely that it would encourage any but the lowest-paid to stay at home. And of course there is a difference between this allowance and others mentioned, in that this allowance is actually opening up opportunities to get others *off* benefits. However, there clearly would have to be an upper limit on how much could be paid out.

The drawback with an earnings-related benefit is that more money is given to people who have more. However, if this were seen as part of the National Insurance system, it would be argued that the higher earners had paid more into the scheme and would be doing so in future. This form of allowance would be taxable, *and as long as tax thresholds were not too low* that would ensure that at least there would be an element of people benefiting from the scheme according to their need, without it being completely irrelevant to the better-paid.

The actual percentage of the earnings paid would have to be calculated so that it was sufficient incentive, while making allowance for the fact that spending more time at home should in itself be an attractive idea to many.

It would encourage parents to share the care of young children – especially because the short-fall in income would encourage the wife to work at least part-time – but would also be a *disincentive* for the couple to work more than is good for themselves, their children or other people needing work. Whereas at present a father may be working forty-three hours a week and his wife twenty hours, if collecting a home-responsibilities allowance he would work up to twenty-five hours, and his wife up to twenty-five hours. Such a scheme would also relieve the strain on those caring for infirm dependants, because it would mean the burden of care in those cases, which is often far less rewarding and more stressful than raising small children, could be shared between husband and wife. For those, usually unmarried women, who are caring alone for elderly, infirm relatives it would mean they could continue more easily to work and enjoy a decent income rather than rely totally on benefits, since they would need to be out of the home only twenty-five hours or so rather than forty. Some now working full-time would choose to be at home more.

A home-responsibilities allowance run along these lines would also be a tremendous help to lone parents. At the moment a serious disincentive for them to work part-time is built into the benefits system. About 325,000 to 350,000 lone parents rely on supplementary benefit while 250,000 work full-time and only 150,000 part-time.

Obviously it can be very difficult for a lone parent to arrange care for her children (more rarely, his) while she works. There are lone parents living in poverty because they feel they cannot leave their children for a full-time job or cannot arrange good care, and there are lone parents working full-time because they feel that they and a child cannot survive on less than £35 benefit a week – but the child may be left alone at times or in poor substitute care.

It is very difficult for a lone parent to follow the usual mother's path of taking a part-time job because supplementary benefit (from November 1980) allows single parents to earn only £4 a week (net of tax, National Insurance, fares and child-care expenses) before the benefit starts being cut back – by 50p for every £1 earned between £4 and £20, and penny for penny above that.

A home-responsibilities allowance would allow a lone parent to work twenty-five hours a week but be paid something within shouting distance of a full wage, and the one-parent addition to child benefit (£3.30 from November 1981) would help to narrow the gap.

There would also have to be changes in the rules governing Family Income Supplement (FIS). This tops up low wages for lone parents working twenty-four hours or more a week – so there is no immediate problem there – but to be eligible for this help the breadwinner of other low-waged families has to work at least thirty hours a week.

And there are injustices to women that this home-responsibilities allowance would not go all that far to correct. For example, although the majority of wives work these days, a married woman (living with her husband) who gives up work to care for a disabled relative cannot claim Invalidity Care Allowance – though a friend (who's not a married woman) of the disabled person who gave up work to care for them could. A wife who cannot work because of her own disability cannot claim disability benefit without extra, more stringent tests than are applied to single women and men, whether married or single. These are not going to be corrected, either, by new regulations being brought into effect to make our benefits system comply with the EEC directive on equality in social security – which will, for example, mean that a female breadwinner will be able to claim FIS – and the cost of bringing them into effect would be enormous.

However, if a married woman who cannot work because she is caring for a disabled relative has a husband who cuts back on his working week in order to claim the home-responsibilities allowance, at least that will mean there is someone else to provide the care for enough hours a week to enable her to work part-time.

A disabled wife whose husband opts for the shorter working

week will at least have the benefit of his help and company for more hours each week.

And a point to be watched by any woman wanting to work is the outcome of the debate about income-tax reform. While the Equal Opportunities Commission want men and women treated equally, regardless of whether they are married – if you earn, you get an earnings tax allowance, but not otherwise – the Conservative government's Green Paper (discussion document) seemed to favour letting a wife pass her allowance to her husband if she doesn't work, which would be a disincentive for many wives to work. Of course, we all believe that mothers at home caring for young children and those looking after infirm relatives should be properly provided for, but this is better done through cash benefits to them, not through a tax allowance which goes to the husband.

Where would the money come from? There are nearly 1¾ million families with children under five, a further two million with children under ten. Of course, the main breadwinner in some of these must be unemployed but only the minority. If the majority worked three days a week or its equivalent a colossal number of hours of work would be freed for those at present unemployed, with a consequent large saving in unemployment and supplementary benefit. We can't gloss over the fact that there would be the drawback that in areas where a smaller percentage of the working population have jobs, fewer hours would be freed, while those are the areas, of course, with the most unemployed. This would imply that some families would have to be prepared to move, which we realize is not easy. However, at least there would be hours of work freed for them to go to.

Also, and this is an important difference, compared with the idea of pushing women out of work, much of the work freed would be 'men's work'.

We are against the idea that women should ever be barred from any jobs, and also believe that jobs in general need re-evaluation away from the idea that any job a man usually does is automatically worth more than any job a woman normally does. However, at present there is often a division in what type of work each sex is prepared to do. It would be a plus to have rather more men's and rather fewer women's jobs freed in this way. Not only would it free jobs for men out of work, jobs they want to do, but it also might actually encourage women to break down some of the barriers. After all, there are plenty of women registered unemployed and the urgency of their need might be an incentive to have a go.

There would be further savings to be made from supplementary benefits, since many lone parents living on supplementary benefit but not looking for work because of the reasons outlined above would get twenty-five-hour jobs and their home-responsibilities allowance would be less than their current total benefit.

Another possible source of funding is abolishing the married man's higher tax allowance. Assuming just pensioners kept it, in 1980–81 this would have yielded £2,600 million a year. Many groups object to the married man's allowance – 55 per cent more than the single person's tax allowance, and based on the outdated assumption that a married man would be supporting a non-working wife at home. These days this is true only in a minority of cases and the vast majority of these could be protected against hardship in other ways – by an increased child benefit and a similar flat-rate benefit for those with other dependants such as elderly and infirm parents to care for.

This benefit – child benefit and one for those with other dependants – could be called a home-responsibilities benefit and would be automatically available to all those with such responsibilities and would be awarded according to the number of dependants, as is child benefit now.

The home-responsibilities *benefit* would replace the married man's allowance – but help people according to their need instead of regardless of it, and without discriminating against those too poor to pay tax, as does the present system.

The home-responsibilities *allowance* which we are proposing would be an earnings-related supplement to this – as maternity allowance was an earnings-related supplement to maternity benefit – only payable to those with such responsibilities who work a shorter week. The allowance would aim to replace the income which would have been derived from working longer hours.

While they are distinct, they are complementary and should be budgeted for together. The fact that one might be seen as a DHSS responsibility and the other as that of the Department of Employment must not be allowed to prevent them being worked out sensibly together.

One allowance isn't going to solve all the long-term unemployment problems of this country, but it could act as a force for change in the right direction, dragging all sorts of attitudes along with it (in the same way as we are afraid that a mothering allowance as suggested by Dr Leach, encouraging women to stay at home full-time, would act as a force in the *wrong* direction way beyond its actual practical effects). It would add impetus to changes which are in any case desirable and it would be absolutely essential that these changes were made if the whole scheme were to work.

We are quite sure employers will be utterly aghast at the idea of an upheaval in their work-force, but actually all we are suggesting is more of the same. What growth in jobs there has been in recent years has been in part-time jobs, because until recently that was how employers could attract the labour they wanted. Employers obviously *can* arrange work along different patterns from the forty-hour week if they want to. Many jobs in the newspaper industry with which we are familiar have already been rearranged into four-day weeks. Clive Jenkins and Barrie Sherman in *The Collapse of Work* point out that it makes more sense to arrange a shorter working week along the lines of three eight-hour days rather than say five five-hour days, to cut down on travelling. In areas like the south-east, where people tend to travel long distances to work, that will be true, but depending on the work and local conditions, five short days worked in overlapping shifts may make more sense in some areas and industries. Whichever is chosen, however, there is a good chance that employers will benefit from greater productivity, since it has already been noticed that people working fewer hours per week tend to work more steadily and concentratedly than those working a forty-hour week. This applies both to routine mechanical jobs, and to 'thinking' jobs – as one job-sharer commented 'our employer gets the benefit of two people's thinking time in the bath each week'. Two heads for the price of one.

Another benefit to employers is that employees working shorter weeks tend to take less time off for visits to the dentist and so on, which they can more easily arrange in their own time, and children's illness is more likely to be covered by a parent already at home if both are working shorter hours.

There might be less chopping and changing in the work-force than they might first expect, too. A young couple with small children trying to build up their home are usually going through their time of greatest economic hardship. They need a home-responsibilities allowance to enable them both to work less than what is now considered full-time, especially since it would be very difficult for them both to work even twenty-five hours a week. But increasingly couples might both choose the twenty-five hour a week option before they start a family, when they can both work pretty freely and have only themselves to provide for, even though they get no allowance for doing so. Also, once the pattern is established, they might keep it up when the children are older and, again, it is easier for them both to work flexibly. It is at least hopeful that as new technology reduces the number of hours needing to be worked, the attitudes encouraged by the home-responsibilities allowance would lead to more people wanting to work fewer hours.

As we have already mentioned, we have a strong feeling that once it was so publicly acknowledged that men as well as women had important home commitments, and that men wanted to work shorter hours as well as women, this would in itself radically alter the position of women in the work-force. An awful lot of their problems are only due to the fact that work is arranged *by* men who don't spend much time at home *for* men who don't spend much time at home. But certainly, tied in with these changes, should be the amendments needed in the Equal

Pay and Sex Discrimination Acts to help women enjoy more truly equal opportunities and pay.

The Equal Opportunities Commission has listed twenty-five amendments. Crucial among these is, for example, that women should be able to claim equal pay for work of equal value without having to find an actual member of the opposite sex doing their job for the same firm in the same place with whom to compare their pay – frequently impossible, since men and women's work is so commonly segregated.

The concept of indirect discrimination, contained in the Sex Discrimination Act, should be included in the Equal Pay Act. This would apply when women are not specifically, in so many words, discriminated against but where conditions are attached to work which effectively make it more difficult for women to comply with the demands. For example, the *Price* v. *Civil Service* case under the Sex Discrimination Act showed that it was indirect discrimination to confine recruitment for certain grades to people between the ages of seventeen and a half and twenty-eight because a large proportion of suitable women candidates were at home child-rearing during those years.

The scope of the Sex Discrimination and Equal Pay Acts should be extended to include provision relating to death and retirement, notably company pension schemes. If women are to share the task of building up pension rights more equally with their partners, then it is essential that they enjoy equal terms under these schemes so that couples' pension rights do not suffer.

The Equal Pay Act should be amended to ensure equal pay pro rata for part-time workers. Without these changes families are still going to suffer too much economically if a man gives up working hours. It may not be too serious a problem while he is compensated by an earnings-related home-responsibilities allowance, but when that ceases it is important that his wife's earnings reasonably compensate for the wages he has forgone. However, it is worth remembering that already women earn more than their husbands in one in seven families. Positive action programmes, to encourage women and men to move into non-traditional jobs, and a rethinking of the economic value of jobs, so that women's jobs stopped being regarded as deserving of lower pay simply because women do them, would be essential.

In *Positive Action for Women*,[2] Sadie Robarts, with Anna Coote and Elizabeth Ball, having studied the affirmative action programmes for women in the United States, put forward a programme for positive action for women in this country.

They suggest that companies should declare themselves to be equal opportunities employers, following this up with a careful and honest statistical analysis of what positions and perks men and women hold and enjoy in the company, and then study how they can redress the balance.

They should re-examine assumptions made when recruiting staff about what are men's and women's jobs, what experience is necessary. For example, it may be customary to fill middle-management jobs from the craft and technical sections, which are predominantly male, rather than from the clerical and administrative sections, which include women, even though their experience may be at least as relevant. They should develop training programmes designed to compensate women for past discrimination and disadvantage, and so on.

This sort of change would be much more likely to happen, too, if home responsibilities were more equally shared, because then more women would have the time and incentive to get involved in trade-union business and see that they accurately reflected and fought for their interests.

So far the unions haven't got very involved in ideas for job-sharing – which could be seen as the precursor for the sort of working pattern we suggest. The impetus has come from individuals anxious to job-share because of personal circumstances, from New Ways To Work (from 1981 aided by a grant from the Equal Opportunities Commission), and from a few employers. Some clearing banks started encouraging job-sharing as a way of attracting married women to return to work – at Barclays Bank some 2,000 out of 50,000 staff share their jobs. The Lothian Health Board estimated that it cost £40,000 to train a doctor and considered that a doctor who has a complete break from her speciality for a few years often finds it very difficult to return to it.

While the clearing banks restrict job-sharing to clerical and secretarial posts, and do not consider – in the absence of having tried it – that a sharer could be given the same responsibility as a full-timer, the Lothian Health Board scheme, in operation since 1975, enables two people to apply jointly for any grade of medical post from house officer to consultant. In 1980 one consultant post, five senior registrar posts and four registrar posts were shared.[3]

Employing more people does entail an employer running into higher overheads – though this may be covered by improved productivity, whether in goods or brain-power. Because National Insurance contributions are now broadly based on earnings, he may not have to pay more in contributions, but there is an increased administrative load, particularly in connection with wages payments – though the more this is computerized, the less important a factor this will be. From the employee's point of view, as long as both partners are paying full pro-rata contributions – which married women in work generally have to do these days – they will end up with a state pension comparable to if not better than the one they would have received if only one full-time earner was paying contributions. Company pension-scheme rules would sometimes have to be adjusted to allow employees working shorter weeks to protect their pension rights – but again the assumption would be that both partners of a couple would be building up a pension, instead of just one.

We need not feel that it is totally impracticable to suggest that such changes could be implemented. Sweden is the country which has worked out the boldest schemes to enable both parents to work and share child-care. Swedish parents already have the right to insist on working only six hours a day until their child is eight years old. Their parent insurance benefit replaces 90 per cent of full wage (up to a maximum limit) for up to nine months following birth (or adoption). Parents may share the benefit, with either the mother or father leaving work to care for the child at home, full- or part-time. The last three months of the benefit may be used by either or both parents at any time until the child is eight years old either as full-time leave or as a proportionately longer period of part-time work. When parental insurance was first instituted in 1974 only 2 per cent of fathers used the benefit. But the proportion has grown rapidly. Take-up for 1978 was estimated at 14 per cent.

Official TUC policy on unemployment and new technology should be adjusted to take account of workers' home commitments and to get away from the idea that child-care is a 'women's problem' – taking the Swedish legislation as at least the starting point for a model.

But probably even more important and immediate in its effects would be if the grass-roots, at branch and factory-floor level, started drawing up demands for annual agreements which included demands for time off for parenting for both men and women which didn't get abandoned early in the negotiating process. Not only generous maternity, but paternity leave at the time of birth should be basic. It is crucial that it is realized, as it is in Sweden, that children don't stop needing care when they are three months old. The problems of combining work and child-care go on for years. An early step towards more equally shared parenting would be if all parents were allowed a certain number of days off per year, or a regular allowance of short days, or flexible working hours. Part-time work should be made available to men and women, and in traditional spheres of work.

At first the take-up by fathers might be rather small – especially if the time off was unpaid – but the Swedish example suggests that the paternal take-up would steadily increase, and so does our experience in talking to fathers in this country.

The same sort of allowance for time off could be negotiated for those with elderly and infirm dependants now. Including this group would also help make it clear that those being given time off were not simply getting an easy skive. And, of course, those without dependants who wanted to put effort into activities outside work could also be allowed time off on similar terms, providing that their time was also spent helping care for others in society who are not able to care for themselves.

As mentioned, we see this as an early plank for negotiation. Eventually most workers will in any case be moving towards a much shorter working week, which certainly will include much more time for straightforward leisure.

And both in the early stages and later ones, women are going to have to find the calm determination to ensure that the result isn't that they combine shorter working hours with child-care and all the work at home, while men combine shorter working hours with increased leisure and the odd game in the park with the kids. We can think of no legislation which can ensure that men take on a fairer share of the housework – though studies do show that younger husbands do expect to share domestic chores more than their fathers did.

Certainly, if men were generally expected to spend much of their children's early years at home, sharing their upbringing, the need would be obvious to make sure they reached adulthood well aware of child-care and children's development. At the moment, such teaching in child-care as is available tends to be treated as a soft option for less academic girls. Even without any of the changes we are envisaging, it is crucial that young people are taught more about parenting in schools – future fathers as well as future mothers. The changes we want would underline the need and make it more likely that it would be satisfied.

Teaching 'parenting' isn't as ludicrous an idea as it may sound. Of course you can't teach someone how to love (though you can help them feel more able to do so), but good parenting doesn't come as naturally as we like to think. If it did we wouldn't need the NSPCC, whose clients aren't child-hating monsters but often confused youngsters who not only love their children but are over-dependent on them, showing them the affection they lacked as youngsters and having totally unrealistic expectations of them. Teaching boys and girls how babies develop means they don't take a nappy soiled as soon as it is put on as a sign of rejection, and they can take informed pleasure in the wonder that is a growing child.

More generally in schools, the expectation of shared parenting should help to break down the barriers to giving girls more equal opportunities caused by teachers' and pupils' attitudes. If what is already reality – that women mostly want to work even though they have children – was better understood and accepted by the girls themselves and those responsible for advising them, more care would be taken over subject choices they start making as young as twelve which can later rule them out from the more profitable types of employment.

The changes we are suggesting wouldn't mean that there would be no need for child-care facilities outside the family. To start with, lone parents will still depend on such help – and even their needs are far from catered for, except with lip service, at present. But having two parents both working and caring in most families would ease the strain. It would mean that they would need outside help for fewer hours, and could afford to make some of their own arrangements, as long as adequate back-up was available to ensure that childminders were properly trained and supported, and that playgroups and nursery classes bore the needs of working parents in mind.

While wonders have been achieved by virtually all-women organizations like the Pre-School Playgroups Association and the National Association of Childminders, we are sure they would welcome the involvement of more fathers in building up local facilities.

More time for parenting would also lessen the pressures which in hard-up families can lead to break-up, with a father out at work all day and the mother rushing out to work at night as soon as he is home to baby-sit. Their time could be more flexibly planned and allow them more overlap. This is a way we really could help to cement families and enable them to give the due love, care and attention to each other and to their children which could avoid so many ills in society today.

We are sure there are going to be those who think that introducing changes which would encourage fathers to spend more time with their children and enable more mothers to spend some time out of the home working belong in Never-Never Land in times like ours, that they would cost too much. In our view, in monetary terms as well as emotional ones, the cost will be too great if we don't.

Appendix: Further Information

If you want to follow up any of the ideas in this book, you can obtain further information and advice from:

Equal Opportunities Commission, Overseas House, Quay Street, Manchester M3 3HN, for anything to do with equal pay and opportunities, and aspects of life – such as parenthood – which may affect these.

National Council for Civil Liberties, 21 Tabard Street, London SE1 4LA, have a Women's Rights Unit which advises on working and individual rights.

Trades Union Congress, Congress House, Great Russell Street, London WC1 (or your own union), for help fighting discrimination or introducing schemes to encourage equal opportunities, leave for parents etc.

New Ways To Work, 347A Upper Street, London N1, for advice on new work patterns such as job-sharing.

Women in Computing, c/o A Woman's Place, 48 William IV Street, London WC2, for women in the industry and those wanting to learn more about new technology and its implications.

Women in Management, 4 Mapledale Avenue, Croydon, Surrey, advise women seeking training – including in new technology – and wishing to advance their careers.

National Children's Bureau, 8 Wakely Street, London EC1, and *Child Poverty Action Group*, 1 Macklin Street, London WC2, for questions relating to children's welfare and development.

National Childcare Campaign, 17 Victoria Park Square, Bethnal Green, London E2, co-ordinate and advise on efforts to increase child-care facilities.

National Council for One-Parent Families, 255 Kentish Town Road, London NW5 2LX, and *Gingerbread*, 35 Wellington Street, London WC2, advise lone parents.

Advisory Centre for Education, 18 Victoria Park Square, Bethnal Green, London E2 9PF, help and advise on problems with education.

National Association of Carers, 77 Dale Street, Chatham, Kent, advises those caring for anyone disabled – children, spouses, parents.

National Council for the Single Woman and Her Dependants, 29 Chilworth Mews, London W2 3RG, helps those caring for elderly or infirm relatives.

(When writing for information it is usually advisable to enclose a stamped addressed envelope.)

References

1. Women under Attack

1. 'Surveying the Cuts', *Poverty*, 47, December 1980.
2. National Children's Bureau Conference, Bath, 1979.
3. S. Weir and R. Simpson, 'Are the Local Authority Social Services Being Bled Dry?', *New Society*, 10 July 1980, Vol. 53, 921.
4. Conservative Party Conference, October 1977.
5. Eyre Methuen, 1979.
6. Dr Christopher Evans, *The Mighty Micro*, Gollancz, 1979.
7. Peter Large, *The Micro Revolution*, Fontana, 1980.

2. Not So Equal at Work

1. 'Fair Care for Children and a Fair Deal for Mum', *Woman's Own*, 17 February 1979.
2. *European Women in Paid Employment – Their Perception of Discrimination at Work*, December 1980.

3. Should Women Go Back Home?

1. 'Fair Care for Children and a Fair Deal for Mum', *Woman's Own*, 1979.
2. Ann Oakley, *The Sociology of Housework*, Martin Robertson, 1974.
3. George Brown and Tirril Harris, *The Social Origins of Depression*, Tavistock Publications, 1978.
4. *Who Cares?*, Penguin Books, 1979.
5. *A Fairer Future for Our Children*, Macmillan, 1980.
6. *Work and the Family*, edited by Peter Moss and Nickie Fonda, Temple Smith, 1980.
7. Orden and Bradburn, 'Dimensions of Marriage Happiness', *Journal of Sociology*, 74 (1968).
8. Lotte Bailyn, 'Career and Family Orientations of Husbands and

Wives in Relation to Marital Happiness', *Human Relations*, 23, 1971, cited in *Work and the Family*.
9. Rhona and Robert N. Rapoport and Ziona Strelitz, *Fathers, Mothers and Others*, Routledge & Kegan Paul, 1977.
10. W. J. Gadpaille, in *Contemporary Marriage: Structure, Dynamics and Therapy*, ed. Grunebaum and Christ (1976), Little, Brown, cited in *Fathers, Mothers and Others*.
11. E. Grönseth, 'Work Sharing, Adaptations of Pioneering Families with Husband and Wife in Part-time Employment', *Acta Sociologica*, 1975, cited in *Fathers, Mothers and Others*.
12. Equal Opportunities Commission, 1980.

4. A New and Improved Sink?

1. D. Piachaud, *The Cost of a Child*, Child Poverty Action Group, 1979.
2. *A Fairer Future for Our Children*, Macmillan, 1980.
3. *Who Cares?*, Penguin Books, 1978.
4. *Mothering*, Fontana, 1977.
5. Hughes et al., *Nurseries Now*, Penguin Books, 1980.
6. Surveys for National Consumer Council and *Woman's Own*, 20 September 1975.
7. Ann Oakley, *The Sociology of Housework*, Martin Robertson, 1974.
8. Paper presented at the annual conference of the National Council on Family Relations, Boston, 1979, cited in *Work and the Family*.
9. 'Fair Care for Children and a Fair Deal for Mum', *Woman's Own*, 1979.
10. *Delinquency and Parental Pathology*, Methuen, 1960.
11. *Absentee Husband in Spiritualist Families, Journal of Marriage and the Family*, 39, 1977.
12. *Guardian*, 1976.
13. M. Young and P. Willmott, *The Symmetrical Family*, Routledge, 1973.
14. *Must Success Cost So Much?*, Grant McIntyre, 1980.
15. Fontana, 1980.

5. The Way Forward: Share the Care

1. Ross D. Parke, *Fathering*, Fontana, 1981.
2. 'Work Sharing: Adaptations of Pioneering Families with Husband

and Wife in Part-time Employment', *Acta Sociologica*, 1975, cited in *Fathering*.

3. *Fathers as Caregivers: Possible Antecedents and Consequences*, paper presented at University of Haifa, Israel, 1980, cited in *Fathering*.
4. *Child-rearing Fathers in Intact Families, Possible Antecedents and Consequences*, paper presented at University of Haifa, Israel, 1980, cited in *Fathering*.
5. *The Four-Day Work Week: Blue-collar Adjustment to a Nonconventional Arrangement of Work and Leisure Time*, Ph.D. diss., University of Michigan, 1976, cited in *Fathering*.
6. Eyre Methuen, 1979.
7. See note 4.
8. 'Fair Care for Children and a Fair Deal for Mum', *Woman's Own*, 1979.
9. Penguin Books, 1979.
10. *A Fairer Future for Our Children*, Macmillan, 1980.
11. Eyre Methuen, 1979.
12. Gollancz, 1979.

6. What Can We Set Our Sights On?

1. Eyre Methuen, 1979.
2. National Council for Civil Liberties, 1981.
3. Industrial Relations Survey and Report 225, 1980.

Index

MORE ABOUT PENGUINS
AND PELICANS

Also published in Penguins

SPARE RIB READER

A celebration of ten years of *Spare Rib*.

'A magazine for ladies who feel that the traditional women's magazines treat them as though they had their brains sucked out . . . It's not shrill or hysterical, neither is it smooth, sleek and totally synthetic – it's just good' – John Peel in *Disc*, 1972

'The toughest, most relevant and most likeable of feminist magazines is two years old. To reach three they're going to need funds, hope and the kind of faith that moves mountains' – Philip Oakes in the *Sunday Times*, 1974

'I used to be a Tupperware groupie – until I discovered *Spare Rib* . . . its sizzling prose blew my hibernating mind . . . and whipped up within me a passionate wish to identify with the growing sisterhood of bold, thinking women' – Val Hennessy in the *Evening Standard*, 1979

'*Spare Rib* has earned its hundredth birthday celebrations' – *Guardian*, 1980

THE FEMININE MYSTIQUE

Betty Friedan

First published in the sixties *The Feminine Mystique* still remains a powerful and illuminating analysis of the position of women in Western society.

'Brilliantly researched, passionately argued book – a time-bomb flung into the Mom-and-Apple-Pie image . . . Out of the debris of that shattered ideal, the Woman's Liberation Movement was born' – Ann Leslie

'A controversial polemic' – *New Statesman*

'Fascinating' – *Guardian*

'Intelligently argued and persuasively written' – *Listener*

'Densely researched study' – *Evening Standard*

'An angry thoroughly documented book' – *Life*

Also published in Penguins

THE SCEPTICAL FEMINIST

A Philosophical Enquiry

Janet Radcliffe Richards

In this important and original study, Janet Radcliffe Richards demonstrates with incisive, systematic and often unexpected arguments the precise nature of the injustice women suffer, and exposes the fallacious arguments by which it has been justified. Her analysis leads her to considerable criticism of many commonly held feminist views, but from it emerges the outline of a new and more powerful feminism which sacrifices neither rationality nor radicalism.

'Intellectually sober and politically practical, yet gay, witty and dashing at the same time . . . It's a model of how to write a book on *any* topic; on a contentious subject like this *it's a triumph*' – *Sunday Times*

WOMEN, SEX AND PORNOGRAPHY

Beatrice Faust

Pornography is a topic that produces feverish responses, but women's reactions until now have been left unexamined. Even the responses of the women's movement have been contradictory. In this major new work, Beatrice Faust discusses the psychology of sexual differences and how they relate to differences in the sexual and erotic styles of men and women and the influence of culture.

In a frank and polemical analysis, Beatrice Faust explores the enormous social implications of these sexual differences, from novels, films and fashion to social behaviour patterns – and rape. She argues that pornography is neither pro- nor anti-woman. But it certainly presents a misleading view of woman's sexuality, and the solution is not censorship but sex education through bona fide erotica and the recognition of differences between male and female sexuality.

Also published in Penguins

DUTIFUL DAUGHTERS

Women talk about their lives

Edited by Jean McCrindle and Sheila Rowbotham

The women in this book are not extraordinary or exceptional, and yet their lives, described here in their own words, are a passionate, often humorous, testimony to the never-ending cycle of the feminine condition. They tell of sexual ignorance, domestic hardship, boring and degrading work, inadequate housing, and sleepless nights with babies. Yet they also talk of freer loving relationships, the pleasures of child-rearing, housework becoming less burdensome, work outside the home more fulfilling. With this they combine an amused awareness of the cultural image of women, so strikingly at odds with the reality of their everyday existence, and a recognition that their lives have changed.

'This moving and densely packed book is an admirable contribution to . . . the breaking down of the silence that still surrounds women's experience' – Margaret Walters in *New Society*

WOMEN'S RIGHTS

Anna Coote and Tess Gill

'An excellent . . . shot in the arm for women's equality' – wrote the *Evening News* when *Women's Rights* was first published.

This third, revised and updated edition is as comprehensive as the first. The new sections deal with changes in the law regarding Maternity Rights, Child Benefit, the plight of battered women and the Equal Pay and Sex Discrimination Acts. Much of the rest of the guide has been expanded and revised.

Also published in Penguins

THE AMBIVALENCE OF ABORTION

Linda Bird Francke

Having gone through the experience herself, Linda Bird Francke set out to discover not only how other women felt about their own decisions to terminate their pregnancies, but how their husbands, or boyfriends and their families felt as well. In interviews with men and women of all ages and all social groups, she describes this essentially human experience and in doing so casts new light not only on one of the most controversial and complicated issues of our time, but also on the emotional and sexual values of our contemporary society.

'Clearly written and compassionate' – *Scotsman*

'Perhaps the most intriguing aspect of Linda Francke's research – and certainly the most original – has been into the effects of abortion on putative fathers' – *New Society*

THE WISE WOUND

Menstruation and Everywoman

Penelope Shuttle and Peter Redgrave

Menstruation – blessing or curse? This book tackles a subject that has been forbidden for centuries.

It is the first study of its kind, and in unveiling taboos both ancient and modern, it will change the way women – and men – view themselves.

'An important, brave and exciting exploration into territory that belongs to all of us, and nobody could read it without a sense of discovery' – Margaret Drabble in the *Listener*

'Peter Redgrave and Penelope Shuttle have researched their subject with unerring diligence . . . It could bring about a major change in our understanding of the sexes' – *Psychology Today*

'An Aladdin's cave of scientific, psychological and anthropological insights . . . all quite irresistible' – *Observer*